VICTOR McLAGLEN MOTOR CORPS

The History of the Oldest Motorcycle Stunt and Drill Team In The World

1935-2014

BY RUTH H. FISHER

The Amazing Victor McLaglen Motor Corps
© 2016 by Ruth H. Fisher

All rights reserved. Printed in the United States of America.

No part of this book may be used or reproduced in any manner whatsoever without express written consent of the author, except brief quotations embodied in critical articles or reviews.

For information:
Ruth Fisher
ruthfisher4@gmail.com
www.thevmmc.com

Book Cover and Interior Design
by Barbara Fail, Studio 14 Productions, Madrid, NM
studio14madrid@gmail.com

ISBN 978-0-9976011-0-7
Ruth H. Fisher
The Amazing Victor McLaglen Motor Corps

Library of Congress Control Number: 2016916574

Acknowledgment

I would like to begin by thanking all the people who encouraged me to write and publish this book. There were times when the task was overwhelming and I was ready to throw up my hands and admit defeat. It was during these difficult times that I was blessed with a letter, or a phone call, or an e-mail, from someone who would remind me of how far we had come, how hard we had worked, how much fun we had, and our continued possibilities for the future. I was, once again, motivated. I persevered and, finally, finished the book. Thanks to each and every one of you for your encouragement and support.

Paula Carrow laid the foundation. She spent endless hours sorting through boxes of materials, organizing the contents, and scanning the data into the computer. Paula set the stage for the rest of the project and made the publication of this book a reality.

The members of the Victor McLaglen Motor Corps – past and present – were with me throughout the writing of this book. They helped to identify former members, they answered questions about particular people and places and types of motorcycles.

"Hey, Bruce, what year is the bike in this photo?" "Scott, where did we leave the rental car at the airport? Was it in Pontiac, MI or Chicago, IL?" This great, fun-loving team – and my second family – were key in researching and providing the information and photographs that brought this book to life.

Throughout the pages of the book, you will witness the artistic and humorous talents of one of our members, Tedd Farrell. Tedd was more than a biker. His humor and artistic creativity were captured in annual Christmas cartoons he shared with his team members. Tedd passed away in 2015, but his artwork lives on in these pages.

My friend, Jacque Heck, edited the first draft and she bled red marks all over everything I had written. Although she excels in grammar and word usage, she knew nothing about motorcycles. I was grateful, therefore, that Patrick Casey stepped in to critique my draft from the perspective of a motorcycle rider.

Thank you to the many photographers: Ken Graeb, Sam Jones, Bing Bengsten, Leo Costa, Bart Perry, and so many others, most of whom I don't know. You made this book come alive!

Graphic arts specialist and expert editor, Barbara Fail of Studio 14 Productions, brought it all together so that we ended up with a professional look for a book that was definitely amateurish when she received it. She made me look good, and for that I am immensely appreciative.

I genuinely hope you enjoy reading this book as much as we all enjoyed writing it.

Ruth H. Fisher

Preface

Many years ago, I started setting aside Victor McLaglen Motor Corps memorabilia – newspaper clippings, magazine articles, pictures, and letters. These all went into a big box, then I added another box, and another . . . until I had quite a pile of boxes. My thought was to someday go through these boxes and do something with all that information. But I didn't have time to even think about that until I retired from my "day job." Then I retired, and had no more excuses.

My motivation was to put all that information into a book, so those stories, pictures, newspaper, and magazine articles wouldn't get lost or just thrown away into a dumpster. There was history that Motor Corps members and their relatives and friends might find interesting. I didn't want it to be lost.

This book is a result of that vision. When my husband, Harry, passed away in 2014, I knew that the time had come to finish this project and get the book published. This book covers the Victor McLaglen Motor Corps from 1935 to 2014, when Harry left us.

Fortunately, the Motor Corps continued functioning after Harry's passing, and is now under the leadership of another generation which, hopefully, will continue the traditions and carry it on into future generations.

I am very proud to have been a part of this fine organization and I know the current and past members and their families are equally proud. We've always held ourselves to the highest standards in the motorcycling community, have strived to project a good, clean image of motorcycling, and set a good example to the young people who watch us. To me, that's an important tradition to hang on to.

I've tried to make this information as accurate as I could, but I'm sure there will be errors found. If there are errors or omissions , it was not intentional.

Ruth H. Fisher

Victor McLaglen Motor Corps
Announcer and Honorary Life Member
April 2016

Just some of the many boxes of Motor Corps "treasures" that needed to be looked at!

Dedication

I dedicate this book to my late husband,

Commander Harry Fisher,

*who was the leader of the Motor Corps from 1978 through 2014.
We had a great life together and his partnership with the team
was a huge part of it. I miss him, as do the members of the Motor Corps
and the many friends he met along the way.*

1935-1939

The Motor Corps was formed in 1935...

"Pyramid"
Top: Lieutenant Jimmy Crawford
Standing: Dale McCullum, Joel Stewart
Drivers: Ray Phillips, Hap Ruggles
Safety: Ernie Eberhardt

This story has been told and retold many times, but the way I heard it was this:

Truman "Nick" DeRush, a stuntman working on a movie set in Los Angeles for one of Victor McLaglen's movies, thought he would strike up a conversation with Victor in between takes. He dragged a folding chair beside Victor's and opened with, "Hey Vic. I hear you have a light horse drill team."

Victor took a swig of his cold drink and said, "Yup." Victor was apparently a man of few words.

Nick continued, "Well, I've seen 'em perform and they look pretty good, but I've got some buddies who can do the same thing – only on motorcycles. What do ya think of that?"

Victor looked at him, a bit more interested now, and said, "You don't say?"

Nick followed up with his pitch, "If I show you that me and my buddies can do the same thing those horse riders do – or better – will you sponsor us too?"

Victor was a lot more interested now. "Show me what you can do, then we'll talk."

So, Nick got in touch with seventeen of his motorcycle-riding buddies, found a place to practice and, a few weeks later, put on a pretty darned entertaining show for Victor. Victor was really impressed, bought uniforms for the entire team and asked his personal business manager, Colonel Kuri, to book shows. The next thing everyone knew, the December 1935 edition of *The Motorcyclist* magazine announced, "The Victor McLaglen Light Horse Organizes Motorcycle Squad".

Since some of the members worked as motorcycle funeral escorts, they already had matching black and white Harleys, so the rest of the team painted their bikes an identical black and white design; and, with matching uniforms, they were ready. That was just the beginning of a journey that has spanned 80+ years . . .and continues today.

Ruth, thanks for keeping the legend alive! There is no one more capable of telling the story of the Victor McLaglen Motor Corps than you. After all, you and Harry were at the helm for 35 years. You were the voice while Harry inspired the team members to do their best creative works – performing on grand old Harleys, reaching back to a more nostalgic era. Together you and all the dedicated team members inspired countless generations to adopt the iron horse sport. Behind the scenes you are still an active voice of enthusiasm and encouragement as the team moves forward towards 100 years.

                            Tom and Barbara Scott, Honorary Members & VMMC Sponsors
                            Former owners of Anaheim–Fullerton Harley-Davidson

I've been riding motorcycles almost my entire life. There are few things about motorcycling that impress me as much as the Victor McLaglen stunt riding team. Go out and ride with a friend and try riding a foot apart at the same speed while keeping the same distance, and you'll find out how difficult that is. Now make that inches and compound it with five other motorcycles and you'll realize how truly amazing this team is. As if that isn't great enough, I've watched Harry Fisher ride two motorcycles at the same time. These riders have dedicated themselves to being the best in the world. The riders of this team are men of great character and I am proud that they made me an honorary Victor McLaglen team member.

                            Steve Schapiro, Honorary Member & VMMC Sponsor
                            Schapiro and Leventhal Motorcycle Attorneys

Ruth, I am positive you have thousands of hours invested in bringing the Victor McLaglen Motor Corps story to the final page, and oh, what a story it is, spanning over eight decades of some of the greatest times in America's motorcycling history. The VM Motor Corps has inspired generations of people to throw a leg over a 2-wheel iron horse because of the wonderful performances of the Motor Corps dedicated team members like Harry, Ruth, Marty, Father Frank, Mark, Scott, and the rest of the performers, past and present.

                            Mark R. Ruffalo, Honorary Member & VMMC Sponsor
                            Owner of California Harley-Davidson

In the late 80s, when I was privileged to participate in my first Love Ride, I was at first curious about a much talked-about motorcycle drill team carrying the name of a famous old-time actor and later fascinated and overwhelmed with just how bloody good these guys were. I became an instant fan and went out of my way to see them every chance I got. After a while, the team made me an honorary member and even let me perform with them a couple times. I'm not sure if it was because I just wouldn't go away and they had to do something with me or what. The fact that they are still rockin' today is a strong testimony of their ability to lure generation after generation of both performers and audiences.

                            Mickey Jones, Honorary Member, Actor & Musician

This is by no means an unfeeling sentiment to greet my good friend, Ruth. It is an enthusiastic celebration for her accomplishment and that of the other "historians" of the Victor McLaglen Motor Corps who took the time and the care to accumulate and to preserve the memorabilia and information that tells the amazing story of the incredible crew of members, rotating through the years and keeping the daring spirit of the VMMC relevant, as motorcycles, the riders, and the industry evolved. No one better or more dedicated than Ruth could have been entrusted with this precious task. Her perspective as the wife of Harry Fisher, Commander of the VMMC from 1979 until his death in 2014, and, as she had become to the team, the voice of the VMMC during their dynamic performances, Ruth's passion for the VMMC has driven her to accomplish this task of love.

Wendy "Wendell" Perry, Writer, <u>ThunderPress</u>

There are not enough words to describe the memories I have made while being a member of this wonderful and historic organization. From the first time I saw the team in 1998 at the Love Ride, I was hooked. I HAD to be a part of what they were doing. Thankfully they let me in, and, well, the rest is history, as they say. A bunch of years later, I became the fourth leader of The Victor McLaglen Motor Corps. Wow! What an honor. I'm humbled that they would entrust me with the future of this team. The team plans to continue to thrill audiences for years to come. We're sure you will enjoy this wonderful book Ruth Fisher has tirelessly and lovingly crafted.

Scott Griffin, Current Commander of the VMMC

For the Victor McLaglen Motor Corps, the 1930s were a whirlwind of motorcycle stunt and drill exhibitions throughout the western United States. Because of their affiliation with well-known actor Victor McLaglen, who had many friends in the entertainment industry and vital connections with Hollywood's promotional agencies, the team became a renowned attraction. From leading the famous Pasadena Rose Parade on New Year's Day, to traveling to the Idaho State Penitentiary to perform for the inmates, the team became a sensation and a much sought-after act.

This is the first team photo, taken in front of McLaglen Sports Center, November 1935. Victor McLaglen center wearing a dark suit. First leader, Nick DeRush, kneeling directly in front of Victor.

Charter members:

Captain Truman (Nick) W. DeRush	**Lieutenant Wayne Fitzgerald**
Sergeant Bob Klein	**Corporal Frank McCartney**
Corporal Stanley Margraves	**Corporal Art Ricks**
Corporal "Hap" Ruggles	**George Alfring**
Getchel (Skeets) Cates	**Bud Cook**
James (Jimmy) Crawford	**Leslie Haserot**
Claude Howell	**Ralph Manshardt**
Charles Roberts	**Joel Stewart**
Bill Swan	**Alvin Thompson**

Victor McLaglen's Light Horse came up with a motorcycle squad and here it is.
Colonel McLaglen is in civilian dress in center background.

The team – looking pretty impressive!

Notice the same stunt being formed in the background.

They practiced at McLaglen Stadium in Los Angeles, California. Although the stadium is no longer there, the postcard below shows a picture of the stadium grounds.

The stadium was built by Victor McLaglen and was located on Riverside Drive, just north of Hyperion Avenue. Costing a reported $40,000 and described as state-of-the-art at the time, McLaglen Stadium hosted a wide variety of events: arena polo, equestrian events, junior college and minor pro football games, lacrosse, motorcycle and midget auto racing, rugby and softball. For a time, it was soccer's primary LA home. But after barely surviving a 1938 flood of the Los Angeles River that undermined and collapsed part of the grandstands, the stadium simply faded from use during World War II. Even its precise location is not known today. It is thought to be either part of the Golden State Freeway, Sunnynook River Park, or the river channel." *

In the first picture, if you look at the bridge in the upper right, you can see a bunch of spectators watching and wondering what in the world was going on! The words "Victor McLaglen's Death Dodgers" was printed on this old picture and I've seen it also noted in newspaper articles. They were known by a few other names too, including "Victor McLaglen Hell Drivers."

*Jim Thurman,"10 L.A. Sports Venues That Are No More", LA Weekly, December 23, 2013

Postcard of the Victor McLaglen Sports Center -1935

Taken from Hyperion Avenue, this photograph shows a general view of the damages inflicted by the Los Angeles River on Victor McLaglen Stadium. (Photograph by F.H. Baalbergen, G.C. Loomer, and A.M. Reece of the Photo Task Force 1938; courtesy of the County of Los Angeles Department of Public Works.)

The river's impact can clearly be seen in this view of the washout under the grandstand of Victor McLaglen Stadium. (Photograph by F.H. Baalbergen, G.C. Loomer, and A.M. Reece of the Photo Task Force 1938; courtesy of the County of Los Angeles Department of Public Works.)

Photo's from Ted Elrick, Los Angeles River (Arcadia Publishing, 2008), ISBN 978-0738547183, pg. 45.

"Ladder Trick" Driver: Nick DeRush, Front: Ray Phillips, Rear: Hap Ruggles, Top: Jimmy Crawford

Victor McLaglen had quite a history BEFORE the Motor Corps

He was a British leading man actor and later a character actor, primarily in American films, and especially in motion pictures under the direction of John Ford.

He was the son of the Right Rev. Andrew McLaglen, a Protestant clergyman, who was at one time Bishop of Claremont in South Africa. The young McLaglen, eldest of eight brothers, lied about his age and at 14 years old left home and attempted to serve in the Boer War in South Africa. However, his plans were botched when he was stationed at Windsor castle where they discovered his age and he was forced to leave.

As a young man, he traveled to Canada where he did farm labor and then ventured into professional prizefighting. He toured in circuses, vaudeville shows, and Wild West shows, often as a fighter challenging all comers. His tours took him to the U.S., Australia (where he joined in the gold rush), and South Africa. In 1909, he was the first fighter to box newly-crowned heavyweight champion Jack Johnson, whom he fought in a six-round exhibition match in Vancouver (as an exhibition fight, it had no decision).

When the First World War broke out, McLaglen joined the Irish Fusiliers and soldiered in the Middle East, eventually serving as Provost Marshal (head of Military Police) for the city of Baghdad. After the war, he attempted to resume a boxing career, but was given a substantial acting role in *The Call of the Road* (1920) which was well received. He became a popular leading man in British silent films, and within a few years was offered the lead in an American film, *The Beloved Brute* (1924). He quickly became a most popular star of dramas as well as action films, playing tough or suave, with equal ease. With the coming of sound, his popularity increased, particularly when cast by Ford as the tragic Gypo Nolan in *The Informer* (1935), for which McLaglen won an Oscar for Best Actor. He continued to play heroes, villains and simple-minded thugs, into the 1940s, when Ford gave his career a new impetus with a number of lovably roguish Irish parts in such films as *She Wore a Yellow Ribbon* (1949) and *The Quiet Man* (1952). The latter film won McLaglen another Oscar nomination.

McLaglen had formed a semi-militaristic riding light horse brigade, a drum and bugle corps, a band, a women's foot drill team, an airplane patrol, and the precision Victor McLaglen Motorcycle Corps, all of which led to apparently erroneous conclusions that he had fascist sympathies and was forming his own private army. The facts proved otherwise and despite rumors to the contrary, McLaglen did not espouse the far right-wing sentiments often attributed to him.

It has been told that one day Victor McLaglen was called to Washington D.C. to explain why he had a military horse team, a military-style motorcycle team, and a small fleet of airplanes. The government officials wanted to know if he was planning a military takeover of the government or some other covert operation. Of course he wasn't. He explained that, "the purpose of his organizations was to promote good sportsmanship and physical education, as well as to always have ready a group of men and women to serve the community, in time of emergencies." These fine teams were established for just those purposes. He also wanted security protection for himself, but I'm unsure if he mentioned that.

Victor (right) and John Wayne, "the Duke," (left) in *The Quiet Man* film.

Victor had two children. His son, Andrew McLaglen, was a well-known director, holding the distinction of directing the most episodes of *Gunsmoke* (1955) and directing episodes of such great series as *Rawhide, Have Gun Will Travel,* and *Perry Mason*. Andrew had two children, Mary and Josh, who are also instrumental figures in the movie industry. Andrew passed away on August 30, 2014. Victor's daughter, Sheila had a daughter, Gwyneth Horder-Payton, who is also a well-known television director for shows such as *Raising Cain, Bionic Woman, Battlestar Galactica, Sons of Anarchy,* and *Hawaii Five-O*.

Victor's acting role in GungaDin, with Cary Grant and Douglas Fairbanks Jr.

Victor had two brothers. His younger brother, Cyril McLaglen, first gained fame as an actor for his role in *The Call of the Road* (1920), then *Balaclava* (1928), *Underground* (1928), *Mary of Scotland* (1936), *The Plough and the Stars* (1936), and *The Black Swan* (1942). Victor's brother, Leopold McLaglen, made quite a name for himself with his expertise as a judo expert, training troops in Great Britain, India, and other countries.

Victor died of heart failure in 1959, at the age of 74, not long after appearing in a film directed by his son, Andrew V. McLaglen. He is buried at Forest Lawn Memorial Park, Glendale, CA in the Garden of Memory, Columbarium of Eternal Light. He had become a naturalized U.S. citizen.

The team knew Victor McLaglen as a very likable guy, always prepared for action, ready for a good time, and just "one of the guys." In the 1950s, the team gave Victor the title "Colonel" and from then on, he was referred to as Colonel McLaglen.

IMDb Mini Biography By: Jim Beaver jumblejim@prodigy.net

THE VICTOR McLAGLEN MOTOR CORPS – WORLD CHAMPION STUNT & DRILL TEAM (EARLY 1940S)
(L-R) Lieutenant Hap Ruggles, Corporal Joel Stewart, Private Don Olds, Corporal Rex Allen, Harland Jester, Lieutenant Ray Phillips, Private Billy Phillips, Private Jack Painter, Private Hubert Phillips, John E. Greenwood, Major Adolph Kuri, Lieutenant Colonel Roach, Major DeRush, Sergeant Dale McCollum, Frank Phillips, Ernie Eberhart, Private Edgar Martinez, Private E. L Bengston, Vern Widdup, Russ Snyder, Victor Lezell, Otto Locke, Harold McElery, H. Bailing, Jim Underwood, 1st Lieutenant Jimmy Crawford, George Alfring, Le Mabling, George Barnett, Harvey Behling

Victor McLaglen

Victor McLaglen, the equipment trailer and the team.
(Note the two men holding up the trailer –Victor was a BIG man!)

Somewhere along the line, they added a uniform that included a white shirt, black tie, and jacket. This is probably their "Class A" uniform, which was worn for special occasions. The "Class B" uniform, included a darker shirt and no jacket and was worn during their regular performances.

The team – with Victor in the middle.

Victor poses with the team – Hap Ruggles on his right and Nick DeRush on his left.

America's sweetheart, Shirley Temple, adorned the front cover of this December 1935 issue of the *Motorcyclist* Magazine. This is the official publication of the American Motorcycle Association (AMA). Inside, on page 26, is the first article about Victor's Light Horse Motorcycle Squad, as it was first known.

Interesting to note in this publication:

AMA's 1940 Safety Report

1937–AMA members traveled 69,753,000 miles
    268 accidents = one accident in 260,027 miles of travel
1938–AMA members traveled 83,567,000 miles
    309 accidents = one accident in 270,443 miles of travel
1939–AMA members traveled 99,469,000 miles
    353 accident = one accident in 281,782 miles of travel
This represented 15,351 AMA club members; an accident percentage of .0229.

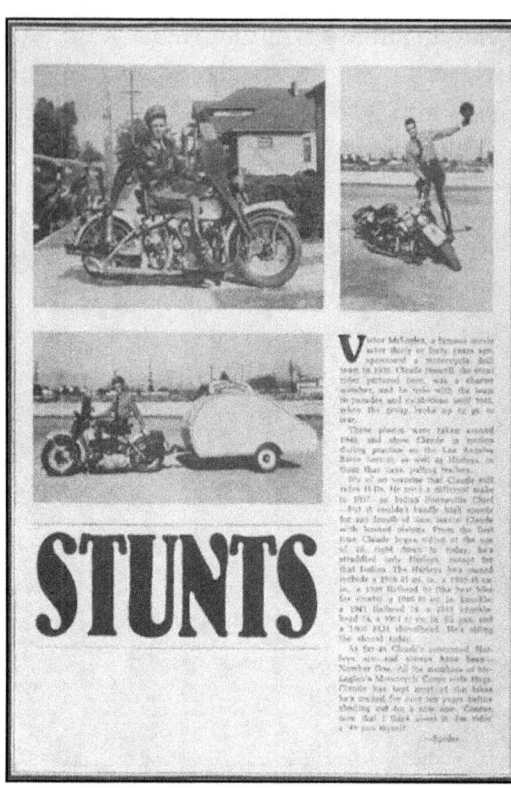

Easyrider Magazine 1978

Victor McLaglen, a famous movie actor thirty or forty years ago, sponsored a motorcycle drill team in 1936. Claude Howell, the stunt rider pictured here, was a charter member, and he rode with the team in parades and exhibitions until 1942, when the group broke up to go to war.

These photos were taken around 1940, and show Claude in motion during practice on the Los Angeles River bottom, as well as Harleys, in them thar days, pulling trailers.

It's of no surprise that Claude still rides H-Ds. He tried a different make in 1937—an Indian Bonneville Chief —but it couldn't handle high speeds for any length of time, leavin' Claude with burned pistons. From the first time Claude began riding at the age of 18, right down to today, he's straddled only Harleys, except for that Indian. The Harleys he's owned include a 1928 61 cu. in., a 1930 45 cu. in., a 1936 flathead 80 (the best bike for stunts), a 1940 61 cu. in. knuckle, a 1941 flathead 74, a 1941 knucklehead 74, a 1951 61 cu. in. EL pan, and a 1966 FLH shovelhead. He's riding the shovel today.

As far as Claude's concerned, Harleys are—and always have been—Number One. *All* the members of McLaglen's Motorcycle Corps rode Hogs. Claude has kept most of the bikes he's owned for over ten years before shelling out for a new one. 'Course, now that I think about it, I'm ridin' a '48 pan myself.

—Spider

The McLaglen team was known by a number of names in those early years: Death Dodgers, Suicide Drivers, Motorcycle Cossacks, Motorcycle Corps, Light Horse Cossacks, Victor McLaglen's Hell Drivers, and you could see them perform for only 50 cents!

The team advertises chains.

They sponsored a Halloween Dance and the admission was only 50 cents!

Two Bikes + 10 Men - No ropes!

Same stunt - Two Bikes + 12 Men

San Diego, California – Pacific Exposition May 1936

From 1935 through 1939, the Corps performed in many shows. One of their highlights took place at the San Diego Pacific Exposition, in Balboa Park, in front of 12,000 spectators. This was six months prior to their World Championship competition with the Mexico City Police Motorcycle Stunt Team.

1937 *Enthusiast* Magazine
"It takes steady nerves, trained muscles, and perfectly balanced motorcycles to do this trick."

1937 *Enthusiast* Magazine
"The Corps comes in to take a bow before the crowd at San Diego after staging a spectacular show of formation riding and stunt drills. Captain Nick DeRush in charge."

1937 *Enthusiast* Magazine
"Colonel Victor McLaglen proudly presents his Lighthorse Troop to an admiring public. Col. Vic is shown on his black charger with his famous Motor Corps in the background."

World Championship Competition
Los Angeles, California
December 6, 1936
Victor McLaglen Motor Corps (U.S.A.)

vs.

Mexico City Police "Squadron of Death" (Mexico)

The challenge was proposed by the Mexico City team leader, Commander Daniel Munoz, and accepted by VMMC Leader, Captain Nick DeRush.

They met at McLaglen Stadium on December 6th and each team had 40 minutes to perform their stunts.

Judges: **Chief of Police James E. Davis, Head Judge**
Gene Biscailuz
Raymond Cato
Jack Snyder

Master of Ceremonies: **Leo Carrillo**
Special Guest: **Renato Cantu Lara**, Mexico's new Los Angeles Consulate

The *Herald Examiner* newspaper said, "Sunday's program is the first actual competition the Mexican daredevils have engaged in on their goodwill tour of America. It is also said to be the first time they have engaged a team able to equal the famed stunts of the Squadron of Death, as the Mexico City team is known."

Officers from the Mexico City police team pose as they prepare for the big competition.

"Axle Ride"

"Swan"

"Speedo"

"Three Men Up"

"Double Side Ride"

"Totem Pole"

Building "The Pyramid"

The McLaglens win the competition!

**Before a crowd of 5,000, the final score ...
America's Victor McLaglen Motor Corps–91 points
Mexico City's "Squadron of Death"–71 points**

The McLaglens accomplished 25 stunts and won the infamous World Championship Trophy!
The local newspaper wrote, "Lou Atkinson climbed aboard the back of Lt. Jimmy Crawford's motorcycle to practice for Sunday's International motorcycle event at McLaglen Stadium. The show will be a daredevil carnival, featuring competition between motorcycle riders from America and Mexico."

"Miss Atkinson will lead a 100-piece band during the festivities."

"Double Side Ride"

"Wheelbarrow Ride"

"Upside Down"

...MBER 7, 1936.—[PART II.]

Americans Nab Cycle Honors

Mexicans Beaten in Dare-devil Carnival by 91-to-71 Score

America defeated Mexico in yesterday's international dare-devil motorcycle carnival at McLaglen Stadium, the screen star's Cossacks winning by a point score of 91 to 71 over the famed "Squadron of Death" from Mexico City.

Judges headed by Chief of Police James E. Davis were loud in their praise of the precision and exactness with which McLaglen's Cossacks went through their twenty-five neck-risking stunts.

Both teams were allowed forty minutes to spring their stunts, and both outdid all previous efforts to entertain the crowd of 5000. It was the first time the Mexicans have been beaten on their world-wide tour.

Victor McLaglen Motor Corps World Championship Trophy
December 6, 1936

Engraved on the front are the names of the Motor Corps members who competed:

Captain Truman (Nick) W. DeRush

Lieutenant Wayne Fitzgerald

Sergeant Bole Klein

Corporal Frank McCartney

Corporal Hap Ruggles

Corporal Stanley Margraves

Corporal Art Ricks

George Alfring

Getchel (Skeets) Cates

Bud Cook

Jimmy Crawford

Leslie Haserot

Ralph Manshardt

Charles Roberts

Joel Stewart

Bill Swan

Alvin Thompson

Years later, the trophy was found in a deceased member's garage. Tom and Barbara Scott of Anaheim-Fullerton Harley-Davidson restored it and it was on display in their store for several years. In 2012, Mark Ruffalo of California Harley-Davidson asked if it could be moved to his Harley shop in Harbor City, California. It is now on display there for everyone to see.

Pyramid
Top: Jim Crawford
Under him: Dale McCullum, Joel Stewart
Motormen: Ray Phillips, Hap Ruggles
Rear: Ernie Eberhardt

The Flying Trapeze
Top Center: Hap Ruggles
Ends: Ernie Aguire, Jimmy Crawford
Driving: Wayne Fitzgerald

On Tour for the First Time

In 1937, plans were made and the team prepared for their first 10-day tour:
Nevada • Utah • Idaho • Oregon

The team traveled by Union Pacific train and used two cars: a boxcar for the motorcycles and equipment, and a pullman for themselves. They departed from Los Angeles, CA and the first stop was Las Vegas, NV.

The guys visited motorcycle dealers in every city where they stopped and the dealers were very generous in helping make the entire trip a success.

In addition, police escorts were provided in every city. The police assisted the team from the time they rolled out of the boxcar to the time they rolled back in, ready to roll to the next stop.

The Schedule

A	Los Angeles, CA	June 4
B	Las Vegas, NV	June 4
C	Salt Lake City, UT	June 5
D	Pocatello, ID	June 6
E	Boise, ID	June 7
F	Baker City, OR	June 8
G	Portland, OR	June 9-13

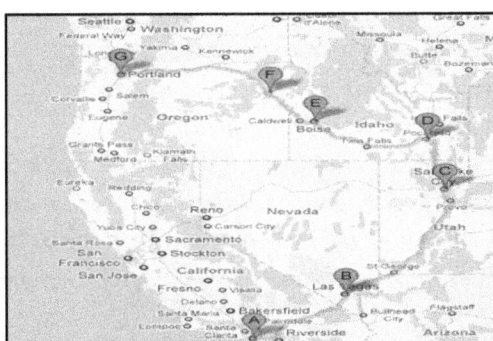

Motorcycles are unloaded from the train.

Las Vegas, Nevada — June 4, 1937

The team arrived in Las Vegas to kick off their first tour. They had only one evening show before they had to leave for Salt Lake City, UT. It was a very successful one.

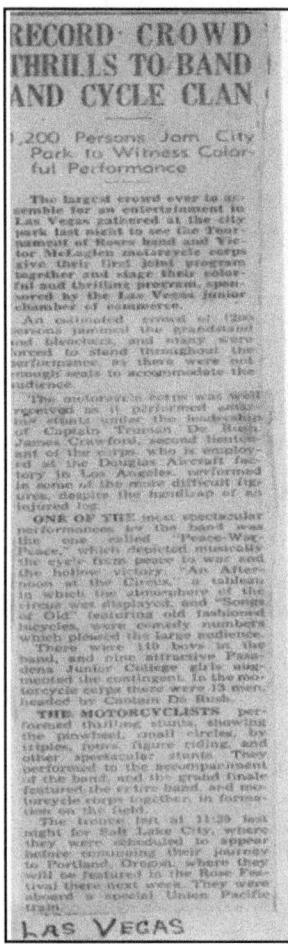

1,200 Persons Jam City Park to Witness Colorful Performance

The largest crowd ever to assemble for an entertainment in Las Vegas gathered at the city park last night to see the Tournament of Roses band and Victor McLaglen Motorcycle Corps give their first joint program together and stage their colorful and thrilling program, sponsored by the Las Vegas Junior Chamber of Commerce.

An estimated crowd of 1,200 persons jammed the grandstand and bleachers, and many were forced to stand throughout the performance as there were not enough seats to accommodate the audience.

The Motorcycle Corps was well received as it performed amazing stunts under the leadership of Captain Truman De Rush. James Crawford, second lieutenant of the corps, who is employed at the Douglas Aircraft factory in Los Angeles, performed in some of the more difficult figures, despite the handicap of an injured leg.

The motorcyclists performed thrilling stunts, showing the pinwheel, small circles, by triples, fours, figure riding, and other spectacular stunts. They performed to the accompaniment of the band and the grand finale featured the entire band and Motorcycle Corps together in formation on the field.

The troupe left at 11:35 last night for Salt Lake City, where they were scheduled to appear before continuing their journey to Portland, Oregon, where they will be featured in the Rose Festival there next week. They were aboard a special Union Pacific train.

"Captain Truman DeRush, head of the Victor McLaglen Motorcycle Corps team, showing one of his stunts, at 40 miles an hour. This is one of the many antics to be displayed in the city park Friday night at 8 o'clock by the 14 members on their motorcycles. The Tournament of Roses band of 115 members and nine beautiful Pasadena Junior College girls will be featured in the program, sponsored by the Las Vegas Junior Chamber of Commerce."

Salt Lake City, Utah — June 5, 1937

The train pulled into Salt Lake City on June 5, 1937. After unloading their motorcycles, the men immediately started entertaining the public with a spontaneous performance. This was followed by a parade performance and then two shows at 2:30 and 8:00 p.m.

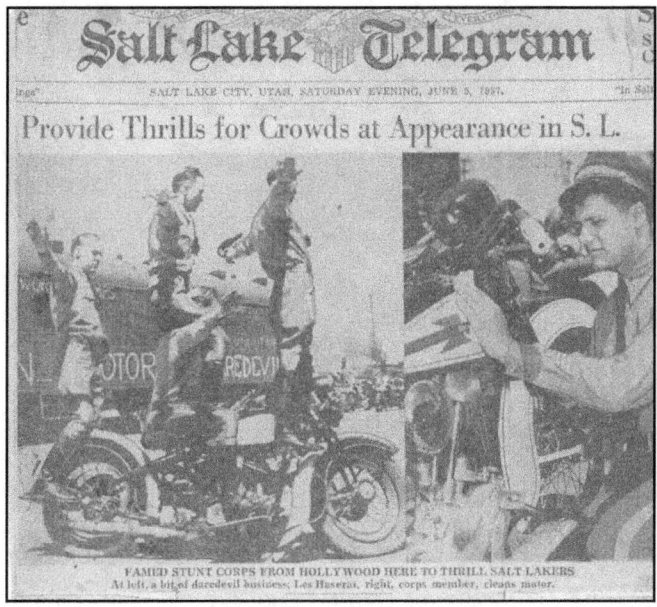

"At left, a bit of daredevil business. At right, Les Haserot, cleans his motor."

First, the parade thru town.

Then a stop at the local Harley dealer.

Pocatello, Idaho – June 6, 1937

The team made a stop in Pocatello, Idaho. The show was at the Idaho Southern Stadium on June 6, 1937 at 3:00 pm.

The admission was only 40 cents for adults and 25 cents for children!

Victor McLaglen Motor Corps stages their "V" formation.

Boise, Idaho – June 7, 1937

Arriving in Boise, Idaho, Monday afternoon June 7, they did what they like to do best, an impromptu show down Capitol Boulevard near Julia Davis Park with hundreds of Boiseans following them. By the time they reached their destination, approximately 1,000 people had gathered. They were scheduled to perform at the Idaho penitentiary later that evening. The picture below was taken with some members of the Boise Police Department.

Dr. M. Sutcliffe, activity director and master of ceremonies of the corps, commenting on the Corps' visit declared, "The boys have absolutely gone wild over Idaho, if you don't mind the slang. Boise is the first city we have visited that the boys really liked. After cruising around town sightseeing for hours today and being treated with the utmost courtesy by everyone, they couldn't help pleading for more time. I'm sure they will remember Boise as one of the best cities ever."

They were scheduled to leave Boise at 9:00 p.m. Monday night, but the guys wanted to see more of Boise. So Joel Priest, Idaho General Agent of the Union Pacific, agreed to hold up their train until 1:00AM. Tuesday morning. They then departed for Baker, Oregon, a little late, but that was OK.

Idaho State Penitentiary – June 7, 1937

The performance at the Idaho State Penitentiary was the first of its kind ever held within prison walls. For some of the inmates, it was the first time they had ever even seen a motorcycle! After the stunt show, a couple of the Motor Corps guys played in the prison band; one playing drums while another did his "Riverboat Shuffle" dance.

After everything was over, the inmates wanted a picture taken with the Corps, so they gathered around with the warden sitting on the motorcycle in front.

Below are some of the stunts the team performed inside the prison walls.

The 1936 version of their "one-legged Ride"

"Swan"
Joel Stewart (Rear)
Jimmy Crawford (Up)
Hap Ruggles (Driving)

"Shoulder Stand"

More stunts inside the prison walls

"2-Motor Pyramid"

"Totem Pole"

Just doing a few drill maneuvers to warm up.

Baker City, Oregon – June 8, 1937

The Baker Chamber of Commerce arranged for the Pasadena Tournament of Roses Band and the Victor McLaglen Motor Corps to stop in Baker, enroute to the Portland Rose Festival. So, on June 8, 1937, they arrived by train and performed at 5:30PM in the street parade and then in an 8:30PM exhibition at the Baker Municipal Athletic Field.

Admission was 55 cents and the money went to pay for the city's new flood lights. According to the local newspaper, "The motorcycle squadron crashed wooden barriers, executed daring stunts and cavorted about the arena with two to seven men on a machine in acrobatic array."

The Baker City directors said that June 8th was one of the biggest days Baker City had seen in years.

There were more than 3,000 people at this performance who paid 55 cents for admission!

Victor McLaglen Motorcycle Corps - 15 Riders

—and—

Pasadena Tournament of Roses Band - 100 Pieces

• •

MOTORCYCLE RODEO AND

BAND CONCERT

BAKER "DEMOCRAT"

• •

BAKER BALL PARK UNDER THE NEW FLOOD LIGHTS

• •

Tuesday Evening, June 8, at 8:30

Admission - - - - - - - - - - - - 55c
Including the Tax

Traveling by Special Train—Enroute to the Portland Rose Festival

Portland, Oregon – June 9-13, 1937

An Oregon newspaper reported, "Victor McLaglen, movie star, will be honorary grand marshal of the Portland Rose Festival floral parade and will appear personally with his motorcycle daredevils at each of the big night shows at the Multnomah Stadium, during the coming festival, according to a telegram received yesterday by **E.A. Burkitt**, president of the Festival Association." It was also noted that the team from Mexico had performed in Portland at the Northwest Police Convention the year before, and the Portland audience was looking forward to the thrills the Hollywood daredevils would give them.

Everyone arrived back in Los Angeles in pretty good shape after a very successful tour. Only four injuries were reported: Stan Gainer, Nick DeRush, Jim Crawford, and Hap Ruggles and all injuries were minor. The boys had a great time but it was now time to return home and their "regular" jobs!

Driver: Hap Ruggles
Front: Les Haserot
Back: John Crawford

Rose Festival Parade

"Defeating the world champion Mexican team in 1936, Victor McLaglen's Corps leads the world in motor stunts. Fourteen men on one motorcycle, one of the 38 different tricks which seem impossible, accomplished only in McLaglen's Corps."

Stockton, California — August 29, 1937

Sacramento Bee, "Stockton, CA, hosted the San Joaquin County Fair in August 1937. The "Death Dodgers" as they were called, performed on the 29th to a record crowd. Later they traveled to Sacramento for the California State Fair."

Five Motorcycle Experts Escape Injury In Mishap

Record Grandstand Crowd Sees Riders Spill On Muddy Racetrack

Grandstand attendants at the California State Fair last night were shouting, "Standing room only," almost an hour before the fireworks and entertainment were scheduled to start.

An American Legion Day crowd quickly filled all the grandstand seats, then packed the space extending from the race track rail to the private boxes to hit an entertainment attendance mark of more than 12,000.

Things didn't always go perfectly, however!

Overdose Of Wetting

One section of the race track which had received an overdose of the nightly wetting down marred the performance of twelve of Victor McLaglen's Motorcycle Corps under the direction of Captain Truman De Rush, but the show presented by the corps brought applause and cheers from the spectators.

Weaving an intricate pattern of red and green traced through the darkness only by the colored lights on the machines, the corps ran into difficulty in an early stage of the maneuvers.

Captain Skids

Captain De Rush skidded on a muddy part of the track and four of the machines ran against each other, turning on their sides. A few slight bruises resulted, but the corps continued the drill after a short delay.

Standing on the seats, pyramiding three high, balancing on one foot, and riding on the handlebars, the corps members sped up and down the track in a trick riding exhibition that showed the result of years of practice.

The corps will present other performances during the fair.

SACRAMENTO BEE

American Motorcycle Association (AMA)

The Motor Corps first became affiliated with the AMA in 1939 when they won their first "Safety Award." There were 496 clubs enrolled in the 2nd Annual Nationwide Safety campaign, conducted by the AMA, and 296 clubs went through the entire year of 1938 without a single reportable accident.

In 1991, Victor McLaglen himself was inducted into the AMA Hall of Fame as a "Motorcycle Drill Team Pioneer."

1939 AMA Safety Awards "Victor McLaglen Motor Corps, national champion club for 1939, together with some of their many and magnificent trophies won through their ability to drill, stunt, and cooperate with police and civic authorities." - March 1940 AMA magazine

Inglewood High School, Inglewood, California 1938

Flaming Twin Tunnels

The flaming twin tunnels is a pretty spectacular stunt, performed in the late 1930s. Two 15 foot long tunnels were set on fire. Then Hap Ruggles would blast through one and Bill Swan through the other at the same time.

This stunt is particularly dangerous because due to lack of oxygen, the fire tends to snuff out the engine activity in the middle of the tunnel leaving the rider right in the middle of all the flames.

Another particularly dangerous stunt is this Human Tunnel. Snagging someone's clothing or clipping their legs when the rider would race through would cause a huge problem!

Santa Anita 1939
"Human Tunnel"

The team led the Santa Claus Lane Parade in Hollywood, California, for many years. The parade originally started in 1928 with just Santa Claus and actress Janette Loff, then ceased operations from 1942 to 1944 due to World War II. It started up again in 1945.

By 1978, the parade had been renamed the Hollywood Christmas Parade in order to attract more celebrities and was broadcast locally on television. In 2007, it changed its name again to the Hollywood Santa Parade.

Member Edwin Phillips recalled that one year after the parade the team went to Palm Springs to do stunts between the races at the Sport Car Races. Then Charles Farrell, who was an actor in the 1920s thru the 1930s, had three of the guys over to his Swim & Racquet Club afterwards for "eats and drinks". Ed said, "he'd also invited the star who played Hopalong Cassidy (William Boyd), which made his girlfriend quite angry as he "shot the bull" with us for an hour." Sounds familiar. That's our Motor Corps!

The Original Equipment Trailer

Nobody seems to know whatever happened to the equipment trailer, but it was used from the beginning of the team's existence until sometime in the 1950s. As you can see, fittingly, it was pulled by a team member and his stunt bike!

Equipment trailer driven by Claude (Chuck) Howell.

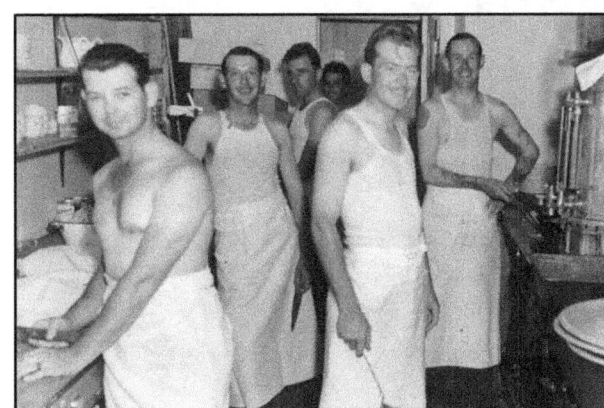

Can you identify these guys? Probably from the tour they took in the late 1930s. If you can identify them send a note to info@thevmmc.com

Believe It or Not – 1936
"All on one" Motorcycle Stunt

By the end of 1939, the team was only four years old and they were performing some pretty fantastic stunts:
- Bill Swan barreling thru fire tunnels.
- Les Haserott hanging onto a rope while standing on a turfboard sliding behind a motorcycle going 40 mph.
- Hap Ruggles piling everyone onto one moving motorcycle and setting a record with Ripley's Believe it Or Not.

The first time they piled everyone onto one motorcycle was in 1936 when fourteen men were stacked on the bike. That was 2,403 pounds on a 600 pound Harley-Davidson motorcycle. It was listed in Ripley's Believe It or Not and Baldwin-Duckworth Chain Corporation decided to use their stunt for a little advertising.

I read that the team got the idea of piling everyone on the motorcycles from watching street cars during rush hour! This was one of the stunts they accomplished when practicing for the competition against the Mexico City stunt team in 1936 and they continued this through August 1939, often times making it their grand entrance into the show arena. It made a pretty spectacular entry, which immediately got everyone's attention.

The Motor Corps was very busy in those early years. They were on television and newspaper news regularly, particularly in the Los Angeles, CA area. Often, they were even in the Movietone news, which was early newsreel with sound.

Three sets of "3-Man Up" for Movietone News.

"Double Floorboard Ride with a Headstand"
Right: Joel Stewart, Left: Hap Ruggles,
Upside down: Jim Crawford, Driver: W. Fitzgerald

Giant "6-Motor Pyramid"

Show Schedule – 1936-1940

TOWN	DATE	WHO FOR	Attendance
	1936		
Long Beach	May	Moto-Speedway	3,200
Monterey Park	May (3 days)	Chamber of Commerce	7,500
San Diego	May	World's Fair	8,500
Santa Ana	June	Promoters	6,800
Ventura	Oct.	Promoters	4,000
Brawley	Oct.	Promoters	5,200
Whittier	Oct.	State of Calif.	600
Los Angeles	Nov.	White Sox Park	3,500
Los Angeles	Nov.	Wrigley Field	9,700
Los Angeles	Dec.	(Met Mexican Police in contest. Score Mex. 71, VMMC 91)	7,800
Los Angeles	Dec.	Fox Movietone News	
Hollywood	Dec.	Santa Claus Lane P'de (2 nights)	197,000
	1937		
Pasadena	Jan.	Tournament Roses	850,000
Los Angeles	Jan.	Universal News	
Long Beach	Feb.	C. of C.	160,000
San Bernardino	Mar.	Promoters	5,000
Los Angeles	Mar.	Wrigley Field (2 days)	48,000
Los Angeles	Sept.	National Air Races	180,000
Los Angeles	???	Electrical Parade (Boulder Dam)	270,000
Long Beach	April	Promoters	6,500
Los Angeles	April	Police Show, Coliseum	87,000
Santa Monica	May	Police Dept.	9,000
Las Vegas, Nev.	June	Chamber of Commerce	11,000
Salt Lake City	June	Chamber of Commerce	7,500
Pocatello, Idaho	June	20-30 Club	4,700
Boise, Idaho	June	Police Dept.	5,700
Pendleton, Ore.	June	Round Up Association	126,000
Baker, Ore.	June	Oregon State Patrol	3,800
Portland	June	Rose Festival Asso. (4 days)	840,000
San Francisco	June	Keazer Stadium	15,000
Los Angeles	June	Knights of Columbus	62,000
Los Angeles	July	American Legion	82,000
Los Angeles	July	Jam Handy Productions (for Chevrolet Motor Co.)	
Los Angeles	Aug.	Gilmore Stadium (Midget Races)	18,000
Los Angeles	Aug.	Shriners	12,000
Stockton	Aug.	San Joaquin C'nty Fair	46,000
Sacramento	Sept.	State Fair (2 days)	120,000
Pasadena	Sept.	B.P.O.E. (Rose Bowl)	75,000
Los Angeles	Oct.	Promoters (Gilmore)	2,000
Los Angeles	Nov.	Police (Thanksgiving Benefit)	11,000
Hollywood	Dec.	Santa Claus Lane P'de	60,000
	1938		
Pasadena	Jan.	Rose Parade and Rose Bowl	900,000
Los Angeles	July	Am. Legion (Coliseum)	73,000
Los Angeles	July	Rodeo, Thrill Circus	65,000
Van Nuys	July	State, McKinley Home	350
Los Angeles	Sept.	Wrigley Field, Circus	23,000
Los Angeles	Oct.	State Hi-Way Patrol	4,000
Montebello	Oct.	State Hi-Way Patrol	1,000
Inglewood	Oct.	Chamber of Commerce	1,800
Reno, Nev.	Nov.	Chamber of Commerce	3,500
Los Angeles	Dec.	Police Xmas Benefit	76,000
	1939		
Pasadena	Jan.	Rose Parade and Rose Bowl	900,400
Santa Anita	July	Sheriff's Barbecue	35,000
Van Nuys	Aug.	Hugh Herbert Rodeo	4,000
Los Angeles	July	Police Show (Coliseum) (3 days)	86,000
Los Angeles	June	Hal Roach Show	400
Los Angeles	Oct.	Thanksgiving Show	5,700
Glendale	Feb.	Scots Day	???????
Los Angeles	Mar.	Promoters (White Sox)	3,500
Los Angeles	June	Promoters (Coliseum) Rodeo	18,000
Pasadena	July	Elks Show (Rose Bowl)	?????
Long Beach	Aug.	City (Parade)	85,000
Los Angeles	Dec.	Xmas Benefit (City)	5,000
	1940		
Pasadena	Jan.	Rose Parade and Rose Bowl	100,000
Los Angeles	Feb.	Arturo Godoy	100
Los Angeles	Mar.	Promoter	
San Bernardino	Mar.	Promoter	

1940 –1949

The 1940s were difficult years for everyone. World War II had been escalating for quite some time and the United States finally joined the effort. This meant that many of the members went off to do their patriotic duty and the Motor Corps was left with not enough men to put on a show. After the war ended in 1945, however, the men returned and the team started performing again.

In 1940, the team was busy performing in lots of shows and parades, and hosting their annual banquet. They ended 1940 with a November 30th **Christmas Holiday Parade**, which was held in downtown Los Angeles, CA. This seven-mile long parade was followed by the "Festival of Bands" event, with 67 various musical acts competing.

November 22, 1940, the Motor Corps led the Christmas parade in Long Beach, California. I could only I.D. Nick DeRush leading and James Parson 2nd row on left

In trying to determine the year this bottom picture was taken, I guessed that it was 1940, the same as the picture above.

To verify, I consulted Bruce Chubbuck. Bruce, former owner of Chubbuck's Harley-Davidson dealership in Pasadena, California and retired member of the Motor Corps, who really knows his motorcycles.

Bruce said, *"The leader is riding a 1941 Harley. I noticed the handlebars are not H-D and thought that they were Flanders bars. I called John Flanders to see when his dad started manufacturing the rubber mounted riser bars. John said that he started in the garage in late 1945. I was looking the cars over and figured that the light gray parked car was a 1940 Chrysler sedan and the dark car could been 1940ish General Motors. The car that you can only see the front wheel at the intersection is a 1941 Ford and there is another one in the parking lot facing out. Then I noticed the license plate on the dark car. It is orange with rounded corners, done only in 1940. In 1941 there was a black strip that went across the top that had California and the year. In 1942 it was orange. In '43, '44 and '45, there was a small plate that covered the year. In 1946, a new black plate with white numbers. So in my opinion, the year of the show was late 1940, as the 1941 cars and Harley's came out in the late summer of 1940."*

Thanks, Bruce. That was interesting.

New Year's Eve 1940 found the team in Santa Ana at the Santa Ana Frolic, where they had won the grand sweepstakes prize the previous year. This event was attended by 65,000 spectators.

Early the next morning, they went to Pasadena, California, where their job was to "spot the floats" for the Rose Parade and ensure the parade did not stop for any reason. This was a tradition that they carried on for the next five years.

In November 1941, they showed their skills at the All Western Band Review in Long Beach, California. They were awarded this Certificate of Appreciation by the City of Long Beach for entertaining approximately 250,000 residents and visitors.

Harlan Jester & Jim Underwood having fun!

"2-Motor 9-Man Pyramid": Captain Nick DeRush straddling the front on the two bikes.

The Victor McLaglen Motor Corps was awarded first place in the 1939 AMA National Club Contest, as shown in the April, 1940 *Enthusiast* Magazine.

ENTHUSIAST Magazine, April 1940
The Motor Corps had a four-page spread and made it on the cover of this February 1949 *Enthusiast* Magazine, shown on the following pages.

On August 16, 1940, the Motor Corps performed to an audience of 75,000 guests at the Los Angeles Coliseum. The event, entitled *A Salute to America*, was hosted by the Los Angeles Police Relief Association and directed by Sergeant Jack Guyot of the Los Angeles Police Department.

Several drum and bugle drill teams and lots of well-known celebrities were on hand to participate in this 6th Annual Police Show. Some of these celebrities included Jack Benny and Rochester, Mickey Rooney, Gene Autry, Andy Devine, Edward Arnold, Jack Carson, Humphrey Bogart, and Leo Carollo.

1. Jack Benny
2. Gene Autrey
3. Muriel Angelus
4. Arthur Lake (Dagwood)
5. Penny Singleton (Blondie)
6. Al Pearce
7. Vera Vague

Hap Ruggles was still writing much of the Motor Corps' publicity, as evidenced in this 1941 *Enthusiast* entry.

JULY, 1941   17

Three 61 OHV Harley-Davidson fans from Eugene, Oregon. Left to right are: Hubert Hill, Ernie Louning and Clint Smith.

big race and have all of you motorcycle riders down here to have a good time. The club members decided to get new blue and white uniforms this year. Then we are going to go out after some of those trophies we have been reading and hearing so much about. Our club would like very much to have other clubs write to us, and let us know what they are doing. Just mail your letters to Archie H. Dedman, Secretary, Lexington Eagles, 367 East Main St., Lexington, Kentucky. So long, and hope to see you soon, if not personally, at least in the mailbox."
Archie H. Dedman, Secretary.

* * *

EASTON MCY. CLUB, Easton, Pa.—"The T. T. race originally scheduled for June 8 will now be held on July 13. Our T. T. track is located at Riviere, 16 miles south of our city on Route 611. We hope it will be a swell day and that many of your ENTHUSIAST readers in our part of the country will bring your buddy or your girl friend, husband, sweetheart or wife and come and have a good time. On May 24 we had a hare and hound chase, in which 15 members and riders took part. It was 24 miles of rough, uphill and down dale going, and when it was all over, they finished as follows: Don Shafer, Bill Diehl, Lew Corriere, George Kleckner, Earland Marx, George Kocher, Frank Geagan, Fred Kocher." *Fred Kocher.*

* * *

VICTOR McLAGLEN MCY. CORPS, Los Angeles, Calif.—"Well, Hollister and the District 36 Gypsy Tour and Rally have come and gone, and through this column our gang wants to thank all of the Northern California riders, the clubs, dealers, officials and the Hollister folks, for it was indeed a pleasure for us to travel the great distance up there and put on our show and to be received with such an ovation. This rally was the best-handled affair that we believe we have ever attended. To all the committees, especially George Harris, Chet Billings, Pop Cohen, Dud Perkins, and the Bay City Club, we salute you. May next year's rally be as good as this one—it can't be better, the way everybody worked.

"A word to Capt. Fred Marshall and his boys who drove from Portland, Oregon, to watch us work. We certainly enjoyed their companionship. The Portland Police Drill Team are an expert aggregation and we were glad we had a chance to be with them. A large bouquet of orchids to the Renard Sisters, who put on a real bunch of stunts at the rally. Hollister will always remain one of our most pleasant memories." *Hap Ruggles.*

* * *

VIKING MCY. CLUB, Lake Charles, La.—"We haven't reported our news for a long time—nevertheless we've been very busy. This time we want to submit a short resume of our activities so far this year. In March we subsidized the DeRidder Ramblers as a branch of our club and had an all day party to celebrate the union and two weeks later they came to Lake Charles where we had a 'Weenie

This photo of Rita Hayworth, Betty Grable, and some of the team was shown on the front cover of the November 1941 *Enthusiast* magazine. Just look at the smiles on those guys.

The team poses for a publicity picture.

Victor's Light Horse Drill Team was still performing and putting on great shows around California and in 1941, they performed along with the Motor Corps, at a charity event honoring the late Howard Jones, football coach at the University of Southern California, who died at age 55. Howard Jones was a member of the College Football Hall of Fame's inaugural class of inductees in 1951. The show paid tribute to his memory and the Motor Corps performed in front of an audience of 50,000 fans at the Los Angeles Coliseum. This event starred three hours of big name entertainment. It was the first event to be held in the Coliseum since Jones' death. Gloria Jean sang the Star-Spangled Banner, and other famous celebrities participated, such as Mickey Rooney, Susanna Foster, Andy Devine, Charles (Buddy) Rogers, Ann Miller, Borrah Minnevitch, and the Harmonica Rascals. Red Skelton was Master of Ceremonies.

According to the newspaper account, "Only mishap of the evening occurred during stunting by two members of the Victor McLaglen Motor Corps. Standing upside down on his hands, Wayne Dunham slipped from the shoulders of Hap Ruggles, who was driving, and was carried from the field with a fractured arm."

January 1942 "Trophy Dinner"
Victor McLaglen Sports Center
Hubie Phillips with a big smile on the right front.

1949 Annual Awards Banquet
Victor and Mrs. McLaglen with Capt. DeRush
in front.

The 1940s were a difficult time. The members did what they could to support the troops, such as perform at USO shows at the army camps, cut back on drills to conserve rubber, and pay their dues to the club in defense stamps. Some of the team members were active in the military and others were busy helping in other ways with the war efforts. So, with the onset of World War II, the Corps disbanded temporarily until the war was over, the boys came home and all was right with the world again.

Enthusiast, June 1945

"Meet John Doe" Movie

In 1941, the Motor Corps performed motorcycle riding drills for a Warner Brothers movie called *"Meet John Doe."* This comedy drama, starring Gary Cooper, Barbara Stanwick, and Walter Brennan, was nominated for an Academy Award for Best Story. You may want to rent the movie, so you can view the impressive performances by the drill team.

Hubie Phillips said, "All we got was $35 and a cold chicken box lunch" for their part in the movie! (But I'll bet they had fun doing it.)

Practicing their 4-Way Crossover at Riviera Polo Grounds for "Meet John Doe" movie

The team lines up at the Riviera Club for a photo.

Marguerite Nichols, a silent film actress in the early 1900s, married Hal Roach, movie producer and director.

Here she is being honored with the title of Lieutenant Colonel of the Victor McLaglen Ladies Troop.

She died a year later on March 17, 1941 from pneumonia.

Mrs Arturo Godoy, Victor, Mrs Hal Roach and Arturo Godoy, heavyweight boxer from Arg.

Colonel Victor McLaglen
invites you to attend the
INSTALLATION CEREMONY
given in honor of
Mrs. Hal Roach
who will be appointed
Honorary Lieutenant Colonel
of the
VICTOR McLAGLEN LADIES TROOPS
at the Light Horse Headquarters
off Riverside Dr. between Los Feliz and Glendale Blvds.
Thursday, April the twenty-seventh
Eight o'clock p.m.

In front are: Sergeant McCollum, left, Lieutenant Crawford, Lieutenant Colonel Mrs. Hal Roach, Captain DeRush, Lieutenant Ruggles and Sergeant Phillips.

After WWII, the Motor Corps started performing full-force again. *Enthusiast* magazine, Feb. 1949

McLaglen Motorcycle Corps ROLLS AGAIN

THE Corps is back in the saddle again —rolling along to fresh achievements and adding an exciting new chapter to an already colorful history. Inactive during the war years, the Corps is operating once more with greater flash, greater splendor and new equipment.

The Corps still carries the original name it started out with, but today, only two of the charter members are still in the organization — Major Nick DeRush and Captain Hap Ruggles. And the present sponsor is the Harley-Davidson dealer of Los Angeles, Rich Budelier.

In 1935 the Corps was formed by DeRush and Ruggles. Frank McCartney, another well-known West Coast motorcycle figure, gave them a hand in getting started. Soon Victor McLaglen, the rugged movie star, incorporated the group as a unit into his McLaglen Lighthorse Troop, and the Corps was on its way. Its reputation grew swiftly. It traveled up and down the Coast thrilling spectators by the thousands. The members practiced hard and long, and gradually added new stunts and maneuvers to their bag of tricks.

When the Corps first began, it served merely as an escort at smaller functions while it gained experience, but it wasn't too long before the boys were able to put on an entire show. The demand for their services grew, and soon they were appearing in San Francisco, at the San Diego Fair, at Hollywood, the Rose Bowl and even beyond the borders of their native

1. This fancy stunt is called "The Belt Hold On." Bill Lewis holds the belts of Fenton and Allum. Charles Griggs is in front, Greenwood in back and Hap Ruggles is pilot. 2. McLaglen Corps, on black and white Harley-Davidsons, leads the "All Western Band Review" parade at Long Beach. 3. Bengston pushes up Ray Phillips.

McLaglen Motorcycle Corps Rolls Again (Cont'd)

state. Each succeeding year saw the Corps improve and expand its show. The constant practice brought the members always a little closer to that perfection of rhythm and timing which they already possessed to an unusual degree. It might be noted in passing, that all during the life of the McLaglen Motorcycle Corps, the personnel has relied on Harley-Davidsons to help them perform their maneuvers.

Among highlights of those early years were their appearances at the world-famous Rose Bowl Parade; at the great Electrical Pageant celebrating the opening of Boulder Dam; at the Los Angeles Policemen's Benefit Show before 60,000 fans, and their historic performance when they were pitted against the famed Mexico City Police Stunt Team, which had built an enviable record by its stunts, also performed on Harley-Davidson motorcycles. The Mexicans arrived in California in 1936 on an extended goodwill

1. The trim uniforms of the Corps are shown to good advantage in the upper photo. Major DeRush is shown on the Harley-Davidson. In front are Lieutenant Ray Phillips (left) and Captain Hap Ruggles. 2. "Two Man Head Stand." Left to right are Costa, Bettleman, Allum and DeRush. 3. and 4. Two more views of the famous McLaglen Corps. Motorcycling needs more such organizations. 5. Ray Phillips walking completely around his moving Harley-Davidson — "no hands."

McLaglen Motorcycle Corps Rolls Again (Cont'd)

THE ENTHUSIAST

tour. Their great reputation as champion stunt artists had preceded them, and when they had arrived, the McLaglen Corps promptly issued a friendly challenge. The visitors smiled and accepted with pleasure.

It was an exciting day when the two organizations met. The stands were packed! For hours the Mexicans and the McLaglenites thrilled the crowd with their difficult stunts and complicated maneuvers. Points were awarded for balance, speed, falls and ability in performing stunts. When the afternoon was over, the McLaglen Corps emerged as victors by a score of 91 to 72. It was indeed a day DeRush and Ruggles will never forget, and that performance is now part of the tradition of the Corps.

With the reorganization of the Corps following World

1. and 2. Photographer Hyman Fink of Photoplay Magazine got these two shots on the night the McLaglen Corps led the Santa Claus Parade. In the first photo are Arthur Lake and Penny Singleton of the movies with Eastin (left) and DeRush. In the other shot, Ralph Edwards, of radio fame, gives the boys a laugh. 3. "Three Of A Kind" — Ray Phillips (front) Bengston and Greenwood. 4. Ray Phillips does a difficult jump from rear stand to seat. 5. "The Horse" — Ed Phillips up, and Harold Bettleman at the handlebars.

War II, the members blossomed out with late model black and white Harley-Davidsons and new blue and gold uniforms, Eisenhower jackets, gold-trimmed pockets, shoulder patches, wings on each lapel, and cadet style caps with gold or silver band on the bill of the cap, depending on the rank of the

McLaglen Motorcycle Corps Rolls Again (Cont'd)

February, 1949

wearer. A white scarf is also worn with the uniform. Breeches are dark blue with gold stripes. On drills and parades, the boys wear chromed helmets. The Harley-Davidsons are equipped with wheel lights, since half of the drills are done in darkness.

The Corps holds at least six practice sessions each month, in addition to its parades and shows. At the present time, the following members belong to the organization: Nick DeRush, Hap Ruggles, Ray Phillips, Otto Locke, John Greenwood, Sidney Allen, James Fenton, Frank Blaesser, Harold Bettleman, Virgil Ervin, Sterling Eastin, Edward Bengston, Harvey Behling, James Parsons, Fernando Palomarez, William Allum, Ken Rayzor, Stanley Kemp, Don Bignell, LeVern Teg-

(Please turn to Page 22)

1. This stunt is called a "Ladder Head Stand." John Greenwood is in front, Sterling Eastin is at the controls, Lawrence Benton is at the rear and Leo Costa is upside down. 2. "Three High." Costa at the bars, Benton and Ed Phillips on top. In the rear is Eastin. 3. and 4. The wonderful balancing qualities of the Corps' Harley-Davidsons are demonstrated by Greenwood (top) and Ray Phillips. 5. Col. Kuri of The McLaglen Lighthorse Troop receives trophy from American Legion. Ruggles and DeRush in background. Braun Photo.

McLaglen Motorcycle Corps Rolls Again (Cont'd)

(From article on previous page)
LaVern Tegland, Rolls Butler, Don Block, Phil Erickson, Bob Hasselbring, Edwin Phillips, William Lewis, Pete Cromer, Lawrence Benton, Lorin Haynes, Elmo Dyerly, Charles Griggs, Vern Widdup, and Leo Costa. They come from all walks of life, but they have one thing in common – enthusiasm, plus a special skill when it comes to handling a motorcycle.

Among recent highlights in the McLaglen Corps' history are the following parades: Santa Claus in Hollywood, March of Dimes, Western Band Review, American Legion, Santa Ana Fun Frolic, Professional Football Opening, numerous charity appearances, and, of course, the most famous of all – the Tournament of Roses Parade. Last fall, when the presidential candidates of both political parties appeared in Los Angeles, the Corps was given a few minutes to put on several of their choice stunts. (That would have been Harry S. Truman and Thomas E. Dewey.)

The spectacular Santa Claus Parade and the colorful Rose Parade give the McLaglen Corps the most strenuous workouts. The night that Santa Claus makes his first triumphant ride down Hollywood Boulevard, the Corps has five minutes to do some of its special drills before the parade "kicks off." Hollywood Boulevard is "all theirs" and the hundreds of thousands lining the Boulevard get a real thrill watching the Corps in action. "And we're thrilled too," says Captain Ruggles. "Who wouldn't be, in front of those hundreds of thousands?"

The parade this year was super – filled with beautiful floats – 20 bands – 300 horses with silver saddles and equipment and, of course, headed by Santa Claus and his reindeer. Movie stars twinkle brilliantly throughout the time of the parade and blonde Doris Day riding alongside Mr. Claus –the lucky guy!

The Corps members go into action at 5:00AM, at Pasadena, on the memorable day of the Tournament of Roses. This year marked their eighth appearance in this great Rose Parade. Incidentally, theirs is the only motorcycle group to work in this parade.

"No stunts on a day like this for the Corps," says Captain Ruggles. "Our job is to escort and to patrol. We are charged with the responsibility of seeing that the floats are in their proper places, and the bands, horse troops and all the other parade aides are in their designated spots. A mountain of pre-parade details to be ironed out is really something to cause despair and confusion, but we're able to handle our job smoothly, thanks to the splendid cooperation we get from all the parade officials and participants. Once the colorful spectacle gets under way, our Corps members patrol up and down the line of march, carefully watching the floats. In case of a breakdown, the crippled float is quickly removed to a side street and the colorful parade moves on without an interruption".

"We're always ready for trouble," remarks Captain Hap Ruggles, "and as a result, it's never nearly as bad as we anticipate. Plenty of preparation beforehand is our strongest weapon."

After more than a dozen years of stunting, drilling and escorting, it might be expected that the McLaglenites have received many tributes, and they have. The trophy case in their clubroom at 4408 West Jefferson Boulevard is crowded with cups and banners won over the years. In

McLaglen Motorcycle Corps Rolls Again (Cont'd)

1939, the McLaglen Corps won the American Motorcycle Association National, Club Activity Contest – the highest honor in American motorcycling circles. Fame has come to the Corps in other ways too. They have appeared before the newsreel camera on a number of occasions and expect to appear in a short movie feature, tentatively titled, "Wheel and Wheels." Many movie stars have been snapped surrounded by Corps members, and autographed pictures from celebrities, in many fields, line the Corps clubroom walls. The members meet on Wednesday nights, after rehearsal, in their clubroom at 4408 West Jefferson Boulevard, where the welcome mat is always out to visiting motorcyclists.

Plans for the future may include trips as far inland as the Middle West. The offers are many, but the members have personal obligations and problems to consider. After all, they have their regular jobs during the week – the Corps is their hobby on weekends. Surely, they deserve to go on a national tour. The entire country ought to see the McLaglen Corps in action. A national tour might inspire other clubs to attempt similar drill and stunt organizations. Crack stunt and drill teams could well be started throughout the country to focus attention on the finer aspects of the sport of motorcycling. The McLaglen Corps has done a magnificent job on the West Coast in gaining the respect and the admiration of the public. Here, indeed, is a challenge to other clubs to follow the McLaglen Corps' example in fostering good public relations. How many clubs will take advantage of this golden opportunity?

When the men returned from WWII and things started getting better on the home front, the team was once again established. Some of the old members rejoined the Motor Corps and also they found a few new riders.

The team made the front page for their performance in Reedley, California.

The team poses for a picture with Captain DeRush standing in the back on his motorcycle.

Safety and Club Influence

By Chet Billings

There is no more kicked around term than "Safety." It has been discussed pro and con by police departments, civic groups, various industries, and by the nation. No matter what the approach, the objective is usually the same; get people to thinking safety.

After a three-year safety campaign on the part of the AMA, and with increasingly better results having been obtained, we can now do a little analyzing as to safety in motorcycling.

In the January issue we published a set of figures released by the AMA. They show, in round numbers, 69,000,000 miles of travel in 1937, the first year of the campaign. In 1938 they show 83,000,000 miles of travel. In 1939 they show 99,000,000 miles of travel. As the miles increased the proportionate number of accidents decreased.

That is all very interesting. In 1937 a certain number of clubs entered a contest to see how far they could travel without an accident. That means first of all that the safety plan had been taken up by groups and not by individuals. Did the same number of clubs travel the additional miles in 1938. No! The added miles came through more clubs joining the contest. More individuals got in on the group plan.

By the same token more clubs joined the program in 1939. As more people entered the contest, although the number of miles turned greatly increased, the proportion of accidents decreased. If we could, theoretically, get every motorcycle rider in the U.S. to join a club, which in turn was entered in the safety contest, the accident rate would be lower, in terms of the miles traveled than within any other group that comes within the field of automotive travel.
(Continued on next page)

The "Totem Pole" in which the west coast representative of the AMA, Chet Billings, accepts an invitation to try a stunt. Hap Ruggles drives and Joe Stewart is middle man. A fourth member hooks a ride on the rear stand. Yes, it Is moving.

AMA *The Motorcyclist Magazine* – March 1940

Safety and Club Influence (Cont'd)

There are no clubs for car owners. Any safety campaign in that field must make an individual sale to each lone driver. There is no contest or brother members to spur this lone driver on to an active interest. The only test he is in is one with several million other lone drivers and the awards are life or death.

Actually motorcyclists have made a very enviable record as far as our overall hundred clubs are concerned. But does the rest of the U.S. know about it or realize what records we really are setting? The answer once more is very definitely no.

There are several reasons. The public does not get a chance to read the figures for one thing. More important than that, if it did get a chance to read the figures it would still see a picture of one lone driver, who by now is in the minority but who gets more publicity for his poor showing than the majority gets for a fine showing.

One careless motorcycle rider in a town can just about offset the good a whole club can do in that town. People don't notice motors when they are ridden the right way. But when they have to climb trees or lamp posts to dodge the one daredevil they naturally have a very vivid recollection of it.

So it seems that if we are to clinch our safety work, we are going to have to do something about the self-appointed hell raiser who seems to think he has to show off.

These same clubs that have helped in the first part of the campaign, can help in the second part of the campaign. If our daredevil friend is just misguided; if down under the surface he has the makings of what might be called a modern motorcyclist, warm up to him and try to get him interested in club work. If he is a total loss, then there are other ways of dealing with him.

The first thing to do is to see that public officials, civic groups, fraternal organizations and all factions that represent the heart of a city's life are informed of the good side of motorcycling. This is a job in itself. It really constitutes an advertising and a service program.

During the past month, the writer was invited to attend a dinner at the Victor McLaglen Sports Center in Los Angeles. The occasion was a formal presentation of the AMA Safety Award won by the Victor McLaglen Motor Corps for 1939.

A number of influential people had been invited to the dinner including a Captain of the California Highway Patrol and other police officers. During the course of the talks that were given, it was printed out what motorcyclists nationally had done to actively work out this matter of safety. The figures which had been run on page 8 of the <u>January Motorcyclist</u> were read. (We reproduced the same figures again in connection with this article.) They were not just read off in a monotone. They were explained.

Then it was brought out that one club turned some 400,000 miles last year without an accident. It was surprising how surprised some of those visitors were to find out what was going on right under their noses, that they had not noticed or stopped to analyze.

In fact, the Captain of the Patrol admitted that although part of his work was safety, he had not realized what a worthwhile endeavor this AMA program was or how much of it had been taking place right in his territory. What he did mention was our daredevil friend. He admitted he had probably judged the many by a few.

The Victor McLaglen Motor Corps turned out to be the national champion club in 1939. That didn't just happen. Attendance figures are necessarily estimated but in many cases these are far too low. For instance, in connection with the Rose Parade in 1939 it shows 1,000,000. Actually close to two million people gathered to see that Rose Parade. And about 87,000 more gathered to see the famous Rose Bowl football game. Not all of them saw the McLaglen boys who helped the Pasadena police, but certainly more than 100,000.

All members of the McLaglen Motor Corps have put in many arduous hours of practice during the past four years. Some of their more sensational stunts are the easiest and some of the less spectacular call for real skill. As may be expected, one member takes naturally to one kind of stunt while the next member may take to another. Each is permitted a certain latitude in this respect. On the other hand, each member must practice until he can become a part of their drill team. Here we see Ray Phillips doing a real rope twirling act.

Ray Phillips

1950-1959

The 1950s brought new faces to the team. In 1953, their leader, Hap Ruggles, quit and Herb Harker, who had only been a member for two years, became the new leader. The '50s also brought in more new members with some of the old members dropping out. New blood can be good for any organization and this new blood was a shot in the arm that was needed. The war had been over for some time and life was getting back to normal. These new riders were energetic and eager to put on shows – just what the team needed.

July 1950

"VICTOR McLAGLEN MCY. CORPS,
Los Angeles, Calif, – We gave a combination drill and stunt show at the Jalopy Races in Culver City June 3. Everything went off fine except that in the "Three-Man-High" stunt Cpl. Phil Erickson dislocated a vertebrae. Glad to report he is improving rapidly though it will be some time before he is able to return to work and to the Corps. Our hats are off to him for his fortitude in carrying on the show in spite of his injury. We are now tentatively planning to make an appearance at the Balboa Stadium in San Diego on the night of July 4 in connection with the Jalopy Races. We plan to give additional drill maneuvers plus extra stunts, for instance the breath-taking "Four-Way-Crossover" and the superb multi-man stunt of stunts "The Sunflower." Let's have fun together on the Fourth."
E. L. Phillips, Sgt, 8432 Minuet Pl., Van Nuys, Calif.

In 1950, the team continued to successfully operate under Captain Nick DeRush, as noted in the April and November 1950 issues of *The Enthusiast* below.

VICTOR McLAGLEN MCY. CORPS, Los Angeles, Calif. — We had our annual meeting banquet, January 21, at the Nite Owl Club in Los Angeles. Merit award trophies were presented to the three top men of 1949 as follows: 2nd Lt. Bill Allum, first place; Cpl. Phil Erickson, second place; and Cpl. Bob Hasselbring, third place. Commanding officer, Major De Rush, announced promotions as follows: Bill Allum from Sgt. to 2nd Lt.; Ed Phillips from Corporal to Sergeant; and Phil Erickson was made Corporal. Herb Harker was elected sergeant-at-arms. 1st Lt. Ray Phillips was re-elected as officer in charge of stunt instruction. Capt. Bengston gave a short talk on plans of the Corps for the current year. He said that we would sponsor a motorcycle hillclimb race May 28 under A.M.A. sanction which should be quite an event as that type of hillclimb is practically unknown in the west. Capt. Bengston, an ex-Marine photographer, had his camera at the banquet. We're enclosing a picture.
        Sgt. Ed. Phillips
        8432 Minuet Pl., Van Nuys, Calif.

April 1950

November 1950

The famous Victor McLaglen Motorcycle Corps, outstanding California stunt organization, snapped in front of the local Harley-Davidson establishment while on a trip to San Diego in July. Riders who have visited this city will be saddened to know that this fine store was destroyed by mid-October.

Article by Gene Jaderquist–March 1951

From the beginning of 1935, members of the world champion Victor McLaglen Motorcycle Corps have been serious riders, interested mainly in developing their abilities to ride in competition events and helping other groups to stage successful, controlled events.

In the short space of one year, they had developed their teamwork to such a high degree that they were able to defeat the Mexico City Police Team in a challenge match for the world championship. Judges for the event were police chiefs and the mayor of Los Angeles. The McLaglen team won by 37 points on superior precision, timing and poise.

Currently the Corps stages shows for parades, benefits, even television. In the past three months, they have made three television shows. Over a year's time, approximately 50 events are rescheduled. Most recent helping hand was extended to the 3-Point Motorcycle Club on its annual Big Bear Run.

Major Nick DeRush, commanding officer of the group since its inception, is especially interested in how to find new members for the Corps. Originally, it was a closed group with just 30 riders, but Major De Rush now wants to expand. Present membership is 22 and the top limit depends solely on the number of qualified applicants. Requirements for membership are not strict. Any make of machine is permitted, but full fenders are required and a standard legal muffler must be fitted. After 60 days in the Corps, successful applicants must paint their machines black and white.

Most of the time, transportation and expenses to out-of-town shows are paid by the sponsors of the show. Training, of course, is free. At present, the average age of the members is about 32, but no preference is shown toward older men.

Major DeRush is working with Lt. Joe Galkin, Disaster and Civil Defense Communications Officer, in the office of E. W. Biscailuz, sheriff of Los Angeles county, on a new program to recruit volunteer riders for emergency work. At the present time, the training program for these volunteers is being set up by the sheriff's office. When completed, each of the thirteen divisions of Los Angeles county will have a small, highly trained nucleus of motorcycles to take control of communications in the event of failure of telephone and radio facilities under atomic attack. Information on this program can be obtained from Major DeRush at 8610 Juniper Street in Los Angeles, the headquarters of the McLaglen Corps.

Members of the Corps will be key men in the civil defense preparations. This is in keeping with the philosophy of service that has been the guiding principle of the group.

1951 Awards Banquet

VICTOR McLAGLEN MCY CORPS., Los Angeles, Calif. –We held our annual dinner in February to award high point members with their trophies. Our club is run on a merit system and at the end of the year our high point members are awarded their trophies. This year, the writer was high point member eligible for the first place trophy. Second place went to Corporal Herb Harker and third to Lt. Phil Erickson. Major DeRush got his trophy for the most members brought in during the year. On March 4, we sponsored a Class B half-mile race at the Corona Race Track. It was so well received that we're having another one in April. We lost our Captain to the Marines. He's been a member since 1937. Captain Bergstrom has been a fine member and we surely will be glad when he's back with us. Due to the armed services taking some of our boys and two others having their motors stolen, we have room for a limited number of members. We are taking an active part in the Civil Defense Program and we have several shows scheduled for this year.

Sergeant Bud Clark
3522 Greenwood Ave., Venice, California

May 1951

Each year, members accumulate points by attending practices, attending shows, and having a clean, safe bike. At the awards banquet, trophies for 1st, 2nd, and 3rd places are awarded to those who earned the most points.

The Victor McLaglen Motorcycle Corps, Los Angeles, Calif., line up for the photographer on the occasion of their annual Trophy Award Dinner. The Corps is run on a merit system. Three high point men received trophies. The three trophies went to Corp. Herb Harker, Sgt. Bud Clark and Corp. Norman Mayer.

Chuck Bruna, Norman Mayer, Bud Clark, Phil Erikson, Bing Bengston, Nick DeRush, Bill Allum, Louie Escabar, Wayne Smale, Herb Harker

(Leo Costa Photo)
The *Enthusiast* June 1952

1952 Awards Banquet

American Motorcyclist Association Safety Award is presented to Captain DeRush on behalf of the team.

Team poses with the Ladies Auxiliary and World Championship Trophy won in 1936.

The team and their ladies.

6-Motor 15-Man Pyramid

Drivers: Herb Harker, Jack Brill
Standing: Newt Fish, Sam Watson Sr., Theron Wilmott, Chuck Schobert Top: Bill Smith

KFI-TV was formed in 1949 by Earle C. Anthony. In the early 1950s, he sold his KFI-TV to General Tire and it became KHJ-TV and now KCAL TV.

The team does a show and Los Angeles television station KFI-TV filmed it for their local news show.

This is the "3-Motor Push-Up" looking a little wobbly and with the stunt almost complete.

The 1950s introduced some interesting new developments. This was the decade of Sputnik 1, the hydrogen bomb, invention of the solar cell, passenger jets, discovery of DNA, the polio vaccination, and ultrasound tests for heart activity.

Harry S. Truman and Dwight D. Eisenhower were United States presidents, the first modern credit card was introduced, the first organ transplant was accomplished, and the "Peanuts" cartoon strip was created. Rock and roll emerged with Fats Domino, Brenda Lee, Connie Frances, Johnny Mathis, Pat Boone, and Ricky Nelson. Then, in the mid-1950s, Elvis blasted onto the scene. With the development of television, the world became more accessible and the Motor Corps had a new medium to promote their shows and activities.

However, in 1953, their leader, Captain DeRush, decided to leave the team, so they had to elect a new leader. This was a first for them. Up until this time, Nick had been their only leader. Nick had led the team for their first 18 years.

After much discussion, they thought maybe they just might have a new leader.

Herb Harker had joined the team in 1951, and they soon discovered that he was an excellent rider; in fact, better than most. He was also good in the drill and an excellent motorman for the stunts. When Nick decided to leave the team, Herb was the likely candidate to take over and he was voted in by the membership. Herb continued to lead the team for the next 25 years.

Herb Harker doing the "Seat Ride"

Herb Harker doing a "Slow Circle"

Ray Phillips makes the cover of the March 1951 *Cycle Magazine*. And it only cost 25 cents!

Victor McLaglen Motor Corps Ladies Auxiliary

The earliest records I could find about the Ladies Auxiliary was a "Financial Record" book showing dues collected in August 1951. This showed a total of nine members:

Della Escobar (Luie's wife)
Elizabeth Harker (Herb's wife)
Eunice DeRush (Nick's wife)
Gaynell Luper
Juanita Thompson
Kay Costa (Leo's wife)
Mary Brunner (Chuck's wife)
Mildred Allum (Bill's wife)
Virginia Mayer (Norman's wife)

Auxiliary cap badge for helmets

Dues were $1.00 per month.

Officers were to be Motor Corps member's wives only. Any member's wife or girlfriend can join the Auxiliary, but officers must be "members' wives only". There were only four officers: President, Secretary, Treasurer, and Points Secretary. All members must be American Motorcyclist Association (AMA) members.

The Auxiliary held meetings the 1st and 3rd Tuesday each month, which coincided with the Motor Corps practice schedule. Members could wear whatever they wanted on meeting nights, but each member was to wear "black slacks and uniform shirts for parades, shows, and meets" according to meeting notes of 1960.

The Ladies Auxiliary was disbanded at a meeting on May 6, 1984 with only five members attending: Vice President Margaret Smith, Lynda Chubbuck, Ruth Fisher, Norma French, and Joan Gerry.

Members in "good standing" at the time were: Nonnie Biscailuz, Barbara Brosell, Dale Carmody, Lynda Chubbuck, Ruth Fisher, Norma French, Joan Gerry, Evelyn Jensen, and Margaret Smith.

Funds in their Treasury were used to pay admission to events where the Motor Corps performed "until the money ran out." Any Auxiliary equipment was given to the Motor Corps.

More 1950's News

The team was incorporated for the first time in 1956 as a non-profit corporation. They had previously been included with the original Victor McLaglen Light Horse Drill Team corporation, but this was a good first step to being an independent team apart from the Light Horse team.

Per the meeting minutes of 12/3/1956, Frank Allen was in Santa Monica hospital (motorcycle accident). The club voted to give him a get well gift of a carton of Camel cigarettes! Interesting sign of the times. In March 1958, a member tried to instill "no smoking" at the annual banquet and have a "smoking period," instead. This went over like a lead balloon!

Strict military protocol was followed in the 1950s. There were plenty of officer designations, promotions to the next level of officer, yearly election of primary officers, stripes and patches on uniforms designating rank. Members referred to as Major Harker, Captain Carmody, etc.

The club was able to negotiate for boots for members at $15 a pair! Eighty years later, these same boots cost more than $200 a pair.

Britches were purchased for $25 in the 1950s, but in 2000, they were over $100, Shirts were $80, and belts were $20.

In November 1958, the team voted to provide all members with a whistle, standardized and purchased through the club. In 1961, the whistles cost 90 cents each. In 2000, they were around $4.

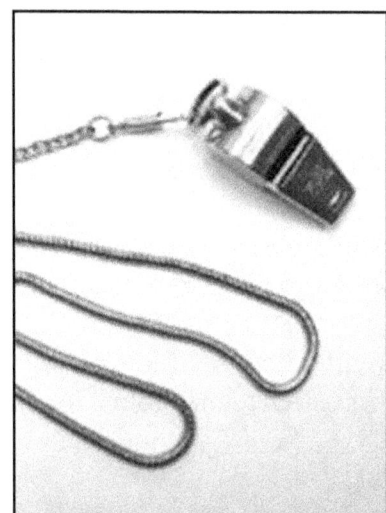

Regulation police-style whistle

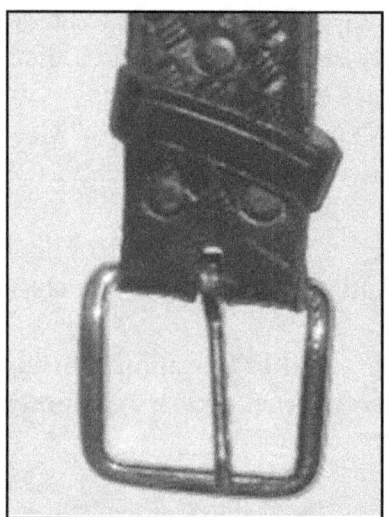

Regulation belt with basket weave

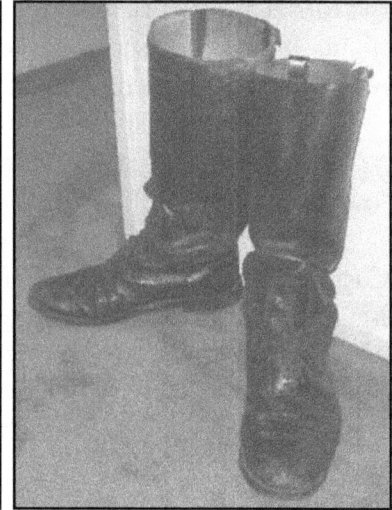

Regulation police-style motorcycle riding boots

The team was also involved in Civil Defense. They met one evening a month to review the Civil Defense Drill and instructions. Each Motor Corps application contained this statement:

Would you, in time of necessity, be willing to serve in a voluntary capacity, in Civil Defense, for as long as you are needed, without thought of remuneration? ___YES_____
Signed _____John Doe_____

They worked with Lieutenant Joe Galkin, Disaster and Civil Defense Communications Officer, in the Los Angeles County Sheriff's office. That office had a new program to recruit volunteer riders for emergency work and the Motor Corps members fit the bill. They would take control of communications in the event of failure of telephone and radio facilities under atomic attack. This was in keeping with their philosophy of service that has been the guiding principle of the group.

They participated in a bomb scare drill during August 1956 and received a commendation from the Civil Defense Committee for their help.

"Crashbar Rear Rack Ride"

Enthusiast **Magazine article, March 1952, page 17**

"VICTOR McLAGLEN MCY. CORPS, Los Angeles, Calif. – *We have completed a very successful year – one of the most successful in the history of the Corps. Last year, we appeared on television several times and put on many other successful shows including several benefit shows for charitable organizations. Last year, we also held two ½-mile dirt track races at Corona. We also helped several clubs with their activities. The most recent was the Big Bear Run at which we controlled the public and traffic for the Three-Point Club. We have received many letters from participants and spectators commenting on the way we handled the event and we want to thank everyone for their fine cooperation."*

Sgt. Bud Clark,
3522 Greenwood Ave.
Venice, Calif.

March 1952

1956 –
Colonel Herb Harker in charge and leading this "V" formation.

1959 –
Back L-R: Joe Perot, Theron Wilmott, Frank Allen, Neil Irving, Sam Watson Sr., Dick Gerry, Ray Watson
Front L-R: Herb Harker, Jack Brill, Lyle Carmody

1.___, 2.___ 3.___ 4. Bud Sindt, 5. Jack Brill, 6. Herb Harker, 7 Bill Smith, 8. Lloyd Freeman, 9.___, 10. Sam Packingham, 11.___

Some members are identified, but not all, as noted.

Per the minutes of October 4, 1958, Motor Corps meeting, Lyle Carmody was asked to contact Howard Hughes to ask for his stated sponsorship. In the October 31, 1958, notes, Lyle said he'd sent the letter. It seemed that nothing became of that attempt and apparently it was dropped.

Per the minutes of the March 17, 1959, meeting, "D. Gerry asked about rumored complaints regarding the club's actions on the March 8th Road Riders Poker Run."

T. Wilmott stated that an unidentified person reported by telephone to Major Harker, that members of the club were speeding and had wrecks. D. Gerry asked whether or not we should send a letter or someone in person to contact the Road Riders. After much discussion, it was decided to wait and see what happens."

Per the meeting minutes of April 7, 1959, "Dick Gerry asked if the club would be interested in watching the Huntington Park Elks do their stunts." Answer "NO." Whew! I guess that showed their feelings about their rival motorcycle stunt team at the Elks Lodge. Maybe that had something to do with Captain DeRush defecting and joining the Elks!

On November 26, 1958, the Motor Corps started leading the Santa Claus Lane Parade in Hollywood, California. They continued leading this event until about 1971. At that time, the lead position began alternating yearly between the Victor McLaglen Motor Corps and the Huntington Park Elks Motorcycle Stunt & Drill Team. That was due to some fancy negotiating by the Elks team leader, Harry Fisher. Harry had been a member of the Victor's until he defected and joined the Elks in 1967. More about that later.

This parade began in 1931, and became a long-time tradition in Hollywood. The name of the event changed a number of times. It began as the Santa Claus Lane Parade, then became the Santa Claus Lane Parade of Stars shown live on KTTV (Channel 11) and KTLA (Channel 5), and transitioned from black & white to color TV in 1965. Then at that time, it was renamed and remains the Hollywood Christmas Parade.

1960-1969

The 1960s brought more new members and more activity for the team. By 1964, they had twenty members and were leading most every parade in Southern California, besides doing infield shows at various events. This decade was full of news: Elvis Presley started starring in movies, Alfred Hitchcock's movie *Psycho* was released, the Beatles arrived from Liverpool, England, the mini-skirt made its debut, and in 1965, the United States started sending troops to Vietnam. The team, however, stayed focused, mostly performing locally in the Southern California area and sticking to their traditional uniform and stunts.

On December 7, 1962, the team performed on the Steve Allen television show at 6:15 p.m. It was taped and shown on December 20th at 11:20 p.m.

The Team Experiences Changes

When Victor McLaglen died in November 1959, the team experienced changes.

Mrs. McLaglen agreed to allow the club to continue using her husband's name as long as they maintained the same spirit and qualities they had under her husband's direction.

Colonel Herb Harker had taken over leadership of the team and, with the help of the other dedicated members, did a great job of keeping the group intact and running smoothly.

During this time, the members' ages ranged from 21 to 57 and, at one point, the youngest was 16. They met every Tuesday in a parking lot at Washington and Main Streets in Los Angeles. In 1964, they were faced with a new challenge. The parking lot, where they had been practicing, was the new site for the Municipal Court building to be erected in 1966. Fortunately, Herb was able to find a shopping mall parking lot in Lakewood, California, and they were still able to practice.

In 1964, a new points system was adopted. They decided this was needed so they could maintain some consistency and interest in the team. A little competition within the membership didn't hurt either.

Points System

Drill on Tuesdays	10
Meeting at shop	5
Stunt Practice	10
Parades in town	50
Parades out of town (30 miles from Los Angeles City Hall)	100
Road Races	50
Socials	5
Club Rides	10
Motor Inspection	10
Uniform Inspection	10

Member must ride his own motorcycle to earn points.

Member does not have to ride his motorcycle to meetings to receive points.

Practice was held at the parking lot located at Washington and Main Streets in Los Angeles during the 1960s.

Getting Ready for Practice.

Mike Catford & Don Snow

"Spread Eagle"
Les Georgeson-Harry Fisher-Cliff Hamer

The wives and girlfriends watch.

"Suicide Split"
Joe Militello & Les Georgeson

Drill "Eight Across" Colonel Harker leads.
L-R: Chuck Spoon, Joe Militello, Harry Fisher, Les Cuppett, Cliff Hamer, Mike Catford, Don Snow

Practice field at Main and Los Angeles

Uniforms – 1960

October 4, 1960 Meeting Minutes – Helmets were added to the uniform. They would be black and white. It became part of the Class A uniform as of September 1, 1962 and they cost $5.20!

On the Class A uniform, a gold braid was worn on the left shoulder. These were issued as part of the uniform and were owned by the club.

Duo Glide motorcycle tie clasps were part of the uniform starting in January 1, 1961. White gloves were voted in on September 11, 1961. Although they were purchased through the club, individual members purchased the gloves as their own personal property. They also bought light bulbs for the wheel lights for 5 cents each through the club.

Chrome bands on members' helmets and gold bands on officers' helmets were used for a short time but this didn't last long. They went back to black and white helmets in 1962. These were purchased and owned by each member and had "chin cups" attached. They would also have Motor Corps metal badges attached at holes drilled into the helmet.

In 1964, they went to a new style tie, these were clip-on ties for safety reasons. If the clip-on tie was caught in the wheel spoke or some other part of the bike or another member, the tie would rip off rather than hang the owner! The AMA Pin was to be worn on the left side of the jacket or shirt and the gold braid was to be worn on and under the left arm.

In 1965, they considered uniform coveralls, however, this subject was eventually dropped.

The July 19, 1966, minutes said that members could buy tires for $22.64 and a rear chain for $5.36.

Wow – How times have changed!

Don Snow shows off his "official" uniform.

The members performed security services at many of the local car and motorcycle races. They each got paid around $5 for the entire job!

On February 7, 1961, Major Herb Harker was promoted to Colonel. I suppose probably that was because Victor had died in 1959 and they didn't have a Colonel in a leadership role. Herb had been previously running the team, but as a Captain.

This promotion resulted in further changes in rank to other members as well:

Capt. Wilmott promoted to Major
Lt. Carmody promoted to Captain
Tech. Sgt. Irving to 1st Lieutenant
Staff Sgt. Gerry to 2nd Lieutenant
Sgt. Ayala to Master Sergeant
Sr. Cpl. Griest to Tech Sergeant
Cpl. Taylor to Staff Sergeant
PFC Jernigan to Buck Sergeant
PFC DeNike to Sr Corporal
PFC Tom Stiltz to Corporal
PFC Schobert to Corporal

Kneeling: Herb Harker, Jack Brill, Lyle Carmody
Standing: Joe Parot, Theron Wilmott, Frank Allen, Neil Irving, Sam Watson Sr. Dick Gerry, Ray Watson.

That same year, the club hosted a motorcycle run. The run started at 9:00AM and went approximately 100 miles. Dick Hutchins, the Los Angeles Harley-Davidson dealer, advised they would need "200 four-cent stamps to mail posters to the dealers and 2,000 three-cent stamps for mailing to riders."

In the meeting notes of July 18, 1961, it seemed that a member was complaining because some of the members weren't doing their part in many of the events of the club, and that he "received no thanks for the things he has done for the club." Member Doc Baum explained, "you can't be an individualist. You must participate as a member of a club. If you want to be an individualist, you shouldn't belong to our club." Colonel Harker further explained some of the background of the club and its reasons for being in existence and that "we must stick together and work as a team". He concluded by providing examples of what can happen when one man lets the club down. Apparently, that satisfied the complainer.

Herb Harker driving

Mike Kenyon

Ed Bengston

Up until 1961, each applicant was required to sign the Civil Defense statement on their application form.

At a meeting of the Executive Board on 9/11/61, it was voted to "make new application blanks and delete the portion about Civil Defense."

March 1964: John Kazian, Sam Reed, Dick Zelenak, Chuck Spoon, Les Georgeson, Sam Watson Jr., Harry Fisher, Les Cuppett, Chuck Caldara, Cliff Hamer, Sam Watson. Sr.

"P-38"
Driver: Herb Harker

Chuck Caldara stands on the back, holding up Joe Dizacomo, while Cliff Hamer is the motorman. In the background, Herb Harker starts the "Backward Ride." June 20, 1963

For the most part, the team's performances were accident-free but for maybe a few bumps and bruises. For instance, there's the black and blue shoulders of the motormen caused by the guys standing on them, and maybe the Suicide Split that caused some damage to a couple of members' feet, or the "Sunflower," that tumbled over at Lake Isabella a few years later. That one's excusable, though. They were performing on a sleet-covered street with more sleet coming down, when a car decided to cut across in front of them! They didn't hit the car, and Mickey Minor had his finger broken in the mayhem that followed. But that was later, and we're talking about 1963 now!

One of the worst accidents occurred in 1964. The team was leading off the San Fernando Fiesta Parade, celebrating the City of San Fernando's 30th Annual Fiesta Week. Sheriff Emeritus Eugene Biscailuz was the honored Grand Marshall, along with his wife, Betty, and children, Michael (10), Mary Ann (11), and Karen (12). Coincidentally, one of the future team members, Ellis Smith, married Margaret Biscailuz, a relative of the Sheriff. Anyhow, a couple of Motor Corps members apparently locked handlebars, causing a chain reaction which caused Gary May, who was riding on the far left of the line-up, to lose control, and slide into the three children. One child suffered a fractured tibia and two others received multiple abrasions. It was a horrible accident that really shook up the guys.

In 1963, they held their annual banquet with Mrs. McLaglen and Business Manager, Adolph Kuri attending. It was big news and the picture was even published in Harley-Davidson Motor Company's *Enthusiast* magazine.

Front Row (L-R): xx, xx, Ruth E. Fisher, Karole Watson, Colonel Kury, Mrs. McLaglen, Liz Harker, Trudy Watson, Jo Cuppett, xx
Middle Row: Herb Harker, Dick Gerry, xx, xx, xx, xx, xx, xx, Cliff Hamer, Les Cuppett
Back Row: xx, Harry Fisher, xx, Ronnie Griest, Kyle Carmody, Sam Watson Sr., xx, George McClellan, Sam Watson Jr., Ray Watson

Getting ready for a show – Colonel Harker in front.

Page 6 -- MOTORCYCLING NEWS -- June 13, 1963

PHOTOS OF THE MISSION TRAILS TOUR

Rich Budelier's Harley shop and the Motor Corps put on the Mission Trails Tour run in June 1963. The run started and ended at the Harley shop, and included about 135 riders.

The way I heard it (and from a very reliable source), the ladies were doing a great job cleaning up. But then when the photographer started snapping pictures, however, Harry Fisher and Joe Dizacomo suddenly became hard workers. When the photographer left, so did they. Slackers!

Captain Lyle Carmody headed up the trophy presentation.

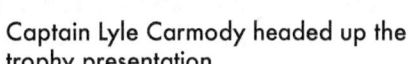

Liz Harker, Tony Ayala and Trudy Watson serve up the spaghetti feed, while rider, Ralph Stohl gladly holds his plate.

The Slow Circles

Harry in 1963 doing his new version of the "Slow Circle" front.

When Harry Fisher joined the team in 1963, he was intrigued by the "Slow Circle." This means riding the motorcycle in slow, tight circles with no hands on the handlebars and feet never touching the ground.

He figured that since he was the youngest, newest member, if he could do that better than anyone else, he'd have more credibility with the team. Harry practiced these "Slow Circles" until he could do them over manhole covers, ditches, holes in the road and any other type of terrain. Then he enhanced them by putting one foot on the floorboard and the other on the seat – one-handed! The "Slow Circle" became the thing to do to show you've mastered riding your bike slowly and in control.

Ray Mehlbaum in 1995 doing the original version of the "Slow Circle".

I have heard Harry tell a new member many a time, "go home and practice that slow circle. Do it until you can do it on any surface. Do it until you can take your jacket off and put it on again while you're still doing that circle – without putting your foot down or putting your hands on the handlebars. Then come back and show me."

Mark Frymoyer doing the "Pivot Slow Circle" stunt. The bike is going around Mark while he pivots on his left foot and others ride in various positions on the bike with Rich Wood going under.

Some took the challenge and ended up doing a stunt that few others could master and becoming very proud of their accomplishment.

Actually, there's a certain bar in Beaumont, California, that boasted about one of our Motor Corps members coming in his back door, doing a "Slow Circle" in the middle of room and riding out the front door, never putting his foot down and leaving a tire mark on the doorsill as he left. I'm not saying who that was, but Harry was very good at doing slow circles! That tire mark was left there for many years and we always visited it when we traveled through Beaumont.

1964 Modern Cycle magazine

Dick Gerry, performing the remarkable "One-Legged Ride".

The "Speedo"

Banquet 1964 –L-R: Cliff Hamer, Les Cuppett, Colonel Kury, Harry Fisher, Lyle Carmody

Front left: Ray Watson
Front right: George McClellan
Center bottom: Harry Fisher
Left top: Frank Horn
Right top: Les Georgeson
Center top: Dick Gerry
Driving: Cliff Hamer, Sam Watson, Sr.

Team Members: 1962-1964

1962	1963	1964
1 Ayala, Tony	1 Ayala, Tony	1 Ayala, Tony
2 Baum, Doc	2 Caldara, Chuck	2 Caldara, Chuck
3 Caldara, Chuck	3 Carmody, Lyle	3 Carmody, Lyle
4 Carmody, Lyle	4 Cuppett, Les	4 Cuppett, Les
5 Denike, Gene	5 Fisher, Harry	5 Fisher, Harry
6 Dizacomo, Joe	6 Georgeson, Les	6 Georgeson, Les
7 Gerry, Dick	7 Gerry, Dick	7 Gerry, Dick
8 Griest, Ronnie	8 Griest, Ronnie	8 Griest, Ronnie
9 Hamer, Cliff	9 Hamer, Cliff	9 Hamer, Cliff
10 Harker, Herb	10 Harker, Herb	10 Harker, Herb
11 Horn, Frank	11 Horn, Frank	11 Horn, Frank
12 Irving, Neil	12 Irving, Neil	12 Irving, Neil
13 Jernigan, Jim	13 Spoon, Chuck	13 Kazian, John
14 Stockwell, Ronnie	14 Stockwell, Ronnie	14 Perry, Bill
15 Watson, Ray	15 Watson, Ray	15 Reid, Samuel
16 Watson, Sam Sr.	16 Watson, Sam Jr.	16 Spoon, Chuck
17 Weldon, Jim	17 Watson, Sam Sr.	17 Watson, Ray
	18 Zelenak, Dick	18 Watson, Sam Jr.
		19 Watson, Sam Sr.
		20 Zelenak, Dick

I'm not sure exactly when the team started putting these wheelplates on their front fenders, but here is a picture of one as early as the 1950s in a show. The team has continued that tradition.

Possible Closure

In 1965, the club faced possible closure. Minutes were written on April 26, 1965, with the following members in attendance: Herb Harker, Tony Ayala, Les Cuppett, Harry Fisher, Kenny Frost, Ronnie Griest, Cliff Hamer, George McClellan, Joe Militello, Jim Swanson, Ray Watson, and Colonel Kuri. They only had 11 members in the club in addition to Colonel Kuri as advisor.

Each person aired his complaints about the club. Then Colonel Kuri spoke, saying that he was very unhappy with Colonel Harker for writing a letter to Mrs. McLaglen. I don't know what was in that letter, but it must have been potent! Colonel Kuri let everyone know that he felt it was improper for the commander to write such a letter. Also, he felt that if the Club re-writes the By-Laws, after they are approved by membership, they must be approved by him before they become legal. He stated that "We must always have by-laws and abide by them." He closed by saying, "You have 60 days to straighten out the club, and if you cannot, we will close out the charter." Whew! Those were some strong words and they got everyone to thinking. I don't know what happened, but apparently, they "straightened out" the club because it didn't close.

In the 1960s, the club had monthly Executive Board meetings and regular meetings every week. All decisions were made by majority vote and several changes were made to the bylaws. For instance:
- Article 28: Membership shall be restricted to men only. (WHAT?!)
- Article 29: At any exhibition of the Victor McLaglen Motor Corps, there must be at least five members present in uniform.
- Article 30: No one other than active members of the Corps shall be permitted to participate in any activities of the stunt team.
- Article 31: No member shall be permitted to wear their uniform in part. Uniforms must be worn in their entirety, except on order of the commanding officer for special events.

The impressive "Spread Eagle" Motormen: Les Georgeson, Les Cuppett and Cliff Hamer; Centers: (left) Joe Militello and (right) Harry Fisher

Modern Motorcycle Magazine – May-June 1965

PRECISION DRILL TEAM PERFORMS THE IMPOSSIBLE ON MOTORCYCLES

Motorcycle drill teams are not the rarest kind of bird on the American scene, but few, if any, can match the split-second precision of the Victor McLaglen Motor Corps. We spent a Sunday morning recently watching them perform on their practice field in down town Los Angeles and found there was little the imagination could dream up that the team had not already tried and, in most cases, perfected.

While the corps likes to operate basically as a team, many of the stunts require fewer members that the current total of 21, and in many cases these are the most spectacular maneuvers.

One of these is the P-38 formation, developed by one of the older members of the corps and his two sons, both in their twenties. Papa sits in the saddle and runs the machine while the two boys hang out to the side in either direction, parallel to the ground. One foot is placed on a peg and the other leg is hooked around the driver's arm. The visual effect is that of a P-38 airplane from World War II.

An even more daring stunt is the Suicide Split, posibly misnamed, since no one has ever been seriously hurt in it. This, however, is no doubt due to the amazing precision with which the group operates.

The Suicide Split requires three or more bikes with riders and two or more unmounted men spread-eagled between them, holding onto the roll bars. Given enough space, the entire team could arrange itself in this formation, with 11 riders mounted and 10 spread between them. Naturally, the younger members are recruited for the hanging-on chores.

Motorcycle is set in motion in second gear at fixed engine speed. To turn, the two men lean in unison.

Left: Ray Watson
Right: Sam Watson, Jr.

Father & sons, all members of the corps, perfected this formation, called the P-38 because of its resemblance to the World War II fighter plane of the same designation.

"P-38" The Watson family! Sam Sr. driving and sons Ray and Sam Jr. hanging out.

Modern Motorcycle (magazine)
May-June 1965

12th Annual Ace of Clubs High Sierra Tour

Driver: George McClellan

Standing On Frame: Ray Watson
Standing On Fender: Harry Fisher

Driving: Les Cuppett
Layback: George McClellan

(L-R) Doc Baum, Sam Watson, Sr., Theron Wilmot, Cliff Hamer, Gene DeNike, Neil Irving, Lyle Carmody, Herb Harker, Tony Ayala, Cliff Taylor, Ronnie Griest, Frank Horn, Delmar, Bill Swan

June 10-11, 1967

Featured attraction at the run was the Victor McLaglen Motor Corps.
Left motorman – Les Georgeson; Right motorman – Cliff Hamer; Center Spread – Harry Fisher

Per Minutes of January 31, 1961, Henry Bloomfield, Jr., President of the Home Ice Company of Los Angeles, saw the team practicing, talked to Herb Harker, and offered his facilities to the team – a parking lot for practice and a room for meetings. Henry also said they could have the use of a gas pump he had on his property because he owned quite a number of shares in Union Oil and got gas for nothing.

This was at 1120 North La Brea, Hollywood, California. After a couple weeks, however, the parking lot wasn't available for practice and it didn't make a lot of sense to drive "clear over to Hollywood" for a meeting room! I guess gas wasn't as expensive in those days as it didn't seem to be an issue! That area is now a huge shopping center.

Driver: Leo Costa, Top: Ray Green

In 1967, Harry Fisher and Johnny Kazian discovered the Huntington Park Elks Motorcycle Stunt & Drill Team. That Lodge bought helmets and uniforms for their members and the team traveled all over the state of California doing shows. That sounded like a good idea to Harry and Johnny.

The duo started to participate in Elks team practices and were having a great time until at one practice they noticed a couple of Victor members watching from the far end of the parking lot. It wasn't long after that when Harry and Johnny both received letters from Colonel Harker saying that they were both dropped from membership. They'd gotten themselves "booted" out!

Well, OK. That settled that and the duo starting riding with the Elks. However, eleven years later, in 1978, Colonel Harker gave Harry a call, said he was retiring, and asked him to take over leadership of the Victor team. Since the Elks team had been limited by Lodge rules to only perform within the state of California, the Victor's had more potential to expand their performances across country. So once again, Harry joined the Victor's. Johnny, however, went on his separate way to a "wing-walking" professional stunt career and a place in the 2004 International Council of Air Shows Foundation Hall of Fame.

Southern California Motorcycling Association (SCMA)

The team became a Chartered Club of the SCMA in December 1969. Ellis (Smitty) Smith was their first president and when he joined the Motor Corps, he talked the Corps into becoming a Chartered SCMA Club. This gave the team more networking possibilities, more exposure for shows, and more potential for new members. A win-win situation.

Motor Corps member, Walt Stagner, became the first SCMA representative for the Motor Corps. Later, member Dick Hill was the representative, and for many years member Mickey Minor took on the task.

The Motor Corps maintained that Charter Club status for many years and supported the SCMA whenever they could with shows and promotional exposure to help increase membership and their charter.

The Motor Corps Finds Sponsorship

Also, during the 1960s, Skip Fordyce Harley-Davidson in Riverside, California, decided to get behind the Motor Corps and help this team move ahead by printing flyers. When Fordyce H-D was sold in 2013, becoming Riverside Harley-Davidson, the Victor's lost that sponsorship.

Motor Corps Picnic - June 16, 1968

The Motorcycle Enthusiast, **November 1963**
"Old and new members of the Victor McLaglen Motor Corps, met for a reunion recently in North Hollywood, Calif. The club, founded in 1935, was sponsored by screen idol, Victor McLaglen whose widow is seated in the front row. Its specialty is performing precision drills on their Harley-Davidsons – an activity which the club has continued through the years."

Front Row: xx, xx, Dick Gerry, Herb Harker, Mrs. McLaglen, Lyle Carmody, Tony Ayala, xx, Howard Jester
Second Row: xx, xx, xx, xx, xx, xx, xx, xx, xx, xx, xx, xx, xx, Bing Bengston
Back Row: Chuck Spoon, Chuck Caldara, xx, Ray Watson, Dick Zelenak, Les Cuppett, Sam Watson, Jr., Sam Watson, Sr., Ronnie Griest, Cliff Hamer, Ed Anderson, xx, Hap Ruggles

Hap Ruggles, xx, xx, xx, xx, Howard Jester, Bing Bengston, Gracie Jester, Mrs. McLaglen

Dick Gerry, Herb Harker, Mrs. McLaglen, Lyle Carmody, Tony Ayala

"Motorcycle Weekly" April 30, 1969 (25 cents)

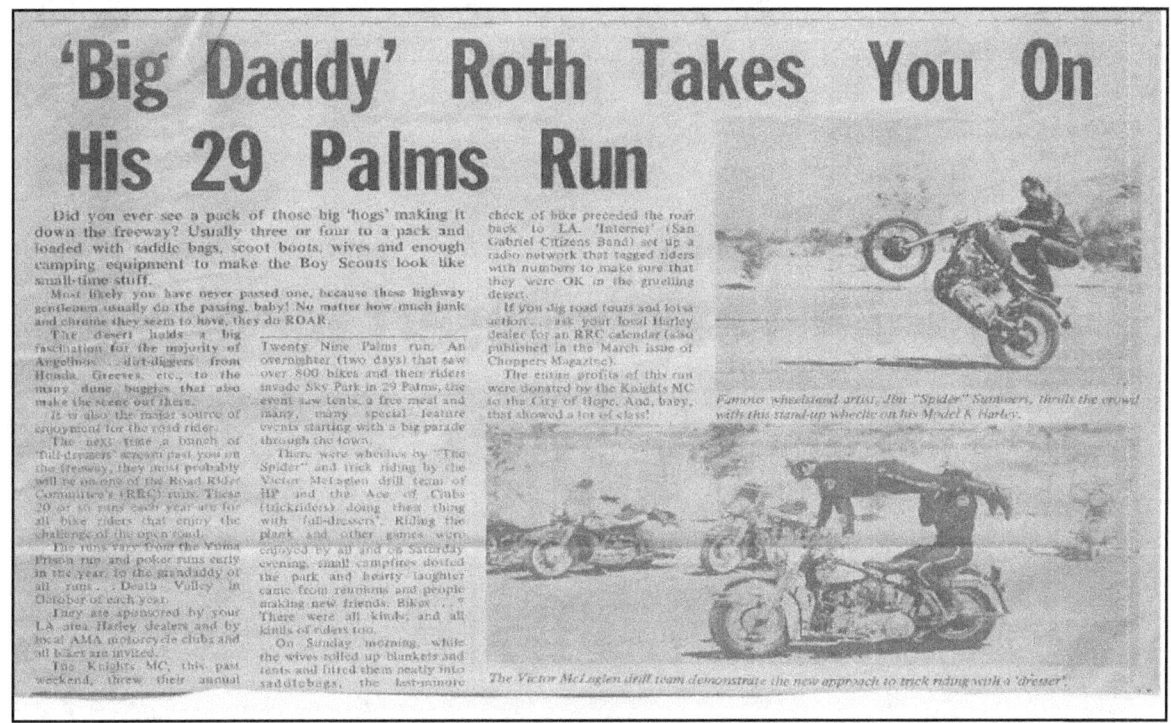

"There were wheelies by "The Spider" and trick riding by the Victor McLaglen drill team of HP and the Ace of Clubs (trick riders) doing their thing with "full-dressers." Riding the plank and other games were enjoyed by all and on Saturday evening, small campfire dotted the park and hearty laughter came from reunions and people making new friends."

1970-1979

"The Victor McLaglen Motor Corps spends great amounts of time and effort in practice.
The results are thrilling stunts such as the "Spread Eagle."
"Standing on his machine, a Victor McLaglen Motor Corps rides between rows of spectators at speed.
The Corps dates to 1935, is named after its original sponsor, the late Hollywood movie star."

The 1970s were exciting. President Richard Nixon resigned, the U.S. pulled out of Vietnam, Teamster President Jimmy Hoffa became missing, Saturday Night Live premiered, the Apple computer was revealed, the Star Wars movie was released, and Elvis died. How can the team compete? But they did. Leader Herb Harker retired from the team and appointed Harry Fisher to take over. Harry brought members and contacts from his time in the Huntington Park Elks Motorcycle Stunt & Drill Team and the Motor Corps rose from a dwindling 5 members to 25 at the end of the decade. Their schedule of events indicated 40 shows in 1979. That pretty much filled up most of their weekends. But wait, I'm getting ahead of myself.

Negotiations with the American Legion

In the early 1970s, the team started negotiating for sponsorship with the Garden Grove Post and the Lakewood Post of the American Legion. Les Georgeson and Herb Harker were the focals for this project, and the negotiations continued for several months.

The team genuinely wanted to retain their name, "Victor McLaglen Motor Corps," but advertise that they were "supported by the American Legion Post." The Lakewood Post offered the use of their hall (when it was available) in exchange for one or two shows. Their 1971 convention was going to be in Los Angeles, so that would definitely be one show. Then, if they did a fundraiser, like a carnival, that would be another event. The American Legion then offered $18 per parade or show, however, they would need an insurance binder. The cost would be approximately $250-$300, which would come out of the team's treasury. Joe Militello was quoted as saying, "Why can't we be paid for parades like the Elks are paid for performing –we are better than they are." Thus began the fierce competition between the Huntington Park Elks Motorcycle Stunt & Drill Team and the Victor McLaglen Motor Corps.

Eventually, that next year, the quest for the American Legion sponsorship was abandoned. On April 6, 1971, a motion was made by Mike Catford and seconded by Tom Evans to not accept their offer. The team voted and agreed to end the negotiations.

1970 – "Sunflower" with Driver: Joe Militello

The Indio Tour

In October 1972, the McLaglen team performed at the 8th Annual Indio Tour in the desert town of Indio in California. There were over 5,300 sign-ins that year and it was touted as "one of the largest gatherings of road riders the nation has ever seen."

"Modern Cycle"
April 1973

Article by George Hays in *"Modern Cycle"* April 1973

Until two years ago, the tour was an AMA sanctioned event, with an AMA card required to sign in. Outlaw riders refused to pay dues to any organization other than their own clubs, so they were rarely seen at Indio. The few who did show up cruised by for a quick look and kept on going. Or skulked around the outer fringes of the run. Then AMA raised their membership fee from $2 to $7 per year. Most road riders refused to go along, feeling that the AMA is unresponsive to the needs of the road rider. The Indio Tour had to have several thousand entrees to cover expenses, so to survive, no AMA cards were required on the 7th and 8th annual tours.

With AMA cards unnecessary, the outlaws began to swarm in. They caused no real trouble their first year, but their raucous behavior and frightening appearance led many of the righteous citizen type riders to mount their full-dress machines and leave in disgust.

On the eighth and last Indio Tour more outlaws appeared, and more "squares" stayed home, making the tour what was probably the largest assemblage of extended forks and long hairs ever seen. You noticed the difference a soon as you got within 50 miles of Indio. Four out of five bikes on the road were choppers. The roadside was lined with choppers, their riders trying to wire their machines back together long enough to make it into Indio. The same old excitement was in the air when you arrived at the Fairgrounds but this time the potentially explosive situation added a hint of fear. This time it was the outlaws who were in the majority, and it was the squares who took a quick look and kept going.

I don't like it," said one rider as he entered the Fairgrounds, "there's the smell of death in the air." Another arrived to put his rare 1917 8-valve Harley racer on display in the line-up of rare bikes, but after one look at the crowd left it on his pickup and departed.

An Indio citizen, viewing the huge crowd of outlaws gathered in front of the Fairgrounds, commented, "It's scary enough just to pass half a dozen of those animals on the road but good God, look. There are thousands of them!"

But the Pacific Coasters, the sponsoring club, were determined to carry on. "We haven't had any trouble with the chopper group up to this point", said President Chuck Myers. "They come to Indio to have a good time, and that's what the run is for. As long as they don't cause any trouble they're welcome."

The traditional program started at 1:30 Saturday afternoons with the parade through town. But this time it was a parade of choppers rather than dressers. Back at the Fairgrounds the Victor McLaglen Motor Corps and the Ace of Club Drill Teams presented their usual fantastic performances of thrilling stunts.

Meanwhile, on the outskirts of Indio, two outlaw gangs were having their own type of competition – a showdown in front of a bar to prove who was the baddest bad-asses of all. Two were shot to death, two stabbed and one was savagely beaten. After the battle one of the gangs was being escorted through Indio by the police when they spotted two members of the rival gang sitting on their choppers in a drive-in parking lot, and decided to even the score. The gang, numbering about 60, jumped off their choppers and charged, pulling off their chain belts as they ran. For several long minutes the mob surrounded the two helpless riders while arms swung and chromed chains flashed in the sun. The gang remounted and rode on, leaving two bloody bodies and two choppers on the ground, one of the bikes set on fire.

Back at the Fairgrounds, everything seemed under control but those who are alert to such things noted that pills and pot were going down along with the beer and booze.

After the dinner the crowd gathered in the stadium for the 'Best Dressed" contests, the beauty contest, and the trophy presentation. It was a problem to find judges for the contests. In years past, this had been done by local law enforcement officers, but this year they were busy trying to keep things under control in town. The crowd in the grandstand behaved like a class of school kids out of control, while Chuck Myers struggled to be heard on the P.A. Occasionally during the program a renegade on a chopper roared through the arena and was rewarded by cheers from the crowd.

Indio next year?" Chuck commented, "I don't know –maybe." But no one seemed to hear or care. After the trophies were awarded the crowd moved into the auditorium for the dance. Later that evening someone rode his bike into the auditorium and across the dance floor while the crowd cheered him on. Chuck Myers managed to get him back outside, but it wasn't long before another chopper roared through the cheering crowd, across the dance floor and center punched an elderly man. Latest word from the hospital is that the old timer will spend the rest of his life in a wheelchair.

At that point Myers told the crowd "If there's an Indio Tour next year, I won't be here." Not long after that someone started punching the band leader and Myers shut the dance down.

Thus died the Indio Tour, America's largest road rally. Many of the runs that still survive seem to be heading for the same fate. Apparently in today's society you can't have a large gathering of motorcyclists without it becoming infested with outlaws and turning into another Custer's Last Stand. The righteous citizen type rides will still have runs, but they will be small and secretive to avoid attracting undesirables. Road riding, for the squares, is becoming a subversive activity.

The Ace of Clubs put on their performance.

The only major catastrophe of the 1970s occurred in a parade on May 28, 1973. The team was performing their "Suicide Split" in the drill portion of their performance when Tylor Hicks hit a bump in the street and went flying off his motorcycle. He was taken to the hospital for further treatment and was released three days later. He still continued to perform with the Corps until 2014, when he retired and had no ill effects from the accident.

Officers in 1974

OFFICERS IN 1974
President: Ellis Smith
Vice President: Bob Keller
Treasurer: Joe Militello
Secretary: Dennis Ferry
Sergeant-at-Arms: Charlie Brown

OFFICERS IN 1975
President: Herb Harker
Vice President: Bob Keller
Secretary: Bob Blanchette
Treasurer: Ellis Smith
Sergeant at Arms: Carman Lachet

The Motor Corps held their 40th annual banquet on March 13, 1975, at Curly Jones Restaurant in Bellflower, California. They had 18 attendees.

Colonel Herb Harker
Ellis (Smitty) Smith
Gerard R. Blanchette
Carl Baker
Ron DeLeo
Donald Warren
Evelyn Biscailuz
Lyle Carmody
Carmen Lachet

Elizabeth Harker
Margaret Smith
Wendi Blanchette
Carol Baker
Lucy DeLeo
Sandra Warren
Harvey White
Dale Carmody
Lori Lachet

"Double Headstand"

The Rivalry Begins

Here's the story eluded to earlier.

In 1975, Harry Fisher (then a member of the Huntington Park Elks Motorcycle Stunt and Drill Team) performed a spectacular stunt at the Rose Bowl Independence Day festivities when he burst through a flaming firewall. The July 5th issue of the *Star News*, Pasadena, California, captured the photo.

The rivalry was on…the McLaglen Motor Corps and the Huntington Park Elks were struggling to book the same shows. And, if the competition wasn't difficult enough, both California-based teams were battling the Seattle Cossacks (Seattle, Washington) who were going full throttle. They had been performing shows since 1938, (three years after the birth of the McLaglen Motor Corps) and they were doing a great job. There were now three teams in the United States displaying exceptional motorcycle tricks and stunts. They were all worthy of leading a parade and performing their spectacular stunts in a way that captivated the audience.

"Double Push-Up"
Drivers: Lyle Carmody, Ellis Smith, Joe Militello

"P-38" Driver" Ellis Smith

Changing of the Guard

Herb & Liz Harker

In 1978, a major facelift took place for the Motor Corps. Colonel Herb Harker decided it was time for him to retire and move to Illinois with his wife, Liz. Wow! This meant, after 32 years, someone else would be in charge of the team. Who in the world would want to tackle such a huge task? That's when Herb had a great idea – he would call Harry Fisher. Harry had been off the team for a few years, however, he had been leading the Huntington Park Elks Stunt & Drill Team. He'd gained lots of experience, booked shows across the state of California, and would definitely be the right guy for the job – if only he could be persuaded. This was going to require some really good, fast-talking! So Herb gave Harry a call and invited him to "stop by sometime." He had something he wanted to discuss.

Well, since Herb and Harry had hardly spoken two words for a dozen or so years (after all, the Elks were competing for the same parades and shows that the Victors were trying to book and Harry had defected to go join the Elks), this phone call was quite a surprise. Curious about what Herb wanted to discuss, Harry said, "Sure. When do you want me to come by?" They agreed to meet the following weekend. Of course, I went along, too. I'm not going to miss this confrontation!

Harry's first reaction was that Herb probably had another Harley he was trying to sell! He couldn't have been more wrong. Instead, Herb broke the news to Harry that he was retiring and asked Harry if he would want to take over and lead the Victor McLaglen Motor Corps. What a shock!

So being really cool, Harry said he'd have to give it some thought and get back to him. The team had dwindled down to a half-dozen members or so, they weren't even doing shows with matching black and white bikes, and the number of shows was down. It looked like there was going to be a lot of work to get things up to speed. After Harry left Herb's house and after a whole half minute's consideration, Harry knew what he wanted to do. Then just to not look too anxious, he waited a couple more days before calling and letting Herb know that he probably could do it! Yes, we did discuss it at home, but it was a no-brainer! The Motor Corps was Harry's passion. And this was my own introduction to the Victor McLaglen Motor Corps, which would become my passion, also.

"The New Gang"

Harry called on everyone he knew who rode a Harley and asked them to come to practice. Once they were at practice and had watched for a few minutes, he made sure they became involved in some of the stunts, standing on the rear rack or the rear fender, following along at the tail end of the drill, or merely sitting on a mini-bike and given instructions on how to do traffic control for safety when the team was doing a major stunt at a parade. They were hooked! It was fun. They got to show off. They were part of a famous motorcycle stunt team – and they learned to ride their motorcycles really well. Most guys went home and practiced riding slow after work every day, slipping the clutch, doing slow circles with their hands off the handlebars, and all with a Cheshire Cat smile on their faces!

By the end of the following year, the team was comprised of 25 members. In addition to performing at 40 shows, every weekend was spent practicing for the next performance.

The Victor McLaglen Motor Corps was back!

1979 was a tremendous year. The Corp performed at 75 events and by Christmas time, had 25 members. The team was written up in Chopper Magazine (twice), Street Chopper Magazine, Chronicle Newspaper, Custom Bike Magazine, FTW newspaper, Cycle News, and many local newspapers from towns where we performed. We were televised on CBS for the Ontario Motor Speedway show, Channels 5 and 11 for the Hollywood Christmas Parade, and Channel 4 for the parade in Echo Park, California. In addition, we had more than 34 intense practice sessions. Yep, we were busy. The riders were sporting navy jumpsuits, white T-Shirts and Motor Corps caps. This was not quite the uniform we wanted, but it would do until we could find a sponsor to acquire more official ones.

Drivers: Roger Davies,
Harry Fisher, Kirby Frymoyer,
Ellis Smith
Standing 1st row:
Bruce Chubbuck, Bob Jensen,
Dick Gerry, xx
Standing 2nd row: Gene French,
Mark Frymoyer
Top: George Anderson
Front Fender: Al Ruiz, XX

In 1978, we gathered for a group photo after practice at the UAW Local 148 parking lot on Pixie Avenue in Long Beach, California.

(L-R) Bill McDonald, Teri & Gene French, Sonny Day, Ellis & Margaret Smith, Harry & Ruth Fisher, Sharon & Roxie Mack, Dale & Lyle Carmody. In orange shirts in the front: Denise Davies and six year old Marty Fisher. (Marty would grow up to be a member of the team and an excellent Motor Man.)

Show helmet

Practice helmet

"P-38 Ladder"
Driving: Ellis Smith, Left: Bruce Chubbuck, Right: Gene French, Back: Tylor Hicks, Upside down: George Anderson

On Saturday, June 17, 1978, the Motor Corps performed at the Golden Age of Motorcycles bike show at the Burbank Golden Mall. Norman Jamison, President of the Southern California Side-Hack Association, wrote, *"Approximately 10,000 people viewed our display (of motorcycles) and over 2,000 watched your group perform. We were amazed as to the magnitude of motorcycle stunts done on those big Harley-Davidsons."* So – only 2,000 people watched the show? What were the other 8,000 doing? I think maybe the performance area must have been in a bad location at the show or something!

However, we had a second chance. In 1979, we did it again. It appeared we had more people watching this time after the audience got word of what they missed the previous year!

1978, the 2nd year of the "reorganization"
Team members:
Motormen: Roger Davies, Harry Fisher, Ellis Smith, Chuck Buckner
Standing: Lyle Carmody, Mark Frymoyer (on top),
Safety (back): Gene French, Kirby Frymoyer, Al Ruiz

The Members

The roster at the end of the year in 1978:

```
DUES PAID BY MEMBERS OF V.M.M.C.

 1. HARRY M. FISHER        APRIL 2, 1978   TO   APRIL 2, 1979
 2. LYLE I. CARMODY        APRIL 2, 1978   TO   APRIL 2, 1979
 3. ELLIS M. SMITH         APRIL 2, 1978   TO   APRIL 2, 1979
 4. ROBERT E. KELLER       APRIL 2, 1978   TO   APRIL 2, 1979
 5. KIRBY A. FRYMOYER      APRIL 2, 1978   TO   APRIL 2, 1979
 6. MARK A. FRYMOYER       APRIL 2, 1978   TO   APRIL 2, 1979
 7. NICK C. OLIVER         APRIL 2, 1978   TO   APRIL 2, 1979
 8. DENNIS J. KATTHOEFER   APRIL 2, 1978   TO   APRIL 2, 1979
 90. THOMAS S. COWEN       APRIL 2, 1978   TO   APRIL 2, 1979
 11. BRUCE CHUBBUCK        OCTIL 1, 1978   TO   OCT.  1, 1979
 10. ROBERT P. GALUSHA     APRIL 2, 1978   TO   APRIL 2, 1979
 12. GEORGE M. ANDERSON    APRIL 2, 1978   TO   APRIL 2, 1979
 13. ROBERT JENSEN         AUG. 27, 1978   TO   AUG. 27, 1979
 14. FOREST C. MOHR        OCT.  1, 1978   TO   OCT.  1, 1979
 15. AL RUIZ               SEPT. 9, 1978   TO   SEPT. 9, 1979
 16. RAYMOND L. BROSELL
 17. NATHAN S. HALL        OCT.  8, 1978   TO   OCT.  8, 1979
 18. AL MACIAS             OCT.  1, 1978   TO   OCT.  1, 1979
 19. RICHARD D. GERRY      OCT.  1, 1978   TO   OCT.  1, 1979
 20. GERALD L. THOMPSON
 21. GENE FRENCH           APRIL 2, 1978   TO   APRIL 2, 1979
 22. ROGER DAVIES          JULY 23, 1978   TO   JULY 23, 1979
 23. ROGER McKINNEY        OCT.  1, 1978   TO   OCT.  1, 1979
 24. DONALD WARREN         OCT.  8, 1978   TO   OCT.  8, 1979
 25. CHARLIE BROWN         NOV.  5, 1978   TO   NOV.  5, 1980
```

By the end of 1978, the McLaglens had 25 members.
The average age of the Motor Corps members in 1979 was 29 years old.

Prior to obtaining the new uniforms, we kicked off the 1979, 3 Flags Classic motorcycle run. This is a motorcycle ride, sponsored by the Southern California Motorcycling Association (SCMA), in which the participants ride from Mexico, through the U.S.A. and into Canada, thus "3 Flags!"

The Motor Corps kicked off the run with a spectacular performance.

Front Row: xx, Al Ruiz Sr, Ellis Smith, Gene French, Lyle Carmody, Tylor Hicks, Walt Hauser, Harry Fisher, Bruce Chubbuck, Willie Abrams
Middle Row: Albert Ruiz, Jr., Bob Keller, George Anderson, Kevin Anderson, Sonny Day
Back Row: Chuck Buckner, Kirby Frymoyer, Nate Hall, Ruben Pantoja, Bob Galusha,
Ray Brosell, Bob Jensen, Dick Gerry, Jerry Thompson, Bill McDonald. Roger Davies

On September 16th, we attended SCMA's Fun Run and performed our show at El Dorado Park in Long Beach, California.

This was followed by leading off the Korean Festival Parade on September 23rd in downtown Los Angeles.

Finally, as a "thank you" to the UAW Local #148 for letting us practice every Sunday in their parking lot on Pixie Ave in Long Beach, we put on a show and provided entertainment for their 2nd Annual Picnic in El Dorado Park, which was held on October 21.

It seemed that November was consumed by Motor Corps activities.

On November 3rd, we led the Bellflower Christmas Parade and did a show at the Bellflower Harley shop. November 23rd we led the Lynwood Christmas Parade, November 23rd led off the notorious Hollywood Christmas Parade and on November 24th the team helped with the Cycle News Barstow to Vegas Poker Run.

December was equally busy, and now we sported new brown, police-style uniforms, which looked especially sharp. The December events included:
- Ontario Time's 500 Race
- Highland Park Christmas Parade
- Downey Christmas Parade
- Southgate Christmas Parade
- Covina Christmas Parade
- Echo Park Christmas Parade
- Motor Corps Christmas party

It was time for the team to recuperate. The riders performed some annual maintenance on the bikes, caught up on some "honey-do's" and revitalized ourselves for the next season of riding.

John Moser

About this time, Harry had a visit from the leader of the Seattle Cossacks, John Moser. The Cossacks is a motorcycle stunt and drill team from Washington state and had been performing at shows since 1938, three years after the McLaglen team got started. John was passing through Southern California and gave Harry a call. They got together for coffee and Harry invited John to come to practice the next day. Harry thought maybe John could give him some pointers on how to do stunts!

John was a good sport and said, "Sure," and the next day, there he was.

So Harry gave John one of his famous "song and dance" stories about how he hadn't been doing this kind of riding long and could sure use some help – and John bought it! His first mistake!

Harry introduced John to the team. John borrowed one of the bikes and showed Harry and the team a few tricks which included standing on the rear rack, slow circles, standing on the seat, riding backwards, etc. John was really an excellent rider. In fact, there aren't many guys who can do what John could on a bike. However, Harry was not just any guy!

Harry grabbed his own bike and warmed up a bit. "Hey, John, is this how you do that riding slow in a circle thing?" " Hey, John, if I stand on the seat like this, is that right?" "Hey John, if I just turn around and ride backward, do you think that'll work in a show?" "Hey, John– Hey, John – Hey, John" – Pretty soon John got the message. He'd been snookered! He realized that Harry and the team were really good riders and he wasn't showing them anything they didn't already know. He was a good sport, though, and everyone got a big belly-laugh out of it. This was the beginning of a great friendship with the Seattle Cossacks.

Unfortunately, John passed away on February 17, 2014 – just one month prior to Harry's death. Undoubtedly, they are behind those Pearly Gates, developing their own new stunt team with all the old members waiting for them and ready to entertain everybody up there! Probably calling themselves the "Winged McLaglen-Cossacks Motorcycle Stunt Team."

"I'll just ride back here for a bit."

"Hey, these guys really know how to ride. I've been snookered!"

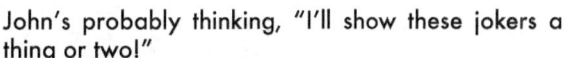

John's probably thinking, "I'll show these jokers a thing or two!"

"Then I'll ride in their little drill."

The team also performed at Trojan Field in Yucca Valley, California, where Harry did the "Board Jump" over the poor prostrate team member at a grand opening at Hutchins Harley-Davidson dealership store in Yucca Valley, California.

Al Ruiz wowed the audience by riding backwards.

Honest – there is a plank that Harry is driving up to "run over" his pal Al!

This is what happens when the top man on the "Pyramid" doesn't duck his head.

EVERYBODY COMFY? – Harry Fisher is always glad to pick up an extra rider or two on his Harley. If they're willing to put up with his unique seating arrangements.

Prior to obtaining the new brown uniforms, the Corps were hooked up with the Interpart Shocks Company and agreed to have their picture on their advertisement.

In 1979, the Motor Corps did over 40 parades, shows and special events, including the Pacific Palisades 4th of July Parade, the Huntington Beach 4th of July Parade, and the Hollywood Christmas Parade, formerly known then as the Santa Claus Lane Parade.

These parades were very hard on the motorcycle engines. Generally, the drills are done at a rate of speed of about 7-9 mph and this often can cause overheating. The parades were hard on the members too. The guy on the top of that "Pyramid" had to climb up there numerous times throughout the parade route and the guy spread out between two bikes for the "Spread Eagle" had to have arms of steel to perform this feat over and over.

Tijuana Police Suicide Squadron

In September we went to Tijuana, Mexico, to perform at the Governor's Palace on Labor Day weekend. This was for a grand send-off to over 250 motorcycle riders leaving on SCMA's Three Flags Run, that went from Mexico, through the USA, to Canada. We were escorted by the Tijuana Police to Benito Juarez Stadium to put on another show for the governor, mayor, police department, and children of Tijuana, in celebration of "The Year of Our Youth." After our show, the Tijuana Police's "Suicide Squadron" put on an exhibition and the entire show lasted some two hours.

The Tijuana Police motorcycle stunt team put on a fantastic show, building human pyramids, riding backwards and doing headstands. Unfortunately, things turned tragic when motorcyclist Jose Malesio Camacho Inzunza was killed. The Mexican team attempted a high-speed jumping crossover. The timing was just a split second off, and Officer Inzunza and Agent Carlos Urrea collided. Agent Urrea was injured, but recovered. Unfortunately, Officer Inzunza did not. The following week, many of the Victor McLaglen Motor Corps members traveled back to Tijuana to attend the funeral services and pay respects to this talented motorcycle stuntman.

The Tijuana Police doing their fantastic stunts.

The Tijuana weekend from member Bruce Chubbuck's prospective in later years.

"There was another incident at Tijuana that happened and is worthy of mentioning. I don't think many were aware of it happening. We stayed at San Ysidro, California, and caravaned to the stadium. We were met at the border by a police motorcycle escort. When we got to the stadium I couldn't see John Moser's motorhome and trailer which had my wife, daughters, and others on board with Harry's bikes and the one I was going to ride (Harry's 33VL) in a trailer hitched behind. I do not remember how I got to the stadium. I know I rode with someone because I was in uniform. I talked to a few motor officers and one pointed to a Lieutenant who spoke English. I told him that a motorhome fell off the escort. He asked what it looked like. I looked up and there it was on the highway. They were on the highway to Ensenada. He told me to, "get on the back of this officer's motorcycle and point them out when you see them." They were going to get off the highway about 7 miles down by going off wrong way on an on ramp. I sat on the radio box of a well worn vibrating Kawasaki police bike with no place to put my feet and I grabbed onto his belt loops. Going code 3 on Tijuana's chuck-holed streets with all the holiday traffic, was terrifying. Not too far down the road, there it was. My wife, Lynda, was kneeling on the engine box between John and his wife and they recognized the brown uniformed passenger (me). We turned around and police-escorted the motorhome to the stadium. Lynda said that the motorhome was the only 4-wheel vehicle being escorted. When the escort motorcycles left, they were out of sight before John was in gear. John knew that being on this highway, they would have to get off at the first opening regardless where it was going. John did exactly what the Lieutenant said he should do. But he was worried the police might be looking for them. Besides that, the police bike in front of him with red lights on made him a little nervous. They were at the stadium in less a half hour and most did not know the motorhome was lost. The event finished in a tragedy and it was after dark when we were escorted back to the border. This time the motorhome went first and we were escorted going the wrong way on an unopened freeway. The escort motors blocked a two-mile long line of cars trying to get back over the border. This time I was in the motorhome and I was standing in the doorway. A man in a green Border Patrol coat wanted to know why we were escorted to the border. John, with his usual charm, told the man "I don't know. Maybe they like us". The man then asked "How many are in there". John said "16". The guy said "Aw sh...Get out of here you're blocking the line".

In November 1979, the team performed for the Huntington Park Elks Lodge Motorcycle Stunt & Drill Team's Poker Run.

From Cycle News, November 7, 1979

"The Victor's laid out a figure 8, a square, a plank teeter-totter ride, and a clothespin game. Winner of the male solo field event trophy was Mark Frymoyer –wouldn't you know it, a member of the Victor McLaglens!

After the field events, the Victor McLaglen's put on a 30-minute performance for the group with a few of their pyramids, chariots, spread eagles, and backwards rides, It was quite a sight to see and was appreciated by all the riders The club was handed a check for their services but it was donated back to the Lodge for the Cerebral Palsy Major Project Fund. The Nuggets received the largest club trophy and the Mixed Breed motorcycle club had the only two members who could successfully do one of the field event games. All in all, everyone had a good time and the riders all agreed that this is one run that they are going to sign up for again next year."

The Victor McLaglen stunt team performed at the Elks' poker run.

Doing a "Headstand" on the gas tank

On Top: Mark Frymoyer
Driving: Harry Fisher, Kirby Frymoyer

From *Street Chopper*, December 1979

ABOVE—The Victor McLaglen Stunt and Drill Team was on hand to give the crowd some thrills with their trick riding techniques. Think the police would frown on this one if they saw it coming down the street.

1ST ANNUAL BIKER ART SHOW

Art works, bikes bikes and live tv to record it

BY JIM PISARETZ

Anyone who knows anything about the motorcycle business knows there's a great deal happening that can be called "art." All you have to do is go to a really good custom show and check out some of the scooters. Not only will you find that the paint jobs are as artistic as many of the things you'll see hanging on the walls of galleries, but you'll find that the style, lines and everything else that went into making the bike was as carefully thought out and planned as some of the best sculpture.

It is true that anyone involved in biking understands this, but few people outside of the sport know that there is an entire art form related to motorcycles and riding. Bob Philips of the MMA of L.A. decided it was time for people to be made aware of fact. He got together with the Pasadena Community Arts Center and they decided to put on a show.

Two galleries provided ample space to display works by David Mann, Gary Little John and others. The tank art, photographs, oil paintings and water colors attracted alot of attention during the day.

Outside on the grounds several hundred bikes were set up to be judged in different categories. Sure they were all riders, but there were some fine looking scooters there.

While the show was going on KNBC set up their cameras for the Sunday Show, a local, live broadcast. The TV people talked to bikers, checked out some of the art work and conducted interviews with people like LACO Bob Lawrence, who started the MMA to run in L.A. years ago, Patricia Zonker, who wrote an anti-motorcycle book recently, Bob "Bitchin" Lipkin whose by line has been floating around the bike mags for years, as well as Phillips and members of the college art staff.

One thing that can be said about the TV coverage was that it got a side of motorcycling across to the public that they didn't know existed before. Who knows, if enough people stand up and take notice of biker related art you might be able to go into a gallery some day and see it displayed along with all of the other "serious" art.

On November 28, 1979, Harry decided that the Motor Corps could partner with the Douglas Aircraft Company (DAC) and maybe get some sponsorship as well as more shows and publicity. He wrote a letter to the President of DAC and pointed out some slogans that could be used, such as:

- "The quiet in the sky – The roar on the ground"
- "Number one in the sky – Number one on the ground"
- "Truly the American Way – The American-made plane – The American-made motorcycle"
- "If it can transport the entire Victor McLaglen Motor Corps, its motorcycles equipment and auxiliary and still have room to practice on the way, it can transport you."
- "McDonnell's DC-10, the Victor McLaglen Motor Corps' DC-10 Stunt"
- "A World Champion likes company"
- "Is there NOTHING safer than flying?"

Harry's letter, the clever slogans and his persistence got him a meeting with the folks at Douglas Aircraft Company. Harry dug out his best (and only) suit, gathered up some pictures, newspaper articles, magazine pictures and anything else he thought would impress them and attended the meeting.

Unfortunately, he received a letter a week or so later from the Director of Advertising stating "our marketing objectives don't seem to be in concert with the values that can be achieved by such a relationship."

Disappointing but, well, you don't know until you try!

Harry, all spiffed up in a suit and tie, getting a security badge so he can enter the Douglas Aircraft facilities

6th Annual Los Angeles Times 500
Grand National Stock Car Race
November 18, 1979 – Ontario Motor Speedway

Daredevil stunts by the famed Victor McLaglen Motorcycle Corps will be another highlight of the show. Formed in 1935 by the late Academy Award winning actor, the club has enjoyed more than 40 years of performing at civic events and parades around the country.

Harry Fisher and Roger Davies perform the "Wheelbarrow Ride" stunt in front of the announcing stage at a parade somewhere in Southern California.

Years later, Stunt Leader Mickey Minor and Dan Welch decided to try this stunt. Only, they didn't do it at practice. They did it with just the two of them on a side street near one of their homes after work – with NO INSTRUCTION!

That following weekend, they showed up at the regular Motor Corps practice field with bruises and bandages and Mickey with a cracked wrist. Harry asked, "What happened?" Mickey sort of sheepishly said, "Well, Dan and I were trying to do that there "Wheelbarrow Ride," and we lost control!" Harry laughed (heck, we ALL laughed) and he said, "Mickey, there is a trick to it, you know." Mickey said, "What's that?" Harry said, "You don't hold onto the throttle when Dan pushes you up. You hold onto the handlebar in front of it. In that way, when you are pushed up, you don't accidentally roll the throttle on and rev it up, get out of control and fall on your keester."

After they learned that little trick, Mickey and Dan did an excellent job with the stunt and incorporated it into the stunt routine at the shows.

Mickey Minor and Dan Welch perfecting their "Wheelbarrow Ride"

Many of the new Motor Corps members came from the Elks team. Harry had a way of talking anyone into almost anything! If you had a Harley, he'd talk you into painting it black and white and riding with the team, even if it's a beautiful candy-apple red or outstanding cobalt blue. If you wanted to join the team, that was the deal – you had to have a black and white Harley.

If you lacked confidence in your riding ability, Harry'd talk you into riding straight ahead in the flag unit for a while until you'd mastered drill riding. If you didn't have a Harley, he managed to get some mini-bikes donated from Hutch, owner of Buttelier Harley-Davidson, so you'd have a ride. You'd ride along beside the stunts in parades as safety to keep spectators out of the way, then eventually you'd work up to getting a big bike and joining the drill.

The trick was to get you watching, then participating in some small way, then standing on an "easy" stunt, then getting more and more enthused until before you knew it, you were a full-fledged member, riding in the drill, doing stunts you never dreamed you could do, and loving every minute of it!

PAID EVENTS

Feb. 17	Carson Parade
May 6	San Fernando Parade
May 12	Fontana Parade
May 27	Brentwood Parade
July 4	Huntington Beach Parade
July 4	Pacific Palisades Parade
July 4	Huntington Beach Infield
Aug. 4	La Habra Parade
Sept. 23	Korean Festival Parade
Oct. 13	Westminster Parade
Oct. 27	Granada Hills Parade
Nov. 3	Bellflower Parade
Nov. 8	Ontario Speedway Infield
Nov. 30	Lynwood Parade
Dec. 1	Highland Park Parade
Dec. 2	Downey Parade
Dec. 7	Montrose Parade
Dec. 9	South Gate Parade
Dec. 16	Echo Park Parade

NON-PAID EVENTS

Apr. 2	Poker Run
Apr. 7	SCMA Blood Bank
June 9	SCMA Blood Bank
June 15	Burbank Mall Side-Hack
June 30	San Diego Veterans Benefit
July 1	SCMA Picnic Show
July 29	Pasadena Art Show
Aug. 31	SCMA Tijuana Show
Sept. 1	Tijuana Year of Our Youth
Sept. 16	SCMA Fund Raising Run
Oct. 13	Westminster HD Show
Oct. 14	H.P. Elks Road Run Show
Oct. 21	UAW Picnic Show
Oct. 27	Van Nuys HD Show
Nov. 4	Yucca Valley HD Show
Nov. 24	Las Vegas to Barstow Run
Nov. 25	Hollywood Christmas Parade
Dec. 1	Covina Christmas Parade
Dec. 23	Sawtell Veterans Hospital

The team's very busy 1979 schedule

Victor McLaglen Motor Corps embroidered on the back. They would be bought at the local Sears or Penney's stores and were inexpensive. Soon we would get our new brown police-style uniforms and look really professional. Then the jumpsuits would be used only for practices.

(Left)
The "Headstand"
(Right)
The "High Pyramid"
Drivers: Kirby Frymoyer
& Ellis Smith
Standing: Jerry Thompson & Sonny Day
Safety: George Anderson
On top: Al Ruiz

The "Floorboard Ride
Stuntman: Harry Fisher

The "Backward Ride"
Stuntman: Al Ruiz

1980 – 1989

The 1980s were even more successful for the Motor Corps. We had 38 members by the time the decade was over and had traveled extensively throughout the U.S. We were written about in many motorcycle magazines and almost everyone who was associated with the motorcycle industry, knew about the Victor McLaglen Motor Corps.

"The High Pyramid"
Motormen: Bob Jensen, Harry Fisher, Mike Betschart, Kirby Frymoyer
Headlights: Albert Ruiz, Sonny Day, Frank Hicks, Mickey Minor
Center: Willie Abrams.
Standing: Gene French, Chuck Buckner, Bob Holbrook, Tylor Hicks
Top: Al Ruiz

In 1980, the team of over 30 members gathered for an Executive Board meeting. The membership was growing and we were receiving more requests to perform than we could possibly accept and disappointed that we had to decline some of the invitations.

It occurred to our members that we could separate into two teams. This would make it possible to accept more invitations, provide a break so members didn't have to work every weekend; and, of course, allow the members to spend a little time with our families. You gotta keep everybody happy, you know!

Although it seemed like a good idea at the time, this plan didn't last long. Splitting up the "family" just didn't make it as much fun. It wasn't too long before we returned to just one team.

GROUP 1	GROUP 2
Al Ruiz, Leader	Harry Fisher, Leader
Kevin Anderson	Willie Abrams
Harvey Behling	Fred Augustine
Ray Brosell	Ken Brown
Lyle Carmody	Chuck Buckner
Bruce Chubbuck	Roger Davies
Sonny Day	Andy Dumont
Gene French	Bob Galusha
Kirby Frymoyer	Dick Gerry
Tylor Hicks	Frank Hicks
Bob Jensen	Bob Holbrook
Al Macias	Ruben Pantoja
Nick Oliver	Albert Ruiz
Ellis Smith	Jerry Thompson

The guys led off the 1980 South Gate Christmas parade in California. It is interesting to note in this picture that the movie, "Touch of Death," was playing at that theater, starring Bruce Lee. I'll bet even Bruce couldn't have made THIS performance any more exciting!

Rene Sevilla climbing to the top spot on the "High Pyramid".

Tylor Hicks in the middle of the "Spread Eagle" with Ellis Smith (Left), and Kirby Frymoyer (Right) as motormen.

1980 South Gate Christmas Parade
The "High Pyramid"
Driving: Kirby Frymoyer, Harry Fisher,
Mike Betschart, Guillermo Sevilla
Standing on seats: Marty Fisher, Bob Holbrook
Standing on shoulders: Al Ruiz, Fernando Camarena
Top: Rene Sevilla
Safety: William Sevilla

On behalf of the Victor McLaglen Motor Corps, Lyle Carmody and Harry Fisher accepted an award at the 1980 American Motorcycling Association (AMA) banquet, presented by Lin Kuchler of AMA.

The Motor Corps, along with Cycle News, also sponsored the 2nd Annual Barstow to Vegas Motorcycle Road Ride and Poker Run. The ride went well – but, mostly, I remember that it was just plain cold that day!

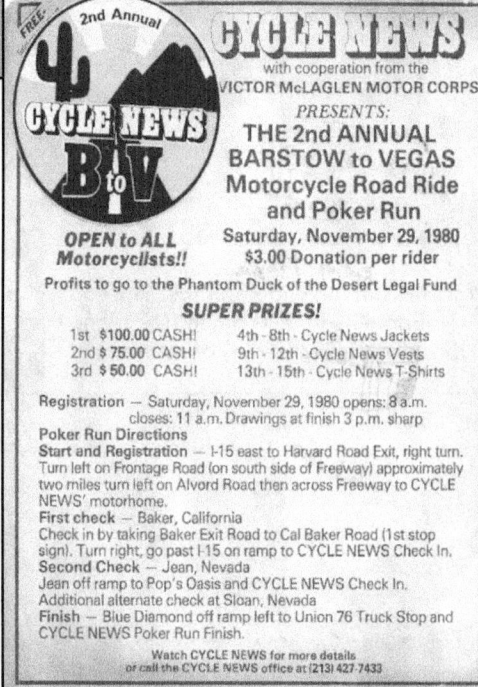

"1980 Montrose Christmas Parade"
Local newspaper - Thursday, December 11, 1980
"Those daredevil stuntriders from the Victor McLaglen Motor Corps, shown above on their Harley-Davidsons, gave a return performance this year in the Montrose Christmas Parade."

By Tedd Farrell

Ruidoso, NM -1980

On October 4, 1980, the Motor Corps traveled to Ruidoso, New Mexico, to perform at the Americade Motorcycle Convention. This trip took more planning and coordination than the newly reorganized team had had to tackle so far, and the guys were really excited.

There were 15 members flying and others who would drive ahead to transport the motorcycles and make sure the lodging and transportation from the airport was all in place and ready.

We contracted SATCO Charter Company in Fullerton, California, to fly the team in two planes, each holding eight members. Then on October 4, 1980, the two groups flew out of Long Beach Airport in Long Beach, California to the Sierra Blanco Airport in Ruidoso, New Mexico.

Plane #1 passengers had to be at the airport ready to go at 4:00AM, stop off in Phoenix for fuel, and arrive in Ruidoso at 8:30AM.

Plane #2 passengers got to sleep in a bit and arrive at the airport at 5:30AM and then arrive in Ruidoso at 8:30AM.

Plane #1	Plane #2	Driving
1. Bruce Chubbuck	1. Fred Auguston	1. Harry and Ruth Fisher
2. Ellis (Smitty) Smith	2. Al Ruiz Sr.	2. Willie Abrams
3. Roger Davies	3. Chuck Buckner	3. Harvey Behling
4. Kevin Anderson	4. Bob Holbrook	4. Ken Brown
5. Tylor Hicks	5. Bob Jenson	5. Andy Dumont
6. Ray Brosell	6. George Anderson	6. Kirby Frymoyer
7. Albert Ruiz	7. Al Macias	7. Dick Gerry
	8. Andy Dumont	8. Frank Hicks

The total price for the 15 people flying? Only $3,675.00! What a deal!

The 21 motorcycles were transported in a commercial trailer furnished by Orange County Van & Storage Company and the truck was owned and operated by one of our members, Kenny Frost.

The members and our families stayed in little rustic cabins. Each cabin had two or three bedrooms, kitchenette, and living room with fireplace, lots of gorgeous pine trees all around and – really quiet. Although Ruidoso is a booming ski area in the winter, it was booming with motorcyclists during this event.

At an altitude of almost 7,000 feet, our riders had a bit of a problem with the carburetors (and breathing); however, they managed to pull off the shows with their usual professionalism. The promoter was happy, the spectators were dutifully impressed, and we all had an absolutely terrific time.

The sponsors for this event were: Southern California Harley-Davidson Dealers Association, Northern California Harley-Davidson Dealers Association, Orange County Van & Storage, and Kenny Frost.

Speaking Requests in the 1980s

The 1980s also brought lots of speaking requests.

- Kiwanis Club of Beverly Hills
- La Habra Lions Club
- Wilshire Kiwanis Club
- Alhambra Lions Club
- Rotary Club of Hollywood
- Exchange Club of La Mirada

I'm surprised that we had time to ride those motorcycles! Although I did find one stunt list from that period that had 33 stunts on it, so I guess we did squeeze in some practices and shows after all!

In October of 1985, we once again made a trip to Ruidoso. This time we stayed in a bunkhouse, which was a lot of fun. The team did 28 stunts at each performance and everyone had a great time.

Baldwin Park Anniversary Parade
January 1981

Bob Holbrook, who was originally a member of the Huntington Park Elks team had joined the McLaglen team in 1980. By day, he had a desk job as a data processing analyst. The people at work didn't have a clue what Bob did on his "off" hours until they read this article in the Hughes Aircraft Company's, Electro-Optical & Data Systems Group's EDSG newsletter!

EDSG'S Real People: Bob Holbrook

Daredevils Bob Holbrook and Evel Knievel have two things in common: they both like motorcycle stunts and flashy uniforms. Holbrook, a data processing analyst at Hughes, belongs to the Victor McLaglen Motor Corps Motorcycle Stunt and Drill Team.

Though Holbrook, who lives in West L.A., said he prefers silver embellishments and stars, the Motor Corps presently dresses in dark brown uniforms similar to the California Highway Patrol's garb. Add a white helmet and a black and white Harley Davidson, and Holbrook looks convincingly like a bona fide cop.

"I'll be riding to a performance and someone will say, 'Hey officer, how do I get to the parade?' Sometimes I go ahead and give directions and they never realize I'm just an ordinary citizen."

Holbrook got involved with the "bike" club about a year ago. Since then he's learned 12 stunts, to which there are basically three aspects: driving, supporting, and the daredevil stuff — such as standing on the supporter's shoulders. All the tricks are done while moving at an average speed of 10 miles per hour.

"The most dangerous stunt I've done is the 'Standing Horse,'" he said. "In it, I leap on the back of a bike as another team member drives by. Then, as we're moving, I climb on top of his shoulders and stand up, holding onto a rope attached to the handlebars."

In addition to stunts, the team performs precision riding — figure eights, crossovers and other, more elaborate routines.

Holbrook performed in about 40 parades this year, including the Hollywood Santa Claus Lane Parade. Most of his weekends are spent practicing for or riding in performances. The Motor Corps has appeared at the San Francisco Cow Palace, the Las Vegas Helldorado Days, and just recently at a Fourth of July spectacular in Cerritos. This September they will be featured in a "That's Incredible" segment filmed at the Ventura Motorcycle Jamboree on Memorial Day weekend.

The club currently has 30 members. For more information, contact Bob Holbrook, Culver City, ext. 7184, or Harry Fisher, the corps commander, at 792-1300.

— Dinah Lahnala

Bob Holbrook (top) and fellow motor corps member Chuck Buckner demonstrate the "Standing Horse" stunt.

11th Aspencade Motorcycle Convention

In October 1981, the team made a return trip to Ruidoso, NM, to perform for the 11th Annual Aspencade Motorcycle Convention.

An issue of *The Ruidoso News* said, "The appearance of the Victor McLaglen Motor Corps, a precision motorcycle drill team of Los Angeles, California, was a parade highlight. These daring-do performers were roundly applauded as they displayed their skills in balancing and in the execution of intricate riding patterns.

The troop performed for an hour at the Chaparral Motor Hotel parking lot later Saturday afternoon. Again, the crowd applauded the performance which was highlighted by balancing exhibitions. In some instances the performers were parallel to the ground, with their jackets just scraping on the paving as the motorcycles moved slowly."

Doing a bit of drill at 7 mph.

A stunt known as the "Swan".

Bakersfield Motorcycle Jamboree

In 1981, we performed in more than 30 parades and shows. This was quite a feat, considering all the members donate their time, equipment, and expertise. Being a member of the VMMC is something we all do over and above our regular jobs.

One of the greatest accomplishments in 1981, was the **23 Men on One Bike stunt**. After attempting to set this record at the U.S. Motorcycle Jamboree in Ventura, California, we hustled back to Brentwood to perform in a parade of 40,000 people. The day was just beginning, however, as we returned (once again) to Ventura for more stunts. More about the **23 Men on One Bike** later.

The Seattle Cossacks were also performing at the Bakersfield Jamboree and the teams agreed to work together to perform even more feats for the crowds. This combination of talents nearly brought the house down. Those Harley riders in the audience really enjoyed the show.

Members attempt their stunt for Guiness Book of World Records: "23-Men on One Bike'

Valley Daily News: "Fiesta Parade kicks off Cinco de Mayo celebration ushering in the annual Cinco de Mayo celebration in the northeast Valley, a Fiesta Parade was held in San Fernando Sunday."

The Seattle Cossacks

Parades in 1981
April 27, 1981

Los Angeles newspaper: "This motorcycle stunt and drill team that performed yesterday was only one of the various modes of transportation from Los Angeles present and past that trucked, or in some cases, ambled down Spring Street from 7th to Temple Streets. The event was the official L.A. Bicentennial "200 Years of Transportation on Parade." Celebrities and community leaders rode in all kinds of contraptions used for transportation in the city's 200 years. The vehicles included an 1800 Conestoga Wagon, a Studebaker Izzer (the last horse-drawn vehicle) the Model A and T cars and modern automobiles."

April 29, 1981

The San Diego Union newspaper: "Uneasy Riders: Members of a Los Angeles motorcycle stunt team "spread their wings" during a recent parade to prove one of two things: (1) That five men can ride a motorcycle, or (2) the team has only one motorcycle."

Notice — Same picture in both stories about different cities and events! Picture supplied by the Associated Press. I think they got their money's worth out of that photo!

The Pasadena Muscular Dystrophy Association Run

Team member, Bruce Chubbuck, the owner of Chubbuck's Harley-Davidson dealership in Pasadena, had a good reason to host his first benefit run. While attending the Las Vegas Harley-Davidson new model announcement meeting, where up-to-date product lines were displayed, Bruce had the opportunity to meet acclaimed actor/comedian Jerry Lewis. Mr. Lewis, National Chairman and 40-year host of the Muscular Dystrophy Association's (MDA) Annual Labor Day Telethon, told the dealers that the MDA was the new company charity and asked for their support.

In May 1981, the Victor McLaglen Motor Corps performed at Bruce's Pasadena Muscular Dystrophy Association (MDA) Run. It was the first benefit run that Bruce had put on and all donations were to be presented to the MDA.

The weather was perfect and the ride spanned over 127 miles of scenic countryside. The run began at the dealership and continued through the valleys of Lake Hughes and the Angeles Forest Highway, before returning to Brookside Park in Pasadena for food, fun and games and a performance by the Motor Corps.

Following the Pasadena Run, Bruce was invited to the Jerry Lewis' Labor Day Telethon to present a check for $1,500 to the MDA. This was a sizable amount of money in 1981 and Bruce said his daughter, Wendy, wanted to be on TV, so she went with him to make the presentation. They were scheduled to present the check at 3:00AM, immediately following a presentation by Oliver Shokouh from Glendale Harley. Oliver's donation was larger, so he was targeted for 2:00AM. For whatever reason, Oliver did not show up, so they moved Bruce into his time slot. There were no cell phones, so Bruce was unable to tell anyone of the time change so they could turn their TVs on. Bruce presented the check and was preparing to tell everyone about the Victor McLaglen Motor Corps when they began asking Wendy questions about motorcycle safety. Bruce said his daughter ruined his big show biz break. "It always seems the pretty girls steal the show," says Bruce proudly. Too bad, Bruce.

As a result of the Pasadena MDA Run, there were quite a few winners. The MDA received $1,500, Harry Fisher won the slow race, Dan Murphy and partner won the egg toss, Bruce and his wife, Lynda, won a trip from Harley-Davidson Motor Company to Club Med in Ixtapa, Mexico, for their Harley shop's support of MDA, and Wendy made her first television debut. I'd say it was a very successful event!

Lynda & Bruce Chubbuck

On June 28, 1981, the team led the 29th Flower Festival Parade in Lompoc, California, and once again, we got our picture in the local newspaper.

"The High Pyramid"
L-R: Driving Chuck Buckner,
Harry Fisher, Ellis Smith, Bob Jensen
Standing –Dick Gerry,
Jerry Thompson, Bob Holbrook,
Gene French
Safety –Roger Davies,
Top –Al Ruiz
June 28, 1981

The Motor Corps led lots of parades throughout the year and ended the season with the Hollywood Christmas Parade on November 29, 1981 and the 34th Annual "Days of the Verdugo's Parade.

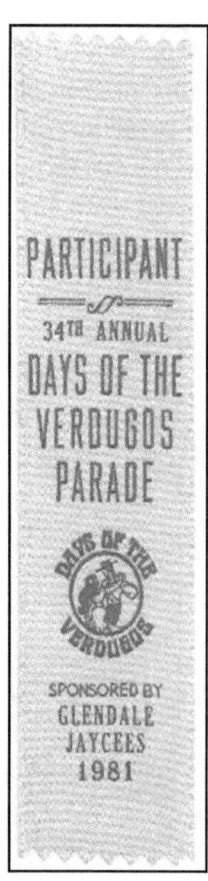

Author Gerald Foster published a book entitled "Cult of the Harley-Davidson" in 1981, and he devoted a couple of pages to the Motor Corps. One, in particular, showed Captain Al Ruiz standing high on top of the High Pyramid.

1981 –"High Pyramid" with Captain Al Ruiz on the top position

"Formed in 1935, the Victor McLaglen stunt and drill team takes its name from the Academy Award winning movie star who promoted the group. Purely as a hobby, the group, all Harley mounted, regularly appear at shows and parades throughout the west. Ages of the group range from mid-twenties to several in their fifties."

Personalized plate on bike that was both used as a flag bike in the Motor Corps and as a funeral escort bike to escort funeral processions in Los Angeles.

In the early 1980s, the team acquired new brown, police-style uniforms and we had publicity photographs taken at the Hollywood Bowl in California.

(L-R) Front Row: Al Ruiz, Harry Fisher, Kirby Frymoyer, Sonny Day.
2nd Row: Albert Ruiz, Willie Abrams, Frank Hicks.
3rd Row: Jerry Thompson, Bob Jensen
4th Row: Dick Gerry, Kevin Anderson, Tylor Hicks
Top: George Anderson

"The Fan" –Big Mike Betschart driving and holding all this upright. Nine guys on one bike. All it takes is one person to let go for it all to tumble down!

In the 1980s, the team obtained sponsorship from Tzubaki Chains. John Linden, Motorcycle Division Manager at Tzubaki, took a liking to the team and showed his support by providing money for travel expenses.

By Tedd Farrell

The Motor Corps started carrying a Tsubaki flag and banner to show off their new sponsor.

Front row: Albert Ruiz Jr., Dick Gerry, Frank Hicks, Sonny Day; Second row: Jerry Thompson, Willie Abrams, Bob Holbrook; Third row: Gene French, Al Ruiz Sr, Tylor Hicks

MEMBERS IN 1982

In the early days after the 1978 reorganization, members wore snazzy blue jumpsuits with

1	Abrams, Willie	17	Gerry, Dick
2	Auguston, Fred	18	Hicks, Frank
3	Behling, Harvey	19	Hicks, Tylor
4	Brosell, Ray	20	Holbrook, Bob
5	Brown, Ken	21	Jensen, Bob
6	Bucknor, Chuck	22	Macias, Al
7	Carmody, Lyle	23	Martin, Alvis
8	Castro, Larry	24	Oliver, Nick
9	Chubbuck, Bruce	25	Pantoja, Ruben
10	Davies, Roger	26	Ruiz, Al
11	Day, Sonny	27	Sevilla, Guillermo
12	Fisher, Harry	28	Smith, Ellis
13	French, Gene	29	Thompson, Jerry
14	Frymoyer, Kirby	30	Virgin, Glenn
15	Frymoyer, Mark	31	Whitesell, Ernie
16	Garza, George		

All-on-One Motorcycle Stunt

To make our big "come back" an even bigger splash, Harry Fisher decided the team needed to set some kind of world record – and thus, the world record "All on One Motorcycle" stunts began.

In order to truly appreciate this amazing feat, it is important that you have a little background into what occurred.

17 Men On One Motorcycle

On April 16, 1974, the Huntington Park Elks Motorcycle Stunt and Drill Team made motorcycling history when they successfully placed 17 men on one moving motorcycle. The feat was shown across the country on KNBC by Ray Duncan, and pictures and letters were sent to the Guinness Book of Records for submission as a new world record.

The total weight of the men and the 1964 Harley-Davidson 74 cubic inch motorcycle was 3800 pounds. The average weight of the men was 179 pounds. The only alterations made to the motorcycle were two braces for the frame and added air pressure in their Goodyear tires. The Goodyear tires were a huge part of this stunt. Their strength, flexibility, and dependability was required.

The sponsors were the Huntington Park Elks Lodge #1415, Kendall Motor Oil, Superior Fast Freight, and Los Angeles Harley-Davidson. LA Harley supplied the four mini-bikes that ride along beside the stunts as safety, Kendall Oil supplied oil for the bikes, and Superior Fast Freight loaned their trailer for transportation.

The Elks team officers were: Manager Doug Patterson, Lieutenant Colonel Secretary/Treasurer Cecil Smith, Captain/Stunt Leader Carl Wicks and – you guessed it, Major/Drill Leader Harry Fisher, who incidentally was the guy driving on this stunt! This was just four years before Harry would leave the Elks and sign on with the McLaglens as their leader.

Members listed on this stunt were:

Dom Buffamonte	Dennis Lausche
Sonny Day	Jim Meek
Harry Fisher	Nick Oliver
Gene French	Al Ruiz
Kirby Frymoyer	Ron Silicki
Bob Galusha	Joe Smith
Walt Hauser	Carl Wicks
Jack Inman	Roger Wilke
Ken Johnson	

20 Men on One Motorcycle!

One of the first things Harry did when he started getting the McLaglen team energized was attempt a new record. He had to "one-up" the Elks team, now that they were the competition!

On May 25, 1980, the Victor McLaglen Motor Corps made history when we put 20 men on one moving motorcycle.

The total weight was 3,842 pounds and the men's weights ranged from 118 to 237, with the average weight being 174.5 pounds per man. The motorcycle weighed an additional 702 pounds and the stunt stayed upright for 17 seconds.

The preparation included adding several pounds of air pressure to the tires and an extension to the rear rack, which was made by member Chuck Buckner.

The motorcycle used was Harry's 1964 Harley-Davidson panhead, which was the same bike used for the 17 man stunt at the Elks. The riders were Harry Fisher (driver), Willie Abrams (front fender), George Anderson, Ken Brown, Roger Davies, Sonny Day, Gene French, Kirby Frymoyer, Dick Gerry, Frank Hicks, Tylor Hicks, Bob Jensen, Al Macias, Ruben Pantoja, Jerry Thompson, Bruce Chubbuck, Kevin Anderson, Nick Oliver, Al Ruiz II, and Albert Ruiz III. The ground support members were Fred Auguston, Harvey Behling, Ray Brosell, Lyle Carmody, Andy Dumont, Bob Galusha, Les Georgeson, Jerry Jackson, Bob Keller, and Ellis Smith.

Lots of practice is needed to put 20 men on one motorcycle and we started out with eight riders and worked our way up. A description of hos that happens is on page 148.

As if that wasn't enough, we completed our performance with a 22-man High Pyramid combined with the Seattle Cossacks motorcycle team and then a spectacular double firewall crash, accomplished by Harry Fisher. That guy does get around, doesn't he?

Created by Tedd Farrell

Practicing the "All On One"
Harry Fisher (driver),
Willie Abrams (front fender),
Bruce Chubbuck (standing up), and
Jerry Thompson (sitting on handlebars).

"22-Man Pyramid"
VMMC and the Seattle Cossacks teams

Harry Fisher crashing the "Firewall"

21 Men on One Motorcycle – Ruidoso, New Mexico

On October 4, 1980, at the 10th Aspencade Motorcycle Tour, the Motor Corps piled 21 men on one motorcycle, just to show what fantastic feats could be done on a motorcycle.

The team was sponsored at this time by the Southern California Harley-Davidson Dealers Association (Tom Scott, President), Northern California Harley-Davidson Dealers Association (Dudley Perkins, President), Ken Frost Trucking Company, and Orange County Van & Storage (Mike Sheldon) for their freight trailer.

A truck carrying 21 Motor Corps Harleys and four mini-bikes arrived on Friday evening. On Saturday morning, the members who had already arrived early met at the truck to begin unloading. The rest of the team was to arrive later by plane.

We drove to the little airport in Ruidoso to pick up the members who flew on the charter planes and I've never seen such a sight! Our guys all walked off those planes with white faces and muttering, "I'm never doing that again!"

It seemed everything was just fine until the planes made their approach – which was up over a mountain and immediately down onto the runway. Apparently, a current dropped them a lot faster than they expected and they all thought they were doomed! Those big, bad motorcycle stuntmen were a little shaken up!

It didn't slow them down, though. The next day, we did a fantastic show and ended by putting 21 men on one bike. It was filmed by television stations in Texas and New Mexico, and for the television show, PM Magazine, which is shown in 50 states. We received a load of publicity in New Mexico.

I found it interesting that Harvey Behling rode rode on the front fender of the 14-man stunt back in 1936. Then re-joined the team in 1980 and rode on the front of this same when they put 21 men on Harry's 1964 Harley at the Los Angeles Coliseum for the Artistry in Iron Show, then again in Ventura when they attempted to put 23 men on that same bike for SCMA's U.S. Motorcycle Jamboree.

Ruidoso News, Monday, October 6, 1980

From the March 1981 issue of *Cycle Guide*:
By George Wegner

    McLaglen Motor Corps – For them, charity begins at the controls of a Harley!

    Picture 21 men in identical, freshly pressed uniforms, jackboots so shiny you can't look at them straight-on. A maze of arms, legs and hands interlocked in highly orchestrated movement. Toes and fingers pulling, feet on shoulders, feet on heads, feet on feet.

    Muscles taut and twisted against the force of gravity. Twenty-one hearts pounding, drowned out by the rolling thunder of a four-stroke vee-twin. A mountain of straining humanity–atop a single motorcycle.

    To the spectator, the sight of 21 men riding a single Harley is enough to etch itself firmly into the memory. To the McLaglen Motor Corps it's just another performance, just one more day in the lives of these motorcycle daredevils.

    But this is more than just a group of precision riders out to dazzle the eye and cause a few heart flutters. This World Championship stunt and drill team works for something more than riding perfection, something that comes to light only after the crowds have gone home – charity. While the team is out risking life and limb to entertain the crowd, they're doing it to aid crippled children's organizations as well. Over the past 45 years, all proceeds earned through public appearances of the Corps above immediate club expenses have been donated to handicapped children.

    In 1935, actor Victor McLaglen first realized the fund-raising possibilities of the Motor Corps and became its first sponsor. The following year, the McLaglen Stunt and Drill Team blitzed the Mexico City Police Stunt Team in the World Championships, taking top honors before a packed house in the Los Angeles Coliseum. It's a distinction they have held to this day.

    Though multi-man, single-bike tricks are the team's trademark, they represent only a small part of VMMC's repertoire. A rundown of the team's stunt routines includes the Backward Ride (at speed), Roman Ride (two motorcycles under a lone rider), Side Ride, P-38 Human Ladder, Double Side Ride, Six Man Stopping Pyramid, DC-10, Hy-Lo Chariot Pyramid (up to 22 riders on four motorcycles) and a host of other two-wheeled acrobatics. As one rider put it, "We can do anything with a motorcycle but wash dishes."

    After you've seen the Corps perform, it's hard to believe that they're not all runaways from the circus, but it's true. There's not a single trained acrobat among them. They're just good-hearted riders who get a kick out of putting on a show and putting smiles on the faces of some handicapped kids. And they work for those smiles. Each member puts in a minimum of six hours of practice each week in addition to scheduled performances, and must purchase and maintain his own machine.

Cycle Guide Article Continued

Commander Harry Fisher is the leader of the pack and the guiding force behind the Motor Corps as it exists today. Fisher first saw the Corps perform when he rode to the Death Valley Tour in 1963 alongside his mother. He was hooked. With the exception of a few years off in the late Sixties to race Class C sidecars and a few TTs as both an amateur and a professional, Fisher has ridden with the Corps ever since. Most of the members started out more or less the same way. They saw the Corps perform, asked a few questions and before they knew it, they were members.

That's no idle spectator-to-stuntman story, either. VMMC is always looking for new members. A phone call to Fisher is all it might take. Of course, it would help if you've got spit-shined jackboots, a polished Harley – and the nerve to ride bull-goose looney through a wall of flames.

– *George Wegner*

As an aside, have you ever seen the team do their Board Jump? It's also a pretty slick trick.

Usually, four guys grab the newest member, or one that has messed up in the drill that day, and lay him on the ground, holding all four extremities. Another member brings over a board that is about 2" thick, 12" wide, and 6' long. One end of the board is laid on the chest of the poor victim and another rider, usually Harry, circles his motorcycle around a few times at the other end of the show area, getting ready to ride up the board and over the victim. Frightened at what is about to transpire, the victim (once free from being held down) throws the board and jumps up. The team, however, is ready for him. He's caught, laid down again and braced with the board. His captors hold him down until the last second. Harry revs up his Harley. He rides up the board and off the other side. There is, of course, applause from everyone watching and relief from the poor victim!

The "Board Stunt" Harry Fisher rides up and over on a board placed on another member's chest.

22 Men on One Motorcycle!

Back to July 12, 1980, the Victor McLaglen Motor Corps made history again when we put 22 men on one motorcycle at the Artistry in Iron event at the Los Angeles Coliseum. Again, Harry Fisher was the driver and he rode his 1964 Harley panhead.

Cycle News
August 6, 1980

On July 13 at the L.A. Coliseum, the Victor McLaglen Motorcycle Drill Team led by Col. Harry Fisher (buried, but at the controls of this Harley-Davidson) set a new world's record by putting 22 men on one motorcycle.

Fall 1980
Enthusiast

The Victor McLaglen Motorcycle Corps set a world record of 22 men on one motorcycle.

$1,000 to the Biker's Fight MD campaign after flying to L.A. from a concert tour stop in Little Rock, Ark. just to preside as Parade Grand Marshall during the Biker's Parade Against Dystrophy

22 Men on One Motorcycle! (Cont'd)

Full dress practice for their attempt at another record stunt.

Note from member Bruce Chubbuck who was on this 22-man stunt and recalling his part in this big stunt.

"I was standing on the gas tank in front of Harry. When Harry started the bike in motion, there were 9 men on the bike. The stunt was tall and skinny. Harry said "Freeze – don't try to correct. That's my job."

They had only moved about 10 yards when Harry said, "I've got it." Then the sidemen started to mount in pairs, front to back. The man on the right was to reach across and grab the left leg from behind of the man standing on the thighs of the man seated on a platform behind Harry. (Huh?)

The left man was to reach across and hold onto the right leg. This went well for the many practices we did. The performance at the L.A. sports arena also went well and we set the record."

The Motor Corps was also successful in completing this stunt on May 24, 1980, at the Motorcycle Jamboree in Bakersfield, California, and again on November 3, 1980, in Ruidoso, New Mexico, at the Americade Motorcycle Tour.

SUCCESS!
22 Men on Harry Fisher's 1964 Harley-Davidson panhead!

This is how you go about piling up to 22 men on one moving motorcycle –

Step #1
First you find some guys who are willing to climb onto one motorcycle. Next you load 9 of them on that motorcycle while it's standing still. Then you ride them around in a big circle, taking up most of the arena.

Step #2
Next, you load on more men, two at a time, one on one side and another on the other side at the same time.

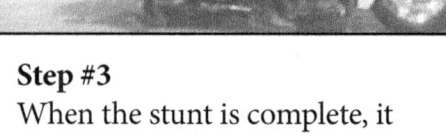

Step #3
When the stunt is complete, it should look something like this –

Step #4
And the celebration looks like this – Commander Harry Fisher is carried around the arena by teammates Al Ruiz and George Anderson

23 Men on one motorcycle!

About a year later, on May 23, 1981, at the Fifth U.S. Motorcycle Jamboree held at the Ventura County Fairgrounds, the team attempted to beat our own record and put 23 men on one motorcycle. Again, with Harry Fisher driving his '64 Harley panhead! There was lots of preparation involved. The event needed to be publicized to attract a larger audience. The team needed to practice to perfect the stunt. Negotiations with the television show, "That's Incredible," was ongoing. The event needed to be filmed and perhaps give us opportunity to obtain more sponsorship.

AMA District 37 Road Rider Newsletter
Motorcycle Jamboree

The 7th United States Motorcycle Jamboree is almost upon us. This is the biggest motorcycling event in California and is sponsored by the Southern California Motorcycling Association. It is also sanctioned by the American Motorcyclist Association for a District 37 Tour Award. Show your AMA card at the AMA booth in the Exhibition Hall to receive your pin.

This three-day event will feature a motorcycle parade through the streets of Bakersfield at 1:00 p.m. with line-up starting at 12:00 noon, continuous-run motorcycle movies, motorcycle judging, games, exhibition hall, two bands Saturday and Sunday, Julie Winfield. The Seattle Cossacks will perform on Saturday evening and the Victor McLaglen Motor Corps on Sunday evening, ending with a combined performance with both teams working together. The SST Trick Team (bicycles team) sponsored by Redline Bicycles will be doing headstands and ramp jumps, the American Trials team will also be performing. The Marines are tentatively scheduled to have their parachute jump team and have a helicopter on display.

There will be a camping area available, so bring your family and look forward to a super weekend. With the support of AMA Dunlop Touring Elite Series, and the Advance Beverage Co., Budweiser distributor for Bakersfield, this event has been advertised nationally and looks like the biggest and best yet. Adult price for age 16 and over $15.00, children under 16 $6.00, age 6 and under free. Get an SCMA, or AMA $1.00 discount and early mail-in discount of $2.00 if you mail in before May 21. This entry fee entitles you to the full weekend's activities, including campground. The Jamboree will be May 25-30th at the Kern County Fairgrounds, 1142 P Street, Bakersfield, California.

See you there.

Harry Fisher
Public Relations Director
U.S. Motorcycle Jamboree

23 Men on one motorcycle! (Cont'd)

Harry did whatever he could to get the most publicity out of this stunt. He wrote letters, talked to editors, and contacted everyone he knew, to talk about this fantastic, world record-breaking stunt that was about to take place.

Harry's picture even made it to the program that was handed out at the Jamboree.

Harry Fisher, our District 37 Road Rider president on his pride and joy 1933 VL Harley as he performed for the Victor McLaglen Motor Corps at last year's Jamboree. Harry is the driving force for District 37 Road Riding and still maintains a job as owner of V.I.P. Motorcycle Escort Service, performs team drill shows with the Victor McLaglen Motor Corps, wants to race off-road desert bikes and flat track if he can find a sponsor who will put him on a machine and a District 37 member who will point him the way. Harry is such a celebrity that he has filled in for Eric Estrada on the famous "Chips" TV series on stunts and riding. Who knows? Maybe he will follow Bruce Penhall on the show and get full coverage in People magazine. Please stop by and get Harry to autograph this souvenir photograph for you.

Then came the day of the stunt. "That's Incredible" television show was there with cameras, everyone had their boots shined and helmets clean, and they were on pins and needles, waiting for the show to start. The team got "big money"–"That's Incredible" sprung for $500!

"That's Incredible" crew starts filming.

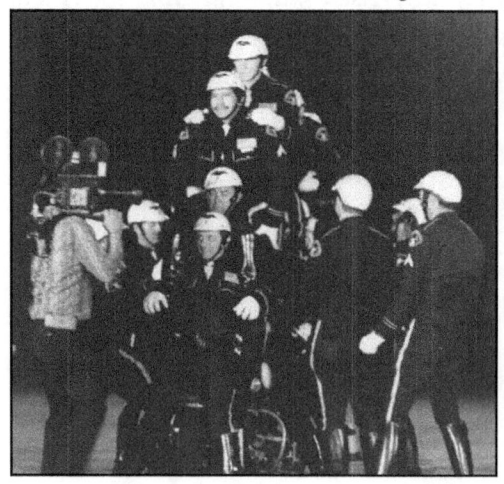

23 Men on one motorcycle! (Cont'd)

First, they were looking good – for about 10 seconds, then somebody or something wobbled and – oops! The problem was that in order for it to be entered into the Guinness Book of Records, it had to be upright for 17 seconds or more. This is what happened after only 10 seconds, so they didn't make the record! However, they did get plenty of media coverage. It made the front page of the *Star Free Press*, *Supercycle*, *Cycle News*, and who knows where else.

The Sunday Star
May 24, 1981

Members on this 23-man stunt were:
Harry Fisher (Driver), Willy Abrams, George Anderson, Kevin Anderson, Harvey Behling, Ken Brown, Chuck Buckner, Bruce Chubbuck, Roger Davies, Sonny Day, Gene French, Kirby Frymoyer, Mark Frymoyer, Dick Gerry, Frank Hicks, Tylor Hicks, Bob Holbrook, Bob Jensen, Al Macias, Nick Oliver, Al Ruiz II, Al Ruiz III, Jerry Thompson

Supercycle magazine

"All on One" Stunt Timeline

17-men	4-16-1974	Huntington Park Elks Motorcycle Stunt & Drill Team
20-men	5-25-1980	Bakersfield Motorcycle Jamboree
21-men	11-4-1980	Ruidoso, New Mexico Americade Motorcycle Tour
22-men	5-24-1980	Bakersfield Motorcycle Jamboree
	7-12-1980	Los Angeles Sports Arena "Artistry in Iron"
	11-3-1980	Ruidoso, NM Americade
23-men	5-23-1981	Ventura Jamboree. Taped for "That's Incredible"

Another interesting tidbit: Harry's 1964 Panhead Harley was used each time –for the 17-Men, 20-Men, 21-Men, 22-Men, and 23-Men On One Bike stunt, each time driven by Harry who was only 5'8" tall and 165 lbs.

In 1982, the Motor Corps was issued a charter as a non-profit corporation in California under the name "Motorcycle Enterprises, Incorporated, dba Victor McLaglen Motor Corps."

In November, they performed in the Circus Circus parking lot in Las Vegas, Nevada, and

December 9, 1982

Mr. Harry Fisher
VICTOR McLAUGLEN MOTOR CORP.
P.O. Box 845
Bellflower, California 90706

Dear Mr. Fisher:

I would like to take this opportunity to express our appreciation of the fine demonstration the Motor Corp. showed to us during the Barstow to Vegas Run held on November 27, 1982.

Spectators commented continually during and after the demonstration and we feel that the Motor Corp. definitely added an additional "Touch of Class" to the event.

I must express our thanks also to the Motor Corp. for their cooperation in working with us in the limited space that was available.

Yours truly,

Mel Larson
Vice President
Marketing/Public Relations

ML:ps

it was a huge success, as per the letter from them below.

The team started off in 1983, with a show in Yuma, AZ, at the 22nd Annual Yuma Prison Run, hosted by the Norwalk Centaurs. Weather was said to be in the low 90s and beautiful, and the Motor Corps had no incidents during the show. Because this is always the first show of the season, it can sometimes be a little rough. Generally, there are new members who are nervous, because it's their first show and they don't want to screw up and embarrass themselves. They don't want to "dump" their bikes, and they want to do everything perfectly. Usually "perfect" doesn't happen, but if they didn't do it perfectly in 1983, at least it didn't get written up in the Yuma papers!

We did our usual parades and 4th of July shows, performed at the U.S. Motorcycle Jamboree and the Love Ride – but then did something a little different. We put on a Halloween Motorcycle Poker Run in October.

The run started out at Chubbuck Harley-Davidson in Pasadena, went about 120 miles, and ended up at the Downey Elks Lodge for dinner, prizes, and dancing. Member Larry Castro was in charge of mapping and created a really exciting route, going through Azusa Canyon, the town of Mt. Baldy, Carbon Canyon, and just a bit of Los Angeles freeways. The price was $7.50 with 50 cent discounts for membership in the SCMA, AMA, HDOA and early mail-ins. It was a pretty good deal.

In November, we sponsored the Barstow to Vegas Motorcycle Race, along with AMA District 37. It was cold, there were icicles hanging on the Yucca trees, and snow and rain which challenged the bikers – You had to be one tough hombre to ride in that race; just to finish was quite an accomplishment!

The Montrose Christmas Parade was a favorite with the team and we led the parade for many years. The parade also featured a "fly-over," with Santa waving at everyone along the parade route. All the shops were lit up with Christmas lights and every light pole was decorated. Lots of jolly good-will and lots of happy kids and families lined the parade route.

After the 1983 Montrose Christmas Parade, we were treated to a little hospitality by the Montrose parade committee.

(L-R) Bob Holbrook, Chuck Buckner, Art Wales, Roger Davies, Ellis Smith, Frank Roberts (founder of the parade), Larry Johnson, Harry Fisher, Bruce Chubbuck.

A very nice article appeared about the Motor Corps in Ozbike *Thunder Down Under* motorcycle magazine, 1983, issue #17 September/ October. All the way from the other side of the world!

The story is slightly distorted from how I remember the history, but it's not far off the mark! No matter – as they say in Show Biz, "any publicity is good publicity!"

What's Going Down

CUNNING STUNTS ON HARLEYS

As seen and photographed by Stumpy on his recent US cruise.

THE Victor McLaglen Drill and Stunt team was originally formed as a result of a bet. Well, you might call it more of a dare really.

Victor, once a contender for the World Heavyweight Boxing Championship and an oscar-winning movie stuntman, was challenged to perform stunts on a motorcycle similar to those he did with his horses. This coincided with the first release of a new massive V-twin motorcycle by Harley-Davidson.

"Box it in" he was heard to say.

Doing amazing feats previously untried on horses and embarrassing his challengers no end, the seeds of a new found motorcycle lifestyle were firmly planted in Victor's future. He started training others and in 1935, the original 17 dare-devil members started performing anywhere they could get paid.

Today, the team is captained by Harry Fisher, President and Congressman of the District 37 American Motorcyclist Association and owner of a motorcycle escort service. They maintain the high standards set down by Victor McLaglen and still perform all over the country.

If you're wondering how the H-D V-twins handle the slow-moving stunts and high temperatures, we were told that some members, aided by aviation oil, actually get 50,000 miles without a rebore. That's a lotta stunts.

The reliability is so good, they're still resisting offers of financial support and better recognition by the riceburner manufacturers. It's a shame the H-D factory doesn't offer it. It'd be great advertising to show prospective buyers just how capable a big twin can be.

By Tedd Farrell

In 1984, EasyRiders Magazine wrote an article about the team leading and performing in the annual Big Bear Run Parade. Big Bear is a part of the San Bernardino National Forest in California, and is a beautiful spot located 7,000 ft. high in the San Bernardino Mountains.

"2-Motor Pyramid"
Drivers: Harry Fisher and Kirby Frymoyer; Standing: Jerry Thompson and Bob Holbrook
Top: Mark Frymoyer

"Speedo"
Al Ruiz, Dick Gerry

"Drill Maneuvers" Harry Fisher, Kirby Frymoyer, Ellis Smith (Smitty)

The December, 1984, *"Free 2 Wheel"* motorcycle newsletter for Southern California published a full page article by Dick Hill, who, by some coincidence, was also a member of the team!

Six people on a motorcycle? Gives a whole new meaning to the words, "Diamond Lane." Actually, six people on a motorcycle is a routine matter for the Victor McLaglen Motor Corps Stunt and Drill Team. If you have never seen them perform, you have really missed something. The Giant Pyramid, for instance, involves four motorcycles. To compliment the four motorcycles are four men standing on front axle extensions, four drivers, four safety men standing in back of the drivers, two or even four men standing on the driver's SHOULDERS. Add to this the option of four men hanging off the back and you have a grand possible total of twenty people involved in just one stunt!

The Victor McLaglen Motor Corps originated back in 1935. Victor McLaglen, a great character actor of the 30s and 40s, originally sponsored a team of stunt people on horseback. Some of those original members, by the way, still turn out to official reunions. Anyway, as the story goes, McLaglen was approached by a group of motorcycle riders with the idea of doing the same stunts on bikes. Why not? "Prove to me you can do it and I'll sponsor you", replied the late actor. Officially chartered by the AMA in 1935, the rest is history. The team went on to win the World Championship for stunt riding when they took the championship from the Mexico City Police Motorcycle Stunt Team. The trophy has been in the possession of the Victor McLaglen Corp ever since. Forty six years!!

The team is now commanded by Colonel Harry Fisher who has reorganized the team and brought together some of the finest stunt riders in Southern California. The aim of the organization is to promote the good, clean positive image of motorcyclists and motorcycling. Each man

Free 2 Wheel article (Cont'd)

owns and maintains his own Harley-Davidson painted black and white police style. The men come from all walks of life and all occupations, from truck drivers to mailmen to machinists and an immigration/deportation supervisor.

The team drill leader takes his riders through loose-order drill and intricate maneuvers in a demonstration of riding skills. One of the highlights is the "Suicide Split," a stunt originated and perfected by the Victor McLaglen Motor Corps. A lone rider charges full throttle, often with the front end high in the air, towards a two-abreast column of riders. At the last possible instant when a collision is unavoidable, the riders in the columns swerve violently to the side and the rider unharmed screams through the small gap. It's a maximum high in excitement and is only a preview of another 18 to 23 stunts to follow.

The show keeps moving with riders performing stunts such as the Rear Rack Ride, Side Ride, Seat Stand, Frame Ride, Slow Circles, Floorboard Ride, One-Legged Ride, and a spectacular one-man stunt called the Roman Ride with one man riding two motorcycles at the same time!

Next comes more fun. The multiple person and multiple motorcycle stunts. The stunts are aptly named. The Sunflower gets its name because the Corps is actually hanging off ALL sides of ONE motorcycle and when it's built, it opens up like a flower. The Speedo is where one person stands on one of the floorboards and battles over who is controlling the darn thing. The P-38 is named after the legendary World War II airplane and sort of looks like one. The DC-10 stunt has more wings than it's namesake, but looks like it could fly. The Pushup shows a Safetyman pushing up another rider. The Chariot looks like the Roman chariot rides. The Single and Double Spread Eagles are self-explanatory. The Stopping Pyramid stops with the Motormen balancing it while keeping their feet up on the floorboards and the crowd counting off the number of seconds they are stationary. The greatest crowd pleaser of them all the six-motor 22-man High Low Chariot Pyramid, and is their signature stunt.

The highlight of an evening show is topped off, when the fire marshals will allow, with a flaming ride through a firewall by a lone rider. Often times in an arena with large crowds, multiple firewalls will be lit so the entire crowd can see.

At that time, Harry Fisher was the only rider in the Corps crazy enough to pull off this stunt. In July of 1983, Harry and C.R. "Sam" Anderson, the unit's clown, rode double through two firewalls. Sam was sitting BACKWARDS on the front fender. The fire marshals almost didn't permit it as they claimed Sam's beard was a fire hazard. After some good-natured negotiating, however, the stunt was allowed.

As a motorcyclist, you owe it to yourself to see the Victor McLaglen Motor Corps perform. They do warn you, however, don't get tanked up on a couple of beers and think you're going to bypass the amount of practice and patience it takes to get things, not only right, but safe.

Yep, it looks like folks are not adhering to the 55 mph rule and that made a good news item in the July 1985 *Easyriders* Magazine. This article was accompanied by an article recognizing the 50 year anniversary of the VMMC. Congratulations, team!

A new report by the American Motorcyclist Association offers some hope to those of us who are tired of being caught between carboning up our engines by running at ridiculously low speeds or spending a lot of time and bucks dealing with speeding tickets.

According to the AMA, the impetus to junk the double-nickel law paradoxically germinated in a National Research Council report praising the 55mph standard as "one of the most effective highway-safety policies ever adopted."

Despite its glowing conclusions, the AMA says, that report "provided clear evidence that the costs of the 55mph limit on up to 31,500 miles of interstates outweigh the safety and fuel-saving benefits, especially in Western states."

Since that report, the AMA notes, significant pressure to repeal or modify the double-nickel has been evident. A few examples are:

— A Feb. 21 U.S. House of Representatives subcommittee meeting at which witness after witness, including a dozen congressmen, called for an end to absolute federal control over highway speed limits.
— The introduction of two bills in the House and one in the Senate to give states the option of a 65 or 70mph speed limit on uncongested rural highways.
— State legislative proposals in California, Iowa, Missouri, Nebraska, New Mexico, New York, Oklahoma, Washington, West Virginia and Wyoming asking Congress to increase the limit on some roads.
— Bills calling for lower penalties for speeding have been introduced in the legislatures of at least seven states.

On a national level, the most significant happening is the introduction of the three Congressional bills cited above. The first, House Bill 693, would allow states to apply to the federal Dept. of Transportation for speed limits of up to 65mph on rural

Crusadin' Rev. Kaiser win

Robert "Rev. Kaiser" Hershberger, whose [...] tion by bar and restaurant owners has fr[...] round in his battle to make Connecticut mo[...]

A superior court judge has ruled that the [...] Opportunities acted illegally in refusing to investigate Kaiser's complaint that he was refused service at a cafe solely because he was wearing biker leathers. After Kaiser refused to leave the cafe, the police were summoned and he was arrested on trespass charges.

According to Kaiser's attorney, the superior court ruling means that the human rights commission will now be compelled to investigate the case and determine if his client was actually discriminated against. If it determines that he was, the cafe owner could face criminal charges and/or the loss of his liquor license.

Fifty years of Harley Stunt Ridin'

The Victor McLaglen Motorcycle Corps recently celebrated their Golden Anniversary with a birthday bash highlighted by the remembrances of dozens of former Corps members, several of whom had been part of the original group back in the mid-1930s.

World-famous for their stunt-riding skills, the Corp has thrilled crowds from coast-to-coast and beyond with their precision formations, motorcycle pyramids, Roman riding (one man riding two bikes), slow circles, and other stunts. Members of the Corp, which was named for its early sponsor the late actor Victor McLaglen, are responsible for buying and maintaining their own bikes and many of them practically live in the saddle — working in bike shops or as funeral escorts during the day, practicing their stunt riding in the evening, and performing in parades or other shows on the weekends and holidays.

One of the high points of the birthday party was the presentation of a commemorative plaque and clock from the Harley-Davidson company. As the Harley rep said, 50 years is a long time and the fact that during those five decades every Corps member has ridden a Harley in every event says something about loyalty — and also the ability of the Milwaukee Big Twins to handle slow-speed precision work as well as fast puttin' down the highway.

These pictures are from about 1978, but that's ok. They were printed in the 1985 *Motorcyclist* magazine and we were happy to see them.

Motorcyclist magazine –August 1985

Jumper: Mark Frymoyer, Spreading: Harry Fisher
Drivers: Jerry Thompson, "Smitty" Ellis Smith

"Front Axle Ride"
Mark Frymoyer

"Backward Ride"
Mark Frymoyer

"4-Motor Push-up" Motormen: Chuck Buckner, Kirby Frymoyer,
Roger Davies, Up: Mark Frymoyer, George Anderson, Mickey Minor
Safety (back): Bob Holbrook, Woody Woodard, Jerry Thompson

In June, 1989, we went to Tijuana, Mexico, to do a show at Juarez Stadium.
Below is a note Harry wrote to the members, following the event.

"For all of you who made it to Tijuana for the infield show, I hope you had as good a time as I did. It was quite an experience to have the uniformed officer with the most brass on his shirt come over to our van at the border and say, "Good afternoon. Are you going to the Hotel La Mesa?" And we didn't know anyone knew we were coming! I didn't catch his name, but he sure was helpful. The hotel people were terrific, too. They gave us fenced-in parking with plenty of security guards, gave the wives a chauffeur (a real professional who drives a taxi in Tijuana – what better training could you have!). Our member Guillermo Sevilla was kind enough to make reservations at a superb restaurant and then made sure we all found our way there and back to the motel again. Joannie Gerry didn't much care for her lobster's eyes staring at her, but I think she managed to ignore him after a while! We all had the VIP treatment by being invited into City Hall and meeting the Mayor. Although I'm still not too sure what he said, I'm sure he was a nice guy! Then we met a new team from La Mesa who honored us with some special words of welcome and we all signed a proclamation to remain friends and to support one another as brother-motorcycle stuntmen. We will be invited down to Tijuana again probably on Labor Day weekend to perform with them and probably attend a barbecue or some other event they arrange. I am looking forward to the event."

Harry then went on to say ---

"Which brings something to mind . . . Please try to make it to practices. It's important! Timing is one of the most important things we must have to perform the drill maneuvers and multiple stunts. We can't develop and maintain our timing if we have people missing from practices. You also need the instruction you will get at practice. You may know how to do a headstand, but do you know how to do it without jostling the bike around? You may know how to ride beside someone, but do you know how to ride beside someone so that when his motor coughs, you can maintain the even ride with the other three guys standing on your bike in a Pyramid? I've been doing this kind of riding for 28 years and I learn something new all the time, so I know that practicing every week will help you all learn something new and get better and better."

In other words, knowing him, I'm sure he was trying to say, "You may be good, but you still need to practice!"

By the end of the 1980s, the numbers had grown to more than 30 members. There were four squads, four color guards, two teenage sons, a medic, mini-bike safety riders, an administrator, and several members who dropped out of the Huntington Park Elks Motorcycle Stunt & Drill team and joined the Victor McLaglen Motor Corps.

Members during the 1980s

Abrams, Willie –Drill/Stuntman
Anderson, George –Drill/Stuntman
Anderson, Kevin –Stuntman
Auguston, Fred –Color Guard/Stuntman
Behling, Harvey –Color Guard/Stuntman
Brosell, Ray –Medic
Brown, Ken –Drill/Stuntman
Buckner, Chuck –Drill/Stuntman
Carmody, Lyle –Mini-bike Safety/Admin.
Castro, Larry –Drill/Stuntman
Chubbuck, Bruce –Color Guard/Stuntman
Davies, Roger –Drill/Stuntman
Day, Sonny –Drill/Stuntman
Dumont, Andy –Drill/Stuntman
Fisher, Harry –Leader/Drill/Stuntman
French, Gene –Drill/Stuntman
Frymoyer, Kirby –Drill/Stuntman
Frymoyer, Mark –Drill/Stuntman
Garza, George –Color Guard

Galusha, Bob –Color Guard/Stuntman
Gerry, Dick –Drill/Stuntman
Hicks, Frank –Color Guard/Stuntman
Hicks, Tylor –Drill/Stuntman
Holbrook, Bob –Drill/Stuntman
Jensen, Bob –Drill/Stuntman
Keller, Bob –Drill/Stuntman
Macias, Al –Drill/Stuntman
Martin, Alvis –Color Guard
Oliver, Nick –Drill/Stuntman
Pantoja, Ruben –Drill/Stuntman
Ruiz, Al Jr. –Mini-bike Safety/Stuntman
Ruiz, Al Sr. –Drill/Stuntman
Sevilla, Guillermo –Drill/Stuntman
Smith, Ellis –Drill/Stuntman
Thompson, Jerry –Drill/Stuntman
Virgin, Glenn –Drill/Stuntman
Whitesell, Ernie –Color Guard
Warren, Don –Color Guard

by Tedd Farrell

"Suicide Split"

If you have never seen the "Suicide Split" performed by the Victor McLaglen Motor Corps, you're missing something exciting.

This happens during the "drill" part of the performance. Usually, the team starts off with a bunch of different drill maneuvers – a column of 2's, then 4's, then break off into 2's again, crossover at the end of the field and come back up. Then, depending on the leader's mood – or space provided – they'll go into single file and make a Figure 8.

Eventually, the leader gets the team maneuvered back into 2's and headed back down the field, away from him. They get themselves into position, by doing a crossover at the end of the field, and head back up in 2's again.

Meanwhile, the leader sits at the other end of the performance area, doing slow circles (really slow, tight circles with hands off the handlebars) and takes his time, waiting for the rest of the team to get into position.

As soon as the first two riders are side by side and heading back, the leader kicks his bike into gear and turns on the throttle full blast, headed toward the first pair of riders. Meanwhile, the pairs of riders coming toward him, turn on their throttles at full blast and run what looks like a collision course right at the leader.

At the last possible instant, the pairs break off – one to the left and one to the right – and the leader rides right down through the center of the column, jams on the brakes when he's passed through the last pair of riders and slides sideways, until he comes nearly to a stop, then slowly rides off back to his guys to finish more drill! Sometimes, this is called "Split the Rail".

The speed of this stunt depends on the performance area. If it's done on the race track with lots of room to work, they will get up to 60 mph. If it's done in a 100x70 ft. space, naturally, the speed will be a lot less. However, no matter how fast or slow it's done, it's pretty terrifying if you're the one facing down the oncoming bikes!

They're all lined in two's, ready for the Drill Leader to come straight at them, splitting down the middle, "split the rail" style

1990-1999

The 1990s were even more exciting for the team. We traveled to the Sturgis Motorcycle Rally in Sturgis, South Dakota. This rally is one of the largest motorcycle rallies in the world with more than 400,000 motorcycle enthusiasts attending the week-long event. We also traveled to Ruidoso, New Mexico, for the Americade Rally, then Red Deer, Canada for another motorcycling event. The highlight was probably the International Motorcycle Shows, though. These are indoor events showcasing all the new motorcycles and accessories and are held across the United States. The Motor Corps was hired to provide the entertainment for these events, so we traveled to nine cities across the country, performing nine shows each weekend. It was one of the greatest experiences that some of us have ever had. Yep, the '90s were exciting for the Motor Corps.

The "4-Motor Chariot"
(L-R) Motormen: Bob Jensen, Mike Betschart, Harry Fisher, Mark Frymoyer;
Standing or pushed up on shoulders: Dan Welch, Mickey Minor; Safety on back: Pat Shanahan, Rich Wood

Leadership members were elected at the 1991 annual meeting. Most were officers who had already served for a few years but some new officers emerged.

Drill Leader	Harry Fisher
Stunt Leader	Mickey Minor
Flag Leader	Bob Nugent
Mini-Bike Leader	Rene Sevilla
Secretary	Frank Hicks
AMA/SCMA Rep.	Ray Brosell
Road Captain	Ted Evans
Sergeant At Arms	Guillermo Sevilla
Executive Board	Jay Cohen, Mike Betschart
Banquet Chairman	Jay Cohen

Practices were held in the rear parking lot of the Huntington Park Elks Lodge. This was a bit strange, since the Huntington Park Elks Motorcycle Stunt & Drill Team had been our competition for several years. Apparently the Elks team had disbanded and, since several of the McLaglen members were Elks Lodge members, we were given permission to use their lot for practice.

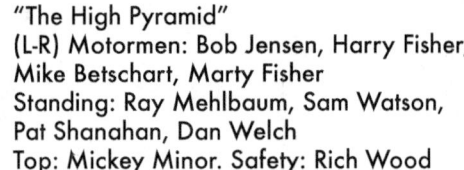

"The High Pyramid"
(L-R) Motormen: Bob Jensen, Harry Fisher, Mike Betschart, Marty Fisher
Standing: Ray Mehlbaum, Sam Watson, Pat Shanahan, Dan Welch
Top: Mickey Minor. Safety: Rich Wood

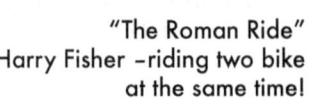

"The Roman Ride"
Harry Fisher –riding two bike at the same time!

In addition to the usual annual performances at the 1991 Yuma Prison Run and the Santa Maria Rodeo Parade, the Victor McLaglen Motor Corps added 19 more parades to the lineup of shows performed in California. Whew!

Cinco de Mayo	Hawaiian Gardens
Cinco de Mayo	Los Angeles
May Festival	Orange
Playdays	Monterey Park
La Fiesta	San Luis Obispo
Hollywood Troops Spec	Garden Grove
Strawberry Festival	Garden Grove
Flower Festival	Lompoc
4th of July	El Sereno
4th of July	Huntington Beach
4th of July	Pacific Palisades
Community Fair	Hawthorne
Corn Festival	La Habra
Old Miner's Days	Big Bear
Independence Day	Santa Ana
Korean Festival	Los Angeles
Stagecoach Days	Banning
Columbus Day	Los Angeles
Hollywood Christmas Parade	Los Angeles

The year 1992 introduced more of the same – parades, shows, and lots of positive publicity in newspapers and magazines.

The team continued to use the Huntington Park Elks Lodge parking lot for their practices and, in exchange for this gesture, the motorcyclists escorted the new Exalted Ruler from his home to the Huntington Park Lodge, where the riders stayed a bit to enjoy a Happy Hour. Yep, there's more to this story than I am willing to tell!

In April 1992, the team rode to Laughlin, Nevada, to participate in the Laughlin River Run, which was hosted by the Harley-Davidson Motor Company.

By Tedd Farrell

1992 Sturgis Motorcycle Rally

A really big treat occurred in August, when the Motor Corps was hired by Harley-Davidson to travel to the famous Sturgis Motorcycle Rally in South Dakota, to perform. We were asked to do four shows. The Seattle Cossack were also invited and our leader, Harry Fisher, and the Seattle Cossacks leader, John Moser, even put together a combined, spectacular performance with both teams.

In preparation for Sturgis, the bikes were loaded up in a 53' trailer, which Harry Fisher transported with his Peterbilt truck.

We took a generator, battery charger, siphon hose, air compressor, and miscellaneous tools, and cases of bottled water. We had it all figured out . . . right down to bringing energy bars in case we ran out of energy.

Plywood was put down on the floor of the trailer and metal stops for both front and rear wheels were installed. Tie-down straps secured the bike, but they were careful not to collapse the forks. A 4"x 6" piece of wood was put under the frame and a 2"x 4" was placed across the seat posts. Four tie-down straps were used for each bike.

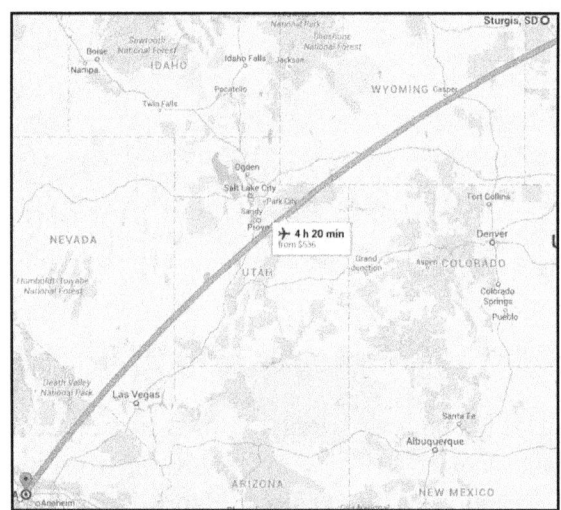

The members were told, "Pack your uniform, boots, belt and helmet in a plastic bin with your name on it, when you bring your motorcycle to load in the truck. This will ensure your uniform remains with your motorcycle and does not get lost in the luggage department at some airport. Also, pack your yellow rain gear, in case it rains. If you are flying, please ensure your luggage complies with the size limitations for carry-on, because we won't be "checking" any luggage. It will all be carry-on. Again, we don't want your baggage to get lost when you need it the most."

We departed from Los Angeles International Airport, changed planes in Salt Lake City, Utah and arrived in Rapid City, at 1:50PM – Mike Betschart, Prisca Betschart, Fernando Camarena, Tedd Farrell, Marty Fisher, Ruth Fisher, Kirby Frymoyer, Dick Gerry, Frank Hicks, Mickey Minor, Bob Nugent, Ron Oda, Ruben Pantoja, Alex Pantoja, Al Ruiz.

We hopped into rental cars and headed to the hotel in Rapid City. Harry Fisher drove the truck and met us at the Holiday Inn.

Sturgis was quite a hoot! The Corps and the Seattle Cossacks, performed at a hotel parking lot in Rapid City. There just wasn't a space large enough in Sturgis with all the riders and vendors taking up space. Of course, Willie G. and Nancy Davidson, were staying in Rapid City anyway, so, I guess it made sense. We didn't care. We were at STURGIS!

1992 Sturgis Motorcycle Rally (Cont'd)

Everybody was nervous. Well, this WAS Sturgis for heaven's sake and their biggest competitors, the Seattle Cossacks, were watching AND the big Kahuna, Willie G. Davidson, Senior Vice President and Chief of Styling of the Harley-Davidson Motor Company and grandson of the original founder, William A. Davidson, was there. Who knows what other VIP might be watching.

All I know is, the professional announcer who was supposed to travel with us, backed out at the last minute and we had no announcer. How in the world were we going to do a great job without an announcer telling the crowd all about us? How are they even going to know who we are?

Well, Harry had a solution – ME! What? I'd never been an announcer. I didn't even know which end of the microphone to talk into, let alone say anything worthwhile and entertaining. But this was an emergency, and there wasn't anyone else standing around, the "show must go on" and I made a mistake when I made direct eye contact with Harry! Long story short, I was volunteered!

So, OK – after I panicked a bit, went into the ladies room, upchucked my breakfast, rinsed out my mouth, put lipstick on, fixed my hair – I was ready.

Our plan was that Harry would line the guys up outside the show area and keep an eye on me. When the show coordinator said it was time, I would give Harry the thumbs-up sign, he and the team would come roaring in, and I would start the introduction and get the crowd's attention. If I ran into any problems, Dave Eady, the current announcer and long-time rider for the Seattle Cossacks, would stand beside me and help. Good plan!

Except – after the thumbs-up and Harry and the team entered the arena, I froze! Absolutely froze. Nothing would come out of my mouth! The only thing I could do was quickly hand the microphone to my (now) best buddy, Dave, and say, "Here – you do it!"

After a bit, I got myself under control and took the microphone back and talked, but before that – what a wimp! Talking on the microphone isn't as easy as one might think, at least not for me. Thus began my new career as the official announcer for the world famous Victor McLaglen Motor Corps.

The trip was a big success and everyone had a great time. We even made it into a Japanese issue of "Hot Bike" motorcycle magazine covering the event. I don't know exactly what they were saying, but presume it must be wonderful! After all, this IS the famous Victor McLaglen Motor Corps!

The two girls in the photo (next page) were Mike Betschart's daughter, Priska, and the other girl in the white shirt is Ruben Pantoja's daughter, Alex. They helped us out by doing some of the stunts. They never actually became members of the team and didn't ride their own bikes, but they did a marvelous job with the stunts, both at Sturgis and again later at the Love Ride. We were really fortunate to have them with us.

1992 Sturgis Motorcycle Rally (Cont'd)

This was the Japanese issue of "Hot Bike"

    Besides our Motor Corps, entertainment for the week included: the Seattle Cossacks Motorcycle Stunt and Drill Team, Waylon Jennings, Willie Nelson, Johnny Paycheck, The Fryed Brothers, Stray Cats, Edgar Winter Blues Band, Savoy Brown, Tinsley Ellis, and Commander Cody and the Lost Planet Airmen. It was quite a lineup of talent.

    On the last day of our Sturgis shows, Harry did a "Triple Firewall Crash"! No, one wasn't enough and two weren't enough – but three?? Well, that would be the ultimate.

    Everything went pretty well except – here's what happened. The three walls are framed with 2"x 4"s and attached to a stand that's covered with plywood; then the redwood slats are nailed horizontally to the upright 2"x 4"s. Then newspapers are crumpled up and stuffed in between the slats. Just before they are lit on fire, they are doused with gasoline. If it's a daytime event, a little oil is added so you can see the smoke better.

    When Harry gives the signal, two guys light their torches, then together, one on each side of the wall, set the wall on fire. At that precise moment, Harry guns his motorcycle and heads toward the fire as fast as that 1964 Harley-Davidson will go. It's a flash fire and timing is everything – too early and the fire isn't big enough yet, too late and the fire will be dead.

    Going through the first wall is tough, because he's basically going into it blind. The flash fire nearly blinds the rider, then coming out of that one directly into the next one, is blinding also. Then you add the third and the poor vision is extraordinary. He just had to start out straight and keep the motorcycle straight and keep the throttle on full blast – no matter what! That was problem enough, but an additional problem was – Harry had his face mask pulled down so he could wipe the fog off his glasses and didn't remember to pull it back up until it was time to go! Like I said, timing is everything, so he took off, got his speed up to about 50 mph – without his face mask pulled up in place!

1992 Sturgis Motorcycle Rally (Cont'd)

I was announcing and nervous as can be, but everything looked OK. He got through all three walls and except for bits of boards hanging onto the motorcycle, nothing much was on fire that shouldn't be. Whew! Little did I know…

So the crowd went crazy, hooting, clapping, hollering, and Harry did his usual ride around the arena, waving. But wait, – when he drove by me, he said, "Afterward, we need to go to the hospital." Sure enough, he had burns on his face that needed treatment. So we snuck off to the emergency room and didn't tell anyone.

What we didn't know, but soon found out, was that two other Motor Corps members were also "visiting" the Emergency Room that evening!

When we arrived, the doctor asked the usual question, "How did this happen?" Well, I never know what Harry's going to say because he never, ever, tells the real truth in these circumstances. His theory is, "If you tell them you got hurt while riding a motorcycle, automatically you get a lecture on how dangerous motorcycles are." So he makes up something. One time when he'd crashed and separated his shoulder, he told the doctor, "I took a swing at my son for mouthing off, missed, and fell down the stairs!" This time his story actually did involve a motorcycle – after all, this was the annual Sturgis Rally, so naturally they'll know his injury had something to do with motorcycles.

This is what he said, "Well, I was trying to start my friend's motorcycle and it wouldn't kick over. So I sprayed some ether on the air filter. Well, the thing backfired, flames sprang up and hit me in the face,"

The doctor looked at him and said, "Would that friend be in here now with the same uniform shirt and a broken finger and second friend, again with the same uniform shirt, here with a cut lip?"

About that time, Mickey Minor came around the corner – surprised to see Harry and Harry obviously surprised to see him! Mickey had hurt his finger during one of the day's performances, but didn't say anything to anyone and showed up in the ER when the shows were all over. Mark Frymoyer was the other member. He'd been showing off for some girls, bending his windshield down when it broke, popped up and cut his lip. The thing is, the guys don't like the public to know that they actually do get hurt now and then. It ruins their perfect-rider image!

But, the jig was up. Harry had to admit what really happened, especially when Mickey told the doctor the truth about his finger, that he'd been performing in a motorcycle show.

Ah, boys will be boys!

"Riding High"

In the early part of the summer of 1992, writer for *Cycle World* motorcycle magazine, Don Canet, decided he wanted to know what it felt like to ride some of the stunts with the Motor Corps, so he contacted Harry Fisher.

"Associate Editor Don Canet poses with Harry Fisher, commander of the Victor McLaglen Motor Corps. Fisher's "motor" is a 1964 74-cubic-inch Harley-Davidson FL Police Special with hand-shift, foot-clutch option. It's rigged for stunt duty with front-axle footpeg extensions, safety rope, beefed-up luggage rack and rear floorboards. Team members purchase and maintain their own machines, Harleys that range from a 1933 VL to a 1989 Heritage Softail. Vintage iron works well for drill team maneuvers; the rocker pedal clutch permits hands-free operation, and an ignition retard controlled by the left twist grip delivers subtle power modulation."

"RIDING HIGH"
By Don Canet

Even with a white-knuckle grip and steady pull against the safety rope, I barely maintain my balance, rocking forward as the two motorcycles supporting our six-man pyramid come to a complete stop. I sway for a moment, like the top of a tall pine in the wind, before regaining both balance and breath.

We remain at a standstill for 10 seconds and without ever touching a foot down, the two motor men below me execute simultaneous clutch engagement, putting the stunt – a "Figure Eight Stopping Pyramid" – back into motion. We proceed to carve another tight figure eight in the parking lot of the Riverside Hotel Casino, located on the west bank of the Colorado River in Laughlin, Nevada.

I'm here as an ersatz member of the Victor McLaglen Motor Corps, riding a fine line between writing a story and filling out workman's compensation forms, trying hard to maintain one of those Rose Queen kind of smiles in the face of danger. Cheers from the crowd – mostly Harley-Davidson riders attending the annual Laughlin Run for a weekend of festivities – bring it all into perspective. My greatest fear isn't pain; blowing it in front of all these people would truly hurt.

Such crowd enthusiasm has been a major motivation for the McLaglen Motor Corps since the Southern California-based motorcycle stunt-and-drill team first began performing more than 55 years ago. The team's heritage dates to 1935 when a group of guys riding out of the Rich

"RIDING HIGH" (Cont'd)

Budelier Harley-Davidson dealership in Los Angeles challenged Victor McLaglen – the Oscar-winning Hollywood actor who sponsored horse drill teams at the time – with the claim that their Harleys could do anything a horse could do. They did well enough to earn not only McLaglen's sponsorship, but his distinguished name, as well.

In 1936, the team challenged Mexico City's Police Stunt and Drill Team to a world championship competition. The spoils went to the Victors, so to speak, and the group's fame was set. The Motor Corps traveled by railroad, performing around the country for the next five years until World War II put a stop to the shows. Operations resumed after the war, but tensions within the group led to a split in 1951, with some members forming a new squad under the Huntington Park Elks Lodge banner. Both teams coexisted until 1978, when a restructure united the two squads once again.

"Due to insurance and lodge regulations, the Elks were only allowed to perform in California," says the team's 46-year-old commander, Harry Fisher – owner of a limousine and funeral-escort service – who took charge of the drill team in 1978, filling the position that Herb Harker had held since 1951. "Now we participate at Elks' functions, we use the Elks' facilities, and some of the money we earn goes to Elks charities, but we're the Victor McLaglen Motor Corps."

I first met up with the Victors last February behind the Huntington Park Elks Lodge, where they were holding their first practice of the 1992 season. Following a 60-day layoff, the guys were getting back into gear by working on the fundamentals. The scene was reminiscent of a ball club in spring training as 15 or so motormen (they don't call themselves "riders") wearing matching coveralls and police helmets, maneuvered their black and white Harley-Davidson motors (never "bikes" or "motorcycles") through a slalom course of orange cones.

After a quick howdy-do with the team members, I was pushed into my first stunt: the "Horse." After a bit of instruction and a dry run aboard a stationary bike, it was time for the real thing.

"Build it!" my motorman commanded once we were underway. I carefully stepped from the small platform mounted over the rear fender up on the shoulders of Harry Fisher, whose 30 years of stunt-and-drill experience boosted my ebbing confidence. I instinctively tightened my grip on the reins, a safety rope that slips onto the handlebar's crossbar. Then –yeeha! –I was up and riding' high as we circled the Elks parking lot. Well, it seemed pretty high at the time.

What followed in rapid-fire order was a succession of stunts with names like the "Shoulder Layback," the "Swan" and the "Pushup." By early afternoon, I felt like I'd taken the Devil's Own Aerobics Class. Then, there I was positioned 12 feet in the air at the pinnacle of the Motor Corps' premier stunt, the "4-Motor High/Low Chariot Pyramid." These guys had me on a learning curve

"RIDING HIGH" (Cont'd)

steeper than the sides of their pyramid. I was truly relieved when the day's session came to a close and I hadn't broken any bones or lost any teeth. After a couple more Sunday practices, it was time to take the show on the road.

What's required to be a member of this elite fraternity? "A motorman needs to be a skillful motorcycle rider, have good coordination, balance and a sense for working as a team member," says Al Ruiz, a 53-year-old machine shop supervisor who started with the Elks team in 1971 and now serves as stunt coordinator for the Victors.

"It requires balance, strength and lots of confidence to be a climber. You have to put your trust in the other members on the stunt," says Mickey Minor, 59, who came aboard in 1985 following a 23-year Naval career. "Being lighter than most of the members, I wind up going up top much of the time."

How specialized are the various roles of the performers? "We have several people who can fill any spot on a stunt. It's important that we remain versatile so that we're not dependent on any one guy to be at every show."

Considering the nature of the team's activities, combined with a busy schedule –performing at some 30 parades and exhibitions a year – the Victor's safety record has been very good. Spills are rare and usually happen at walking-pace speeds. "We stress that our people be qualified in doing stunts in practice before using them in a performance on the street. We worry a lot about safety," says Commander Fisher.

The oldest Motor Corps member is Dick Gerry, 72, and at 30, I wasn't the youngest. Marty Fisher, the CO's son, became a team regular three years ago at age 14. "I've been around it since I was about 4. I would hang around practice and, during a break, my dad would put me on the headlight and do a slow circle," says the high school senior who recently made the transition from the McLaglen mini-bike squad onto the full-size motors. "I've filled in whenever they've needed me, riding the headlight or front fender. I went up on shoulders a few times, but fell once and hit my head. Now, I prefer to be a motorman, seat man, or safetyman."

One stunt we (thankfully) wouldn't be repeating during my stint with the team involved piling 21 men onto Harry Fisher's Harley while he rode in a large circle. "Taking part in the 22-man stunt is easily the most terrifying thing that I've ever done on a motorcycle," recalls 61 year-old Bruce

Chubbuck, the West Coast Harley-Davidson fleet manager who joined the team in 1978 as a liaison officer between the Motor Corps and Harley-Davidson. "The team has never had any official ties with the factory, although Harley has helped finance several trips, including Daytona and Sturgis," says Chubbuck.

"RIDING HIGH" (Cont'd)

Although the men on the team perform as professionals, nobody is getting rich. "We're a voluntary organization." says Fisher. "What money we make performing is used to cover our expenses and our banquet at the end of the season. What's left over goes to charity." Listen to Motor Corps members talk about team camaraderie and spectator appreciation, and it's clear that they love what they do.

"The start of the Hollywood Christmas parade with all the millions of people there is quite impressive, but most of all I enjoy performing in front of our peers – bikers – because these people have a better understanding of what we're doing." says 59-year old Bob Jensen, a welder by trade. Does crowd response have any effect on the 14-year team veteran? "During our big finale, the 4-Motor High/Low Chariot Pyramid, I like the sound of the crowd. They're really cheering, which makes you feel like you've done a good job," Jensen says.

As we went through the program before a crowd of 5,000 at Laughlin, I hadn't figured on stage fright being such a factor. Hell, back in the Elks parking lot, I had my part pretty well wired in the seven stunts I'd be performing in. But here, in front of a live audience, with the intense, non-stop action of one stunt following another, I was stressed to the limit. But Bob Jensen was right. The crowd's enthusiasm came to a head during the grand-finale stunt, and my anxiety disappeared as a I proudly waved the Cycle World flag from my position on the pyramid. As we rode out of the demonstration area in a two-abreast column, through a gauntlet of smiling, cheering faces, I got a taste of what it is that keeps members of the Victor McLaglen Motor Corps coming back for more.

The team also had support from Tsubaki Chains–free chains and expense money to take trips. John Linden, executive at Tsubaki, was instrumental in securing this deal and it was very much appreciated by the guys.

"Our man in the Corps. Canet's uniform includes a breakaway, clip-on tie, not a bad idea when climbing around a moving motorcycle"

The "4-Motor High/Low Chariot Pyramid" always brings a huge response from the crowd. Canet is on the right flying the Cycle World flag."

In 1992 the team once again led off the Huntington Beach 4th of July Parade.

"3-Motor Push-up"
Motormen: Bob Jensen, Mike Betschart, Kirby Frymoyer

Then we performed at the Ventura Fairgrounds in California and made it into the local newspaper.

"DC-10"
Driver: Mike Betschart
Safety on back: Sam Watson
Top: Fernando Camarena
Handlebars: Tylor Hicks
Front Fender: Mickey Minor
Sweeper on back: Al Ruiz

Another interesting show the team did in 1992, was the Christmas Parade in Lake Isabella, Kern Valley, California. It was COLD! In fact, it snowed while we were performing.

The street had snow and sleet on it, and the team just kept right on doing stunts and drill maneuvers. After all, that's what we were there for. No wimping out! Harry was leading and he said something about "the show must go on," and no one dared contradict him, I guess.

Harry was driving, so of course, it was HIS fault!

The stunt was the "Sunflower", you know, one motorcycle, four guys hanging out the sides?

Well, apparently it doesn't work well when there's sleet on the street to start with and a car decides to cross over right in front of you.

Harry put on the brakes, the bike slid sideways and, well, you see what happened.

So, this was where the "Blooper Award" was born and it was presented as a surprise to Harry at the Annual

Awards Banquet that next year!

The good news? They once again made their way onto the front page of the local newspaper!

Dick Gerry, Mike Betschart, Mickey Minor

Given any thought to washing your bike?

In 1993, we performed in Newhall, California, for the 4th Annual Accessories Unlimited Harley Ride and Street Rod Show.

LEFT:
Motorman: Mike Betschart,
Front Left Side: Ray Mehlbaum,
Front Right Side: Mark Frymoyer,
Back Left Side: Dick Gerry,
Back Right Side: Ruben Pantoja,
Front Safety: Bob Jensen,
Middle Safety: Rich Woods,
Topman: Troy Lee.

BELOW:
1993 Pacific Palisades
4th of July Parade
Motorman: Harry Fisher
Safety on back: Tedd Farrell
Horizontal: Mark Frymoyer

One of the events we performed at in 1993, was the Laughlin River Run in Laughlin, Nevada. How much more fun could you have? The casinos, the great restaurants, thousands of other motorcycle enthusiasts – and we get to show off in the parking lot of the Colorado Belle Casino Resort.

"Speedo with Human Ladder"

Reno, Nevada

In September of 1994, the Motor Corps went to Reno, Nevada, for the first time to perform. It was windy and cold and the parking lot that was used for the performance was a great place for the blowing sand to get in your face and in the engines. Fortunately, no one had a problem and the shows were a success. The bikes were transported in a 53 foot trailer pulled by a very impressive Peterbilt truck and the team was looking first class, which of course, they were.

Several years later, we returned to perform for Street Vibrations, a motorcycle rally that's held each September.

This event was very interesting. The performance was held on the main street, in front of one of the major casinos, and we had no sound system. This posed a problem as to how I would announce the show. The issue was eventually resolved. I was to use a microphone which was connected to the casino's PA system. I had to stand in the circle in back of the dealers where the pit boss hung out. I couldn't see the street, let alone the Motor Corps show, so how was I suppose to make any sense on the mike? I had a stunt list, but they don't always follow it. How would I know when they started or completed the stunt or if they fell down, or – then Claudia Watson, wife of team member Sam Watson, had a great idea. She would stand at the doorway with the stunt list and watch the show. She would send signals to me by holding up her fingers for which stunt was being performed on the list, #2, #6, etc. I'd catch her signal, look at the list, and announce just as if I really could see what was going on! The gamblers at the tables and the dealers in the pit sure looked nervous, though. I'm sure they wondered what I was up to and if it was the reason why they were losing!

Dan Welch was riding a Flag Bike, which is a motorcycle with a flag pole attached and either an American Flag, state flag, or Motor Corps flag flying. The Flag Bikes usually ride in front of the group. Dan's flag was flying high and he rode under the entrance overhang at the casino -you know, the kind that has hundreds of light bulbs in its ceiling? Well, after Dan got through, it had a bunch of broken and missing light bulbs and there was glass everywhere! Guess that flag pole was a tad too tall.

The team salutes the audience after their show.

60th Anniversary Awards Banquet

In 1995, we celebrated our 60th Anniversary, and held our annual Awards Banquet. Members attending were:

Drill Team:
Mike Betschart
Les Ellis
Tedd Farrell
Harry Fisher
Marty Fisher
Mark Frymoyer
Dick Gerry
Frank Hicks
Bob Jensen
Ray Mehlbaum
Mickey Minor
Ruben Pantoja
Rich Wood

Flag Unit:
Bruce Chubbuck
Keith Noe
Bob Nugent
Pat Shanahan
Dan Welch
Don Warren

Mini-Bike Safety Unit:
Allan Betschart
Troy Lee

Announcer: Ruth Fisher
Medic: Ray Brosell
Lifetime Member: Bill Lomas

91st Huntington Beach 4th of July Parade

Well, not every show went perfectly that year and not every stunt was flawless. Someone asked me once if I had a picture of the High Pyramid collapsing and of course I said, "It rarely happens and if it does, we sure wouldn't want to keep a picture of it!"

Just when I thought our secret was safe, up comes a picture from the archives of the Los Angeles Times of – you guessed it – the High Pyramid collapsing!

It happened at the 4th of July Parade in Huntington Beach, California, in front of more than 200,000 spectators standing on the sidelines and, since it was televised, who knows how many viewers on TV around the world saw this mishap. Oh my, apparently these guys aren't perfect after all! I don't know what the excuse was but probably something to do with a spectator crossing the street in front of them, a cotton candy vendor getting in the way, the wind was not right, a gum wrapper blew into the drivers' eyes – or whatever excuse they could think of at the time.

200,000 Show Their Holiday Colors at 91st Huntington Beach Parade
CHRISTINE COTTER / Los Angeles Times

Another Firewall Crash

In 1994, Harry did a Firewall Crash with journalist Robert Hough onboard. I don't know if this had anything to do with it or not, but the journalist quit Cycle World soon after this stunt!

The Victor McLaglen Motorcycle Corp. practices its stunts to minimize any risk to not only the riders, but the spectators as well. And, kids, don't try this at home!

Riding On The Edge

Some Harley riders aren't quite content with the open road.

photography by
Brett Hatch and Alan Keller

Stunts are, by their nature, inherently dangerous. No one knows this better than the people performing them.

Ironically, though, one of the best ways to minimize the risk associated with doing a stunt is to practice it over and over until it can be performed perfectly and precisely every time.

That's the goal of stunt riders like the members of the Victor McLaglen Motorcycle Corp.

- continued on page 24

Despite their reposed positions here, the VMMC riders don't take their stunts or their safety lying down.

We're not exactly sure what the point of this stunt is ... but it sure doesn't look like anything amateurs should attempt.

MOTORCYCLE MILESTONES   Collector's Edition 1995

For a number of years, the team performed at the Bikers Against Diabetes (B.A.D.) Ride and, sure enough, 1995 was no exception. Usually Larry Hagman (of "Dallas" and "I Dream of Jeanie" fame), Peter Fonda (of "Easy Rider" fame), the Willie G. Davidson family, and actor/musician Mickey Jones, are the celebrity special guests. But countless others participate to raise funds to stamp out diabetes.

"The High Pyramid"
Motor men: Bob Jensen, Harry Fisher, Mike Betschart, Marty Fisher
Side Chariots: Ray Mehlbaum, Mark Frymoyer
Seat men: Sam Watson, Tedd Farrell
Safety man in back: Rich Wood
Top of the Pyramid: Mickey Minor

By Tedd Farrell

Ruidoso, NM

In 1995, the team went back to Ruidoso for the Americade Motorcycle Rally. The motorcycles were trucked and the members either flew or drove.

The motorcycles were all carefully placed into the 53' trailer – and they all arrived without a scratch!

Once again, we were given lodging in cute little cabins. One had five bedrooms with a main living/dining/kitchen area. It was a really spectacular setting with great hospitality. (And my introduction to the state where I would be living many years later when I retired!)

By Tedd Farrell

Member Marty Fisher celebrated his 21st birthday in a great log cabin in Ruidoso, NM with mom, dad and members of the team. And look at that – drinking Pepsi and not beer. How in the world did that happen to a college guy on his 21st birthday?

Marty Fisher & Mom, Ruth Fisher

RIGHT: Everybody gathers round for a little cake and friendly "ribbing" for the 21-year old. Mickey Minor, Dick Gerry, Ruben Pantoja, Tedd Farrell, Sam Watson, Cheryl Woods, Claudia Watson, Bob Jensen, Ruth Fisher and Mike Betschart

BELOW: Mickey Minor, Les Ellis, Mark Frymoyer, Joyce Ellis, Mike Betschart, Rich Wood , Mark Frymoyer, Sam Watson, Bob Jensen, Marty Fisher

The cake with, of course, a motorcycle theme!

International Motorcycle Shows (IMS)

1996 was another fun year. The team were asked to perform at the International Motorcycle Shows (IMS) – which meant they went to nine (that's 9) cities across the country, performing nine (that's 9) shows each weekend. There's an entire section of this book that tells the story, one of the more interesting being the shows in New York City. We performed at that venue in front of 30,000 fans who were attending the Northeast's largest motorcycle indoor show.

The motorcycles were trucked from city to city, with Harry Fisher and Tex Harris driving, and the remainder of the team (14 members were chosen to travel) who flew in, did two shows on Friday, four shows on Saturday, and three shows on Sunday. We rushed to the airport after that last show and flew home so we could be at work the next morning! Check out Appendices B and C for more of the story.

We did the same routine over and over a total of 81 times, and by the time we finished that last show in Denver, we could practically do those stunts in our sleep! (And I got really good at announcing, too.)

In the year 2000, we performed for the IMS tour again. This time, we knew what to expect and were ready for it. And again, we got better and better. We would arrive on Friday afternoon, perform nine 20-minute shows throughout the weekend and depart on Sunday evening right after the last show. It was fun and we loved it.

Motor men: Bob Jensen, Harry Fisher, Mike Betschart, Marty Fisher
Standing middle row: Ray Mehlbaum, Tex Harris, Sam Watson Kirby Frymoyer. Top: Dan Welch
Safety in back: Pat Shanahan

Canada

In 1996, in addition to our other shows, we also went to Canada. It was a great trip, but the toughest part was getting INTO Canada! The rest of the team flew in, but Harry and I were in the truck, transporting the motorcycles.

We thought we had all our paperwork in order, lists of all the bikes with their VIN numbers, proofs of insurance, registrations, notes from the stunt bike owners, that we had permission to transport them into Canada, etc. We had a very detailed and complete Bill of Lading. Harry had all his log book sheets up to date. He said all the "Yes, Sir" and "No, Sir" answers politely, and I had the biggest smile on my face –but they still didn't want to let us enter their country!

They seemed to think we were there to "work," and they wanted to see our work visas. We tried and tried to explain that we weren't "working," we were just supplying the entertainment for the charity event and none of us received compensation.

Then they found out that the rest of the team was flying in, so they put their best border patrol agents on that end of things, at the airport. Harry had called one of the members and gave him a "heads up" to ensure each member knew to say the right words –we were receiving NO compensation, which was very true.

Our team members at the airport fumbled through all the questions and seemed to be doing OK, until the agent discovered that one of our members had an outstanding warrant. Yikes! We hadn't counted on that happening –and the member didn't either. It seemed, he thought he'd taken care of it, but apparently, all the documentation hadn't been posted, so he was stopped. Fortunately, Frank Hicks, one of the other members, was a retired U.S. Border Patrol Agent, and Frank vouched for him, so the agent accepted that and let them all through. Whew!

Meanwhile, Harry and I were still trying to get the truck across the border. We'd arrived there around 8:15AM and it was now 4:50PM. Finally –an agent told us to come with him and he took us to a supervisor who was sitting in one of the offices. The supervisor took one look at the paperwork and another look at us and said, "Oh, I know these guys. They're OK." He stamped the papers and we were done! I don't really know if he knew who we were, or it was just that it was almost quitting time and he wanted to go home. Regardless, we were finally allowed our admittance into Canada.

We arrived with the truck and motorcycles and met up with the rest of the team, finally. The shows went well and we all had a terrific time. Canada is beautiful and the people were very hospitable –once we got over the border.

One of the highlights for Marty and me was going to Edmonton to see the statue of hockey's great Wayne Gretzky. Marty was playing hockey for San Diego State at the time, so the Fisher family was way into hockey!

The "Light Show" at this event in Canada was interesting. Since the sun is still shining in June (even at 11:00PM) in Red Deer, Canada, the parade of bikes with all their accessory lights on, rode into the big convention hall, which was darkened.

We finally made it after staring at this sign all day! Harry and Patches, trying to be patient.

The flag bikes flew the American flag, the Motor Corps flag (left) and the Canadian flag (right) for this show

Windows were covered and all the lights were turned off. The parade of bikes entered the front door, single file, drove around next to the wall, crossed in front of the stage and then drove out the side door. Of course, the Motor Corps being what it is –and Harry being how he was – our bikes had their wheel lights turned on and we drove into the building like the others, then left the parade of bikes and drove up a ramp onto the stage. Our guys did a really tight Pyramid and a couple other stunts, before hitting the ramp and exiting the building. Show-offs!

As usual, we had a great time. The team loaded the motorcycles into the transporter and headed to the airport and back to California, to work the next day, Harry and I climbed into the truck and started the journey back home.

What a great trip!

And we were able to see the statue in Edmonton of the great hockey player, Wayne Gretzky (L-R): Ruth, Marty & Harry Fisher

Victor McLaglen Motor Corps

MOTORCYCLE STUNT AND DRILL TEAM

Harry M. Fisher, Commander • P. O. Box 845 • Bellflower, CA 90706 • (213) 920-2768

June 24, 1996

To The Members,

Our trip to Red Deer, Canada was VERY successful (in spite of the trouble getting across the border and through Customs at the airport!).

The truck made it there with no mishaps, (the scenery through the Rockies and Montana was just gorgeous - You all should have seen it!)

The field events went well and our participation in the parade through the country-side, our show and the "light show" inside were all just perfect. They were very pleased with us. In spite of Mike's front wheel slipping on the sand just before the ramp, (sand imported by Dave Eaddy), and Dan almost catapulting right up into the rafters off the scissors, and a couple of our guys catching one of the Canadians coming out of control down off the ramp with all his lights glowing, - - WE DIDN'T EVEN FALL OFF THE STAGE!! The "Grand" Pyramid looked just great circling the dance floor and drew a standing ovation from the crowd.

Dick and Marty hold the record for "Highest stack of beer cans"! This was proclaimed by one of the bar tenders, so it must be true! Marty learned the trick at S.D.S.U.!
I think we all had a super time, eh? And it was all for a good cause.

Thanks to everybody who made the Grand Opening of Anaheim Yamaha. Our shows went very well and it was good to see Rich out and around again - as well as Kirby. Thanks for the support, guys.

The videos will be ready and handed out this weekend at the Tipper's Picnic Show, so be sure to have $5 for each one you asked for so we can get our bills paid.

See you at the next show!

Harry

Harry

Harry's letter to the team afterward

Big bang for the buck
Variety is the spice of "ground-level thunder '96"
by Reg Kittrelle

We—that's you and us—have this deal going concerning "*ground-level thunder.*" Our part of the deal is to put together the most for the least. That is, the most fun, for the least money. And your part? You have to show up. Well, it's a little more complicated than that: Actually, at least 6,000 of you have to show up. You'll be happy to know that, by doing your part on September 7 and 8, we were able to do at least half our part; the part that says "...for the least money." For the third consecutive year, our basic ticket price was kept at a measly five bucks. As far as "...the most fun" part is concerned," well, that's up to you to decide.

To help in that decision, here's a recap of what happened: As in previous years, "glt" was held at that 88-year-old fruit stand on Highway 152, eight miles inland from storied Hollister, California. Casa de Fruta, as it's named, is an oasis of touristy things like a restaurant, a winery, a petting zoo, an RV park and several other "...and a"-type things to make a road-weary traveler stop and loosen their wallet.

See *glt '96*, page 24, col. 2

Victor McLaglen's Col. Harry Fisher puts the heat on *Thunder Press* publisher (see page 29)

Harry Fisher and Reg Kitrelle crash the "Firewall"

Great balls of fire, indeed!
Our publisher gets a firsthand lesson in fire safety

By Reg Kittrelle

"*Aren't we overdoing it a bit?*" *I idly thought. I mean my leather jacket, full coverage helmet and gloves . . . I'd forgotten my gloves (No problem; I'd just hold my hands in closer) . . . would be more than enough protection. So why are they zipping me up in this silly jumpsuit? And what's with all this fire retardant stuff that Ruth, Harry's wife, was spraying on me? And the tape around the wrists? And what was that Harry just said about my ponytail?*

Several months ago Harry Fisher, commander of the Victor McLaglen Motor Corps, and I reached a deal wherein the Corps would perform at this year's "Ground-Level Thunder." As kind of an afterthought, Harry said it might be possible for him to perform his seldom seen firewall stunt along with the regular program. "That's great!" I told him, "Nothing like adding a little twist to the show." "Of course," he added, "you'll be on the back of the bike."

I checked out the "wall." No big deal; just a couple of uprights strung together with several dozen one-inch lath strips. What the hell, I figured a healthy sneeze could break through it. No problem. "You nervous?" asked Marty, the youngest Fisher and newest Corps member. "Nope." Why should I be nervous? All I had to do was hang on. Harry'd done this stunt many times before, and was an accomplished stuntman motorcycle racer – and older than me. I figured the last one was important, 'cuz if he'd been going around doing stupid things, he wouldn't have lived this long. No problem.

Earlier in the day, Harry suggested we try a few practice passes. "We'll have to do it at about 35 mph," he said in answer to my question. He brought out one of the rigid Harleys, and we made a couple of fast walking pace passes with me perched on the rear rack and hanging on to the front seat edges. No problem. "You ready?" he asked over his shoulder. Assuming I said yes, he nailed the old Harley and pointed it at where the wall would be later that evening. The up-till-then smooth grass suddenly became a washboard which the rigid rear only touched on occasion. My butt lost contact with the rack – then found it too abruptly, slamming my head into Harry's back and causing my eyes to question their rightful sockets. "Maybe we ought to use a bike with suspension?" I weakly asked. Harry concurred, and went off to find a newer model of the Corps' motors. I, in turn, was left, briefly, to ponder how lucky I was that I didn't want children. Another pass with some suspension under us proved to be a piece-o-cake. No problem.

"Harry Fisher and a would-be crispy critter"

All bundled up and sprayed down – and still trying to figure out what the fuss was all about – I was ready to do it, when Marty suddenly decided that I needed more neck protection. "Better safe than sorry." chimed in Ruth. Finding a handy towel, Marty stuffed it around my neck. No problem.

Wandering off, I left Harry to practice his passes. Returning a bit later – Harry had left – I found Kathy Halsey anxious to point out a new divot in the grass. "Know what that is?" she asked. Hoping I didn't, I answered "no." "He went down," she said with a smile. Seems someone had walked in front of Harry's bike and he went down to avoid them; he wasn't hurt. No problem.

Climbing on behind Harry, we rode the hundred yards or so out to the wall. Turning the last corner, we were confronted with a sea of people. All right! This is going to be fun! That wimpy wall was about 75 feet distant, stuffed with balled, gasoline-drenched newspapers. We made a couple of slow passes and then took up the starting position. Mistress of Good News Halsey appeared with a jug of tequila, but I couldn't figure out how to drink it through the full-coverage helmet.

Then they lit the wall. Problem.

The wimpy wall suddenly became a blazing inferno, rocking the crowd back on its heels and sending – I swear! – heat licks around Harry and I (OK, so it was probably fear sweat). My mind raced: Was there enough fire retardant on me? Were my wrists taped? Is my ponytail tucked in? Did I . . . Harry slammed the throttle open, and with a slight slewing we headed for what was sure to be my last barbecue. Tucking behind Harry like a noontime shadow we whapped! Into the wall and through it. What a rush! Drunk with a bit of euphoria, it took a moment for me to realize that my crotch was on fire. No problem, I just reached down and removed that bit of burning lath.

With the fire out (including a pesky one that persisted atop the engine, just beneath the gas tank) Harry rode us back to the doused wall and up to Kathy and her bottle of tequila that she again offered us. Grabbing it, I sucked it dry. Sorry Harry, I needed that drink!

In 1997, the team was asked if we wanted to do an advertisement for Uplift Custom Cycle Lifts. In exchange for using their picture, each participant would receive a free lift.

Of course, these guys would do it for something FREE! Therefore, prior to our performance at the Legends of Motorcycling show at Del Mar, California, we attempted to put our High Pyramid on four lifts.

Building the Pyramid "static" is just not exactly the same as doing it when the bikes are running, so behind where you can't see – four members are sitting on the fenders to balance the bikes on the lifts! I think I was one of those.

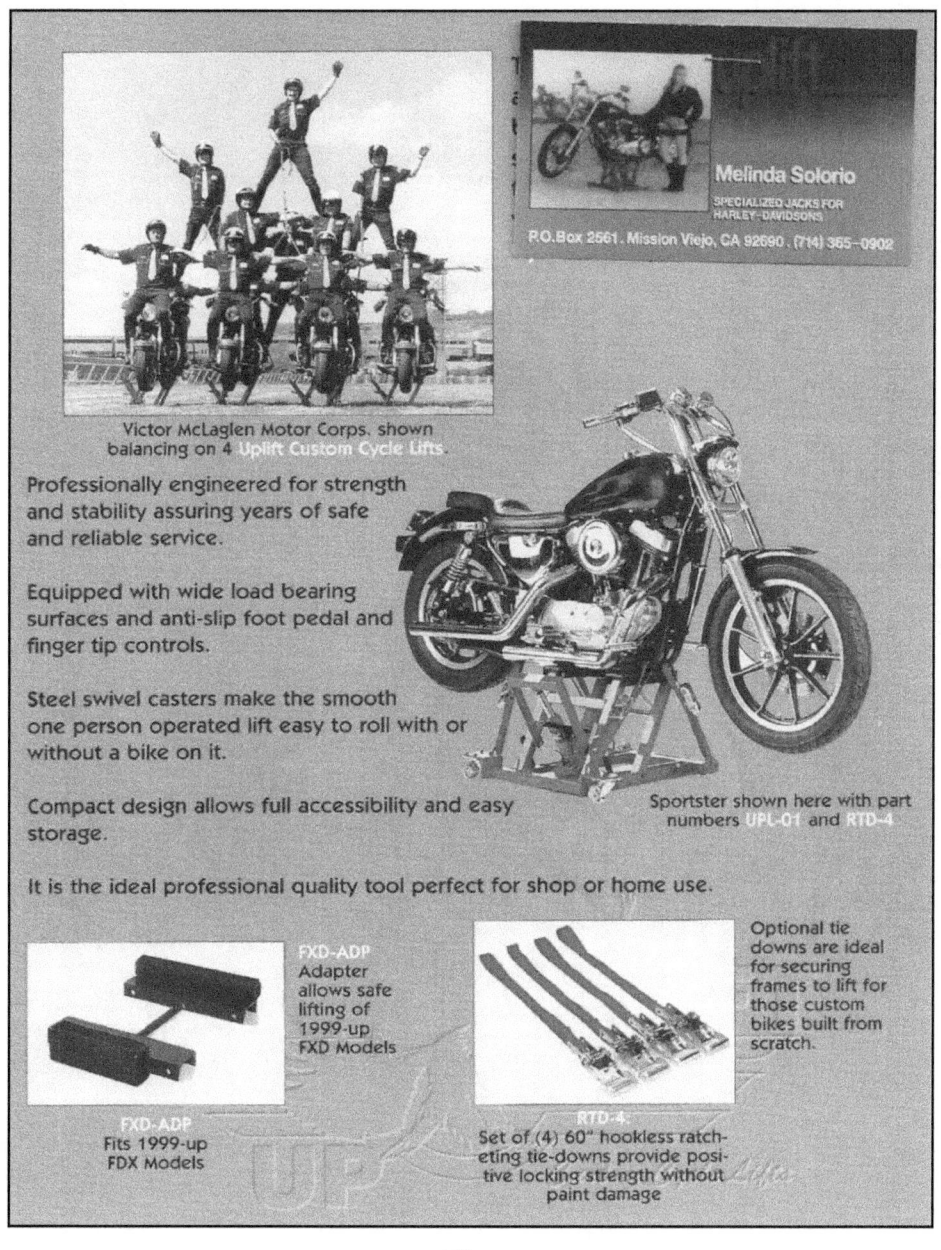

In 1997, a write-up about the Motor Corps showed up in one of the police magazines. I don't even know why. Maybe because we have black and white motorcycles? Maybe because the police motor officers would enjoy reading about the skills that our team exhibit? Maybe because somebody knew somebody who writes for the magazine! You just never know why these things happen sometimes.

2000-2009

A new century and the team was doing more traveling and getting stronger than ever. In addition to our regular local (California) shows, we performed at the Americade Motorcycle Rally in Lake George, New York; the Tennessee State Harley Owners Group Rally in Memphis, Tennessee; the American Motorcyclists Association's Vintage Motorcycle Days in Pickerington, Ohio; and Street Vibrations in Sparks, Nevada. We voted into membership our first woman rider and held an awards banquet where we invited the "old timers" who had been members in decades past. We were doing well.

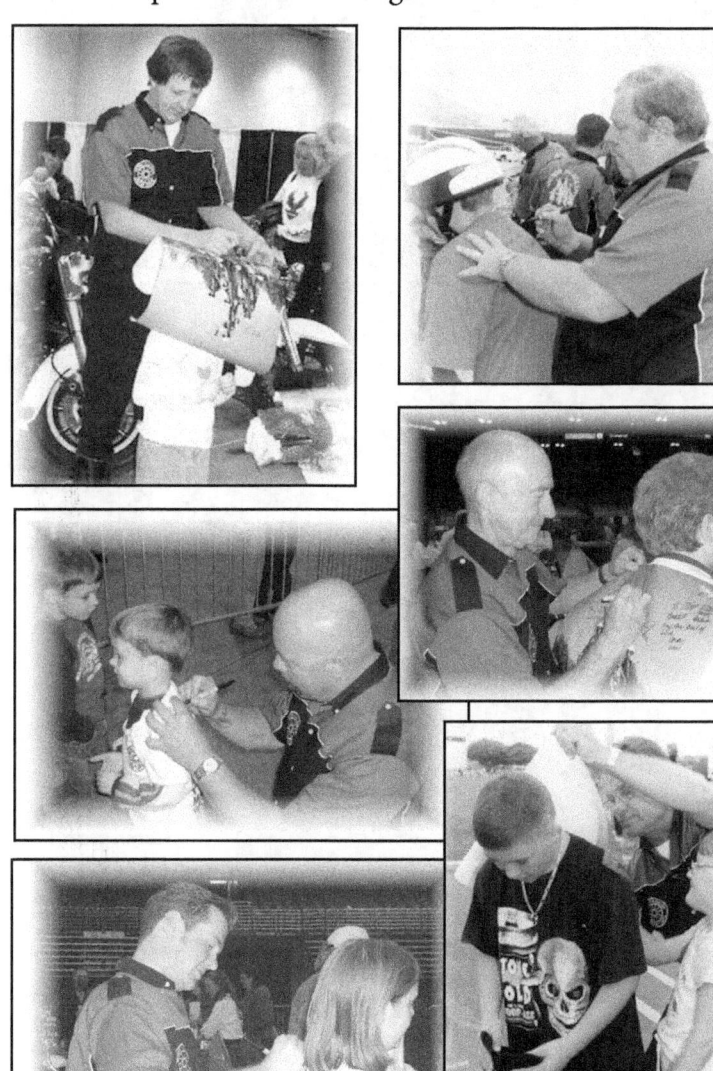
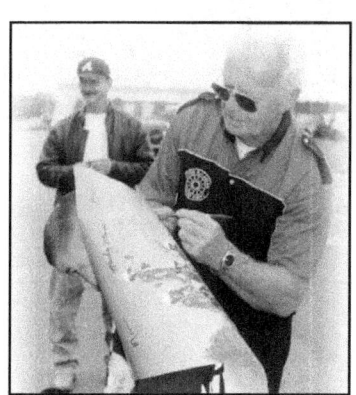
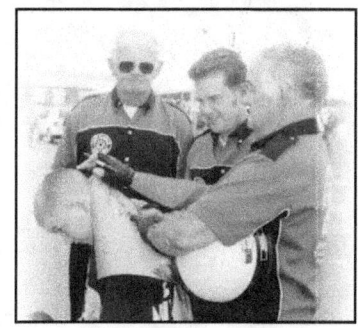

Americade, Lake George, NY

In 2000, the Americade Tour was held at Lake George, New York, and we traveled across country once again. The motorcycles were transported in Harry's truck and the members flew. Lake George is absolutely beautiful, with lots of green trees, green grass, flowers, and shrubs. And the reason why all those things stay green is because it RAINS! This weekend was no exception. It rained almost all weekend, and we didn't have rain gear, but Harry had a solution – black trash bags. They're cheap, they all match, and one-size-fits-all! We put on great performances, nonetheless.

The transporter is parked at the site.

Marty Fisher models the new trash bag rain gear!

The team is ready.

It's raining and our bikes are getting really wet.

The team lined up –rain or not!

New, Professional Pictures

In 2001, we decided we needed new, professional photographs of the stunts and team members. After all, how could we publicize ourselves if we didn't have pictures? Our new member, Maria Willers, had a friend, Sam Jones, who agreed to do the job. Sam was a writer for a local motorcycle magazine and, as you can see below, he's a photography wizard, too.

"High Pyramid –Front"
Motormen: Sam Watson, Harry Fisher, Mike Betschart, Marty Fisher
Standing on Front Crashbars: Jake Elmore, Mark Frymoyer
Short Chariot: Tylor Hicks, Jeremy Norton, Art Wales
Safety: Maria Willers, Moe Elmore
Top: Mickey Minor

"High Pyramid –Back"
Sitting on rear fenders: Bruce Chubbuck, Bob Nugent, Frank Hicks

These are some more of Sam Jones' pictures, which were used numerous times for publicity.

"The Speedo" Maria & Mark

"Totem Pole" Mike, Sam, Mickey

" Human Ladder" Mike, Marty, Sam, Mark, Mickey

"P-38" Mike, Jeremy, Art

"Fan" Mike, Art, Sam, Mickey

"DC-10" Sam, Moe, Art, Tylor, Mickey

"Sunflower" Harry, Art, Moe, Marty, Jeremy

"P-38 Human Ladder" Harry, Tylor, Art, Mickey, Moe

Make-A-Wish / Pediatric Brain Tumor Research Foundation

The team has always been a big supporter of the Make-A-Wish Foundation and, on several occasions, we were able to provide entertainment for a fundraiser event.

In fact, at a "Ride for Kids" event in Torrance, California, I met one of the "kids" who received a wish. Ride for Kids is a fundraiser for the Pediatric Tumor Research Foundation. After the show, all participants of the event were given sack lunches by the Honda Motor Company –which were very good, by the way. Some ate their lunches sitting at tables under a tent, but I opted to sit on the grass with a few other Motor Corps members. Just as we were getting settled down to our scrumptious lunch, a young man of about 14 years old came over and asked if he could join us. He was one of the Pediatric Brain Tumor kids, who was there as a guest of the event. Of course, we were honored to have him eat with us. Just to make conversation, I asked him, "what do you like to do for fun?" And he replied, "Well, I dabble in the stock market some." Right away, I knew that I wasn't talking to just any kid –and probably I would have trouble keeping up a conversation with this bright kid! So I said, "Great. Do you make any money with it?" And he said, "Well, sometimes. Do you happen to know about the Make-A-Wish Foundation?" Of course I did, so he explained why he brought it up.

"Last year I was given the opportunity to have my wish come true. I wanted to ring the opening bell at the New York Stock Exchange and they let me do it. "

Now, I don't exactly remember where the conversation went after that, because I was too much in shock to say much. I mean, what do you say to a fourteen year old who's hobby is "dabbling" in the stock market? I definitely didn't know much about the theory of relativity, or the facts on global warming, and I sorta figured he would be more interested in something like that, than how the Lakers were doing this year, or if Harley would come out with a new belt drive bike next year. What an interesting young man.

"Half P-38" Marty & Bruce

The team lines up.

Rip's BAD Ride

For many years, we performed for Rip's B.A.D. Ride. That's "Biker's Against Diabetes" (B.A.D.). The originator, Rip Rose. was a biker photo-journalist for Easy Rider magazine and succumbed to diabetes in the year 2000. But, in 1997, he had an idea to rally bikers together, to make money for research for this dreaded disease. The first show was at Glen Helen Pavilion in Southern California and the Motor Corps was there exhibiting our skills. The venue moved to various other places, so we subsequently found ourselves performing on grass in a lot of places, complete with gopher holes! It made for a very interesting stunt show.

Lots of celebrities: Peter Fonda, Mickey Jones, Larry Hagman, Willie G. Davidson and his wife, Nancy Davidson, and daughter, Karen, attended this event. Several had diabetes themselves or had a close friend or relative who had the disease. Of course, the Motor Corps wanted to contribute. This was a good fundraiser for the Diabetes Foundation and we were ready to do our part.

At one of these events, Rip's motorcycle was being auctioned off. I was talking to team member, Mark Frymoyer, when Mark suddenly saw someone he knew on the other side of the crowd and waved. Well, Mark didn't know it, but he'd just bid several thousand dollars on Rip's bike! I said, "Mark, you just bid on the bike." His face turned white! Fortunately, someone else bid higher so he was off the hook.

2001 -"The DC-10"
Driver: Sam Watson
Safety: Moe Elmore
Top: Jeremy Norton
Handlebar: Tylor Hicks
Front Fender: Mickey Minor

2002 -"The High Pyramid"
Drivers: Sam Watson, Harry Fisher,
Mike Betschart, Marty Fisher
Chariots: Sue Hutchings, Tylor Hicks
Safety: Maria Willers, Scott Griffin,
Mark Frymoyer; Top: Mickey Minor

CHOC Ride

We also did several shows for CHOC, Children's Hospital of Orange County in Southern California.

"The Scissors"
Driver: Mike Betschart
Safety: Sam Watson
Handstand: Jeremy Norton

"The Roman Ride"
It looks like Harry's heading for the 405 Freeway with his two bikes!

Practice – Every Sunday

Practicing Drill August 11, 2002

When the drill starts getting a little rough and the new guys don't know what to do, or when a new maneuver is being learned, the team walks through the maneuver. They line up, the Commander blows the whistle and the riders trot out in their Nikes and Reeboks and do the cross-overs, socks, figure eights, or whatever the leader decides is needed. Then when they mount the bikes and go through these maneuvers, they stand a better chance not to have an accident. I gotta tell you, our guys can ride those bikes a lot better than they can walk and trot!

There's also the Cone Game, which is often played at practice. The riders divide up into two teams. One is on one end of the field and the other on the opposite side. The orange cones are lined up between them and a tin can is placed upside down on the middle cone. Each team rides down opposite sides of the cones, aiming for that tin can. The first one to get it, carries it to the next cone and places it on top. The opposite team tries to get it and bring it back to the next cone nearer their home base. This goes on until one team is able to get the can all the way to the last cone, on their side of the field.

It's fun and a great way to develop skills in riding with one hand, keeping your bike going slow while leaning over and picking up or dropping off the tin can. That is, of course, until someone gets ticked off, because someone else cheated. But then, that's another story!

The "Can Game"

In the July 2000 issue of *Hot Rod Bikes*, Commander Harry Fisher was interviewed. It's lengthy but I've included the entire article here because it tells the story of Harry's involvement and also a lot of the history of the Motor Corps.

Colonel Harry Fisher

AN INTERVIEW WITH THE LONGTIME LEADER OF THE VICTOR McLAGLEN MOTORCYCLE CORPS

PHOTOS: FROM HARRY'S COLLECTION
COPY: K. RANDALL BALL

Harry Fisher, a short, stocky, well-preserved 54-year-old lifetime motorcyclist and stunt drill team leader for more than three decades, is a mild-mannered trucking company owner who refuses to let a spectator down. There is more about Harry in the words he uses than in the overall description. A hard drinker and constant rider, he's a leader who likes a new challenge, is always concerned about his teammates, and prides himself in a high level of family integrity. You won't find Harry badmouthing anyone—his life has been too much fun.

HRB: How did you get involved in stunt riding and the Victor McLaglen Motor Corps?

Harry: I grew up in a motorcycle riding family. We all had Harleys, and my mother taught me how to ride a motorcycle. I had a 125-cc Harley (and I got a

Colonel Harry Fisher (Cont'd)

165 cc later). We use to do business at Chubbuck's Harley-Davidson. My mother found a bike there that she wanted but it had a hand clutch and a foot shift, and the one she owned had a hand shift and a foot clutch, so we traded motorcycles. We rode to Death Valley on the Death Valley Run. I was a pretty good rider, but she beat me through Stove Pipe Wells, so I guess I wasn't that good after all.

Anyway, I saw the Victor McLaglen Motor Corps show there and they were doing some slow circles. It was extremely impressive to see them bring the handlebars to the full lock position and roll in a circle. So I asked my mother if she knew anything about the team. She said, "I think I know the guy who has a dealership who runs it." That was Whittier Harley-Davidson, owned by Herb Harker.

We checked it out. I went to several practices, they voted me in, and I've been riding in stunt groups ever since. That was in 1962. Ultimately, Rich Budelier and Dick Hutchins were the driving force behind the Motor Corps.

The Motor Corps leader from 1935 to 1955 was Nick DeRush. Nick was the sales manager for Rich Budelier. It became the Victor McLaglen Motor Corps in 1935 when Victor McLaglen, the actor, gave everyone a leather jacket after they proved the Motor Corps could perform as well as the Light Horse Drill Team Victor had started.

In 1936 the Victor McLaglen team challenged the Mexico City Police Motorcycle Stunt Team and won. The trophy is still at Fullerton H-D in a big case with all the original members' names etched on it. The competition was held in the Los Angeles Coliseum in December. Some guys did solo tricks dressed as clowns. There were only the two teams around at that time. The competition was a one-time event. We won it and kept the trophy.

Tell us about stunt riding in the mid-'60s.

We lead a lot of parades, went to the Lone Pine Run, 29 Palms, and Death Valley events. That was the circuit at the time. We rode our bikes to the events, rode in the field meets, rode in the show, and just had a good time—it was a lot more casual back then. We did some stunts but no pyramids, which was one of the things I always wanted to do because I remember as a kid the RKO news at the theater showing the Mexico City Police Team doing a big pyramid.

I left the Corps in 1967 when they caught me practicing with the Huntington Park Elks. I got booted out. The Elks did a pyramid and the guy at the top, Johnny Kazian, offered to teach me. He was a professional stuntman. He ate fire at some events, and wing walked on airplanes. I didn't believe him about the wing walking, so I rode down to the airport at Huntington Beach and there he was standing on the wing of a bi-plane flying over the airport. Next thing you know we were doing motorcycle-to-airplane transfers. He was a colorful guy, and I learned how to do a pyramid.

Then the Mexico City Police Motorcycle Stunt Team came to Los Angeles for a Latin American Festival that the LAPD had. Our government wouldn't allow them to bring their bikes into the country, so I loaned them four hand-shift bikes, and a couple of friends of mine also had some to loan. Afterward, the team invited me to go to Mexico City as their guest as sort of a thank you, so I told my boss that my great uncle was sick and I had to go to Mexico to see him! I went down for two weeks and rode with the team and took a lot of pictures for reference. I fell down more times in that week than ever in my life.

When I came home we worked on what we do today, which I think is very good.

Although there are only a couple of stunt groups now, there were a bunch in the '60s?

There were several: The Ace of Clubs, the Elks, the Motor Corps—all in the Los Angeles area—and the Cossacks from Seattle, but they stayed in their area (they started in 1938). At the time, we just performed at local events, although our motorcycle team had the privilege of spending some time on the road in the late '30s, before the war, touring Idaho and Washington. At the time, they loaded their bikes on box cars for the trip. They performed at fairs, fairgrounds, and horse showgrounds.

When did you leave the Elks and return to Victor's group? What were you doing with the Elks prior to returning to Victor's group?

In 1978 I came back. But before that, the Elks lead the Rose Parade two years in a row. Because I was an Elk at the time, we were involved with several

Colonel Harry Fisher (Cont'd)

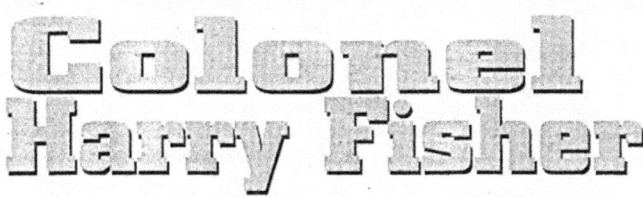

charities, including the Piggy Bank Ride, picnics, etc. We escorted the Rose Parade floats at night; they then allowed us to ride in the front of the parade the next day, which was, of course, with no sleep. It would rain, be windy, and sometimes cold as hell. We rode 52 miles in a 7-mile parade, without stopping. We could never hold the parade up, just rode back and forth, back and forth. There was a walker in front of us setting the 2.5-mph pace. That took place in '72 and '73.

We also lead the opening of the Ontario Motor Speedway, and were the flying-V escort for Evel Knievel when he jumped 19 cars. We were also in the movie with George Hamilton as Evel Knievel.

The Elks have an annual baseball game at Anaheim Stadium where we performed in the pre-game show, which reminds me of a story. One of our guys, in the Elks tradition, enjoyed his drink. Well he pulled up to the curb and fell down and we picked him up and he fell down again. Well, we got to the parking lot gate and they were going to charge us admission to go in. I didn't handle it too well. I shot through the gate and circled around the booth a couple times with the team following, but we got busted and had to go explain to the head honcho what we were doing before we could perform.

Tell us how and why you left the Elks and went back to the Motor Corps.

Around 1976 I moved, making the traveling distance to practice a big factor. I was working hard and dropped out. Herb called up and told me he was going to retire and asked if I was interested in running the Victor McLaglen stunt team. So I took it over. At the time, there were only four existing guys left on the team: Les Jorgenson, Herb Harker, Smitty, and Bob Keller.

The Elks Lodge was having a problem, so that team disbanded anyway. So when I took over running the Victor McLaglen Corps, the remaining Elks guys came over and we got the team going again under the Victor McLaglen Motor Corps name and started practicing in Long Beach. We had no uniforms at the time, but we started training. Then Bruce Chubbuck got involved. He had a Harley dealership in Pasadena and thought it would be fun to join our group, so we picked up a few more members. We thought that one of the simplest things to do as far as uniforms are concerned would be to get helmets, but it was by far the hardest thing to wear. We couldn't hear, they covered our face, they were a pain in the ass.

In 1980 we performed for the Motorcycle Jamboree in Bakersfield. We were on the road again and it felt good. We did three of those Jamborees, and I was even the chairman one year. I've been on the Love Ride Committee practically since its inception, and in 1992 we brought the Cossacks down to perform alongside our team, then at the end we had a group show. We worked in the parking lot and it was late in the day and not a lot of people got to see it, but we ended the show with eight bikes and 42 people on a pyramid going around the parking lot—it was spectacular. It definitely was the biggest stunt of that type I've ever been involved with.

Tell us about the first year after you re-energized the Corps again.

We primarily practiced. The next year we started doing parades again. We practiced every week. We did 20 parades. In 1980 we did 10 infield shows and about 40 parades; that year we had the competition in Tijuana; and in 1981 we went to Ruidoso, New Mexico. Then we were asked to go to Daytona and Sturgis.

Tell us about the Mexican motorcycle stunt team fatality.

We had some interesting rules at the event. The main rule was that the first time someone fell off, the meet was ended. This was a program for kids at a baseball stadium, Benito Juarez Park, in Rosarita Beach, Mexico. As it turned out, it was OK if they fell off. We did our stunts and no one paid much attention. John Moser from the Seattle Cossacks was there with his bike and he did this rear rack to seat stand jump, and that seemed to impress the kids. Then we started building more pyramids and sunflowers and they really started watching. Then the Mexican stunt team got onto the field, but halfway through their routine the bikes started to crap out, so they borrowed a couple of ours.

Colonel Harry Fisher (Cont'd)

Well, they got to the eight-way ramp jump where the person drops a hankie and they go for it. But the hankie wasn't dropped properly on a single motion. So a couple of them started and a couple didn't, and it caused a head on, in-the-air type wreck. The guy riding my motorcycle was killed. It ended the meet on a bad note, but prior to that it was an excellent day down there.

Three days later we went back for the funeral and escorted the limos to the grave site where we attended the services. After that, the Tijuana Suicide Squad was disbanded. One of the fellas on the squad, Guermo Sevilla, came up and rode with us for a while.

Thankfully, we've never had another mishap like that one.

That's incredible, but you must have had some other nicks and dings from time to time.

Sure. One time in Sturgis we did a pyramid and a three-firewall crash. As we were setting up and I was waiting, it was hot so I pulled my mask down. Then suddenly they lit the walls and gave me the signal. Well, I didn't have time to fix my mask up over my face correctly, but away I went. At the first wall, I hit a burning splinter that went right through my plastic face shield and burned my face. Well, I went through all three walls, shook some hands, and then rode to the hospital.

I have a code that I never wanted to be a motorcycle accident statistic. It's all right to get hurt, but just not on a motorcycle. So when the doctor asked me what happened, I told him that I brought my bike to Sturgis and I've been spending all week trying to start it. I just didn't have any luck. Well I filled the carb with gas, hit the starter button (even though I had a 1951 kick-start bike), and it backfired and burned my face. So the doctor treated my face and I get up to leave because I was in a hurry to go to a party. I asked the doctor how Meredith Minor (who was also in the emergency room) was, and he asked me how did I know Minor. I said that he broke his finger on the starter button. Actually, he broke his finger getting off a pyramid stunt. Another team member was in a different room for some reason or other. It looked like old home week. Because we didn't want the injuries to reflect on the team, we all snuck into the hospital individually.

How did the '80s treat the new revived Motor Corps?

The biggest thing was the trip to Daytona. That was a major move for us. We worked very hard, but one of the toughest obstacles was finding an announcer. That has always been a tough one. Dave Eades' wife, Paula, was the announcer for the Seattle Cossacks, so I talked my wife into helping us. The guys felt that without an announcer we don't have a show—quite frankly that's the truth. If you go to a race it's the guy on the microphone that helps make the race exciting.

We used to talk a parade announcer friend we know into going along once in a while, but he was usually too busy to go very often. Then Dick Hill, a team member, did the announcing for some time. He was an editor for *Black Biker* magazine. He kind of quit announcing when he divorced his wife because her boyfriend didn't like Hill much and sent him a package that blew up his house. That's when my wife started announcing.

Tell us about the bikes that made you famous.

All Harleys. I've had two, my '51 and the '64. My son rides the '64 and I ride the '51, which originally had a sidecar on it and was owned by Schaeffer Brothers Printing Company. Mom bought it from the company and rode it until 1955 when she had a bad accident. My uncle rebuilt it for her; from '59 on, it's been in steady use. It has traveled close to 500,000 miles (the '64 has between 250,000 and 300,000). Both bikes have been rebuilt plenty of times. The real ass-kicker is the heat produced with riding the bike slowly, the pyramids, the Roman rides. In 1981 I set the record having 22 people on the '64.

Was there a particular stunt that the team mastered in the '80s?

The biggest thing was putting all the people on one motorcycle. We practiced three times a week perfecting the balance, working on the camaraderie, knowing when team members were jumping on and off. I think the thrill of doing it was great. I always wanted to take 22 people for a ride right down the 605 freeway!

We started with the Elks group piling on 17 people. KTLA came out to cover it. When we put the Motor Corps back together we put 17 on again, then added more to make 21 at the motorcycle Jamboree, then 22 at the Artistry in Iron show in Los Angeles. We were going for 23 with the television show "That's Incredible," but we were at the fairgrounds on a really rough track in Ventura. We had everyone on, but then fell, so we didn't make the show. They had us all wired for sound, but when the guys started cussin' and stumblin' on the rough surface, it probably wasn't proper enough for the show.

We were in the *Guinness Book of Records* until a Japanese group piled 49 on a running motorcycle. We probably have the weight and distance record, but it's not recorded.

When the '90s rolled around, your core group had been together more than 10 years and was well rehearsed. What changed about this decade?

Going to Milwaukee for the 95th Anniversary was a highlight. We rode in a parade in Buckhannon, West Virginia,

Colonel Harry Fisher (Cont'd)

then went to Lake George, New York, then over to Milwaukee. We became a well-oiled machine. The routines became second nature and we just enjoyed the heck out of traveling around the country doing our stuff.

I have a big wall calendar in my office to watch the dates and promote. I have my trucking company, and can afford to haul the bikes around to more events. Now we can hit more dates in more places than ever before.

We went to the Pomona 1/2-mile to perform. We were representing Tsubaki

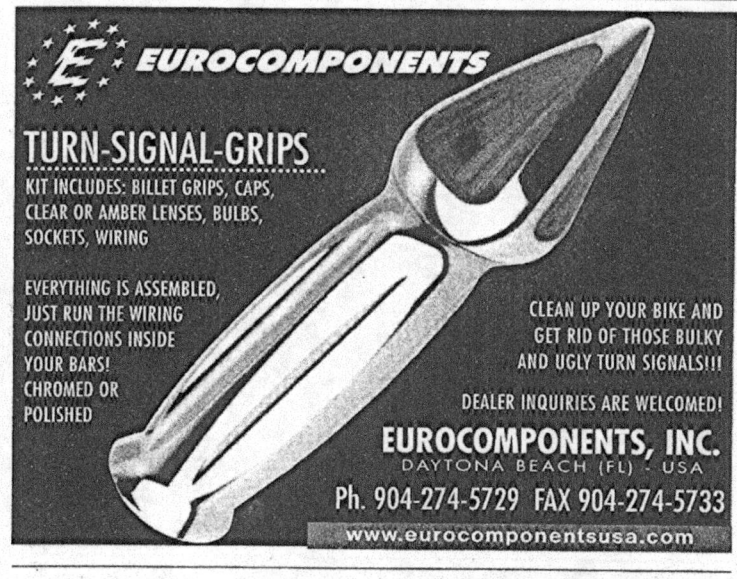

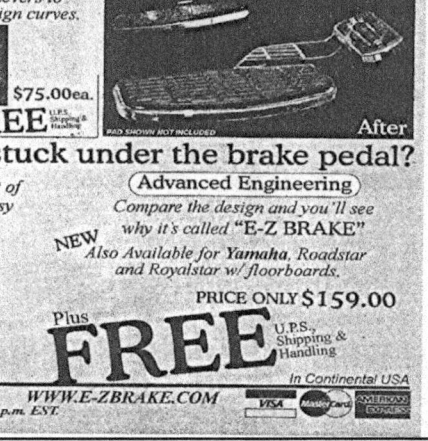

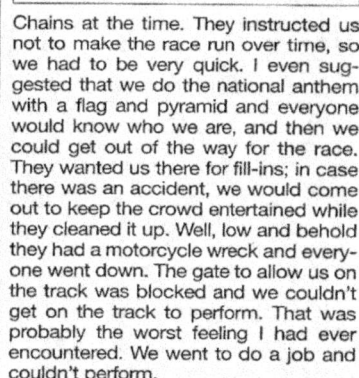

Chains at the time. They instructed us not to make the race run over time, so we had to be very quick. I even suggested that we do the national anthem with a flag and pyramid and everyone would know who we are, and then we could get out of the way for the race. They wanted us there for fill-ins; in case there was an accident, we would come out to keep the crowd entertained while they cleaned it up. Well, low and behold they had a motorcycle wreck and everyone went down. The gate to allow us on the track was blocked and we couldn't get on the track to perform. That was probably the worst feeling I had ever encountered. We went to do a job and couldn't perform.

Del Mar was a truly rewarding venue to play at for a couple of years. Bobby Bishop and the San Diego Antique Motorcycle Club did a hell of a job for a lot of years—now that's changed.

We can do three shows a day. Two is comfortable and one is gravy. We did four shows a day in New York. Generally spectators rotate, so we're performing in front of a new audience every time. But people don't often treat us like the real deal. We usually lose money on every event, yet we've been performing for 40 years or more.

Have you had any accidents on the street?

I recently fell off my motorcycle when a woman pulled in front of me, but it was not as bad as the time a car didn't stop at the stop sign and hit me. I had no idea what happened—I was just out. Well, I get into the hospital and this doctor who

Colonel Harry Fisher (Cont'd)

hated motorcycles comes up to me and asked, "You ride a motorcycle?"

I said, "I guess so."

"Did you just ride and fall off?"

"Yep, that is what I did," I said. I had no idea. I didn't know I was on a bike and got hit. Hell, I didn't know who the hell I was. So they rush me to the MRI. The doctor was irritating me, but I still didn't know what happened and he continued to ask me questions. So I got the MRI. When I came out of the donut, I remembered what happened. Of course the doctor was gone by then. I had a broken rib and they wanted to keep me all night and give me morphine. I refused the morphine and the pain pills.

When the doctor came back, he thought I was some sort of idiot. The doctor starts going off about me being old and out of shape with hardening of the arteries and high blood pressure, and he also said I was about ready to kick it. I got real upset, so I said, "Doc, I need to check out. I'm going to a funeral home. They've got more to offer me there. They've got music and a comfortable room, a nice place to lay down. I need to leave. You don't have anything to offer me."

I was finished, out the door—no clothes, no nothin'. Fortunately my son had picked up my bike and came to the hospital and rescued me. I don't know how the hell I would have gotten out of there otherwise. Wrapped in a sheet I guess.

How do you perceive the change in audiences throughout the years? What is the change a reflection of?

Motorcycling has changed. When we started out everyone was in clubs and all wore club uniforms. Then we went to a pretty rough looking group. Now we've come to a stage where a lot of guys are forever motorcycle riders and others who like to dress the part and only ride once in a while.

We performed at American Honda and were treated just as well as at the HOG Rallies. It's based on skill. The audience appreciates more today what we do than they have in the past. Years ago you had to kick start the bikes and you didn't have instruction courses like the Motorcycle Safety Foundation. So if you wanted to ride, you had to go for it, ricochet off the curb, and ride through the neighbor's fence.

The early riders were also more of a muscular group than the rider of the '90s. My accountant bought a bike recently. The guy has never even mowed his lawn, let alone ridden a motorcycle. He went to the store, bought a motorcycle, a helmet, a leather jacket, boots and gloves, and away he went. Years ago, you had a motorcycle jacket, some engineer boots, and a pair of Levi's—that was your clothing. No one bought all the apparel in one place.

Do you think the Motor Corps should change its look annually?

We haven't got to the stage of painting the bikes, but we are in the process of changing the uniforms. A drawback is the police-type uniform. In the earlier years it was kind of a plus because we served as escorts and that was kind of the look for the '50s.

Now we go to the circus to research our outfits.

We need strong shirts that look sharp, but they must also be something your partner can hang onto. It can't be light color because if your partner steps in oil then on your shoulder it will look a mess. Yeah, we're looking at coming out with a new look. But annually? Probably not.

We're planning more stunts, too—more riders on a single bike and stuff. Much of our future depends on getting a corporate sponsor. I don't know how much more we can do or how many more out of town places we can get to without some financial support. **HRB**

HOG Rally, Nashville, TN

Driver: Sam Watson, Jr.
Top: Art Wales; Handlebars: Bruce Chubbuck
Front Fender: Mickey Minor; Safety: Jake Elmore

In 2003, we traveled to Memphis, Tennessee, to provide entertainment for the Tennessee State Harley Owners Group Rally. This was the first big show where we traveled without our leader, Harry, to ramrod.

The motorcycles were, once again, shipped by a transporter truck and the members arrived by air. We stayed at the Park Vista Hotel, in East Memphis, and put on a heck of a show right there in the hotel parking lot! Mark Frymoyer, our Assistant Drill Leader, led the drill and the only mishap was when Sue Hutchings took a tumble and ended up with a huge bruise on her butt! All in all, though, considering that the parking lot was on a tilt and that slant had to always be taken into consideration, the shows went very well, we met a lot of terrific people, got to experience that great southern hospitality, made the front page of the local newspaper and went home happy.

We also took time to take in one of the local sights. This particular sight was Elvis Presley's "Graceland" home and it was well worth the trip and the time. I didn't expect to see so much that depicted what a wonderful man he was. Elvis was a legendary musician and a big humanitarian, too. I was amazed to see large numbers of local organizations to whom he donated large sums of money, like the local Boy Scouts. What a guy!

We just HAD to visit Graceland!
Mark Frymoyer, Sue Hutchings,
Scott Griffin, Darlene Griffin,
Bruce Chubbuck, Mickey Minor,
Ruth Fisher, Marty Fisher

WWW.FULLTHROTTLEUSA.COM   **FULL THROTTLE**

ELVIS:
The King Of Rock N Roll Sure Loved To Ride!

Part 1 of 5
BY: EVAN WILLIAMS

Sometimes it's not easy to be a motorcyclist. Avoiding random lane-changers, road rage psychotics, and just run-of-the-mill geranium brains in two ton steel cages all help make motorcycling a pastime for the alert and skilled cyclist. All bike enthusiasts know the feeling - it's a jungle out there.

But for the moment, let's pretend you are not. Let's crank up the time machine, and set the controls for 1976 and the location for Memphis, Tennessee. You are the King of Rock-and-Roll and lifelong bike enthusiast, Elvis Aaron Presley, AMA member number 94587.

Speaking of jungles, let's say you're lounging in the Jungle Room at Graceland, and decide it's time to go for a ride. You give call out to your girlfriend, Ginger Alden, and ask her not to fetch you another peanut butter-and-banana sandwich, but your leather jacket, because you two are going for a ride. And when the King decided to go for a ride, nothing could deter him.

"Don't forget where he came from," Elvis's guitarist Scotty Moore told the Memphis Commercial Appeal. "Elvis was still a kid when he died. He never grew up. It was usually things he hadn't had a chance to do when he was growing up."

If you were Presley, you'd stroll over to the garage, and decide which toy you would fire up for a ride into Southhaven. It could be a vintage chopper, or a Honda Dream, or perhaps a trike. But most likely it would be a Harley Dresser that Elvis preferred. "Most of the bikes he had that I saw him ride, the FLH, the dressers, police-type bikes, were bigger and close to the ground," says Ron Elliot, the proprietor of Supercycle, a Memphis bike shop were the King took care of his (motorcycle) business. "They were more predictable and handled better (than some of his other machines)."

But first, we'd look for a member or tow of our entourage, the Memphis Mafia, to ride along with us. "Elvis was real big on getting a lot of his friends to ride with him ... I guess it was hard for him to go anywhere by himself. The fans just swamped him everywhere he went, even down here (in Memphis)."

You've had health problems over the past few years, and you're not getting any younger, but it all fades away on your bike. The promise of the open air hits you as you roll down the hill and out the Graceland gate, maybe head towards the Circle G ranch you own right across the Mississippi state line. You are reminded of the early days, when you first bought that little Harley stroker when the money started rolling in. Of the wild California times, when you and the guys (and girls) rode up and down the coast. About getting one day away from touring in the early '70s, and coming back to ride downtown in Memphis.

You are wearing an open face helmet, but onlookers invariably know it's you. They all double take, wave or look for their cameras, and more than a few have trouble keeping in their lanes. If anything, the frenzy fans show at concerts is increased when they see Elvis on the streets. To circumvent the hoopla, most of your riders are at night, like this one.

Looking around at the neighborhood, you'd remember that this place was a quiet little neighborhood when you bought Graceland in the 50s, but twenty years have brought plenty of commercialization to the area. The smells of magnolias have been replaced with urban exhausts, but the ride still replenishes energy to your psyche.

As the ride ends, you realize it's never quite long enough. You roll through the gate and feel a twinge of sorrow. Perhaps now is the time in your life to cut back on the constant touring and relax a bit. Enjoy life, ride your bike more. You've told others that you want to make this tour your "best one ever", but part of you wonders why you can't give it a break. Perhaps delve into some serious film roles, and spend more time with your daughter, Lisa Marie.

But it wasn't meant to be. Two days later, Elvis would be dead and his fans would be in a mourning period that to this day really hasn't ended.

He may have been a Superstar, but Elvis was just like us. He was a bike nut and enjoyed nothing more than getting out on the open road to clear his mind. Elvis could often be seen motoring around the streets of Memphis, or Los Angeles during his movie days. "He rode a lot; cold weather, warm weather, whenever he was in town," says Ron Elliott.

Look for Part 2 in our November issue

November 2002 issue of *Full Throttle* did a great article about Elvis, written by Evan Williams, which started us thinking about visiting Graceland the next year.

On January 25, 2003, we held our long-overdue Awards Banquet. It was a pretty lavish affair held at the Phoenix Club, in Anaheim, California, and a few of the Old Timers were our special guests: Tony Ayala (1959-1965), Chuck Caldara (1961-1964), Roger Davies (1978-1985), Les Ellis (1993-2000), Warren Farrell (1985-1987), Gene French (1978-1981), Kirby Frymoyer (1978-1995), George Garza (1982-1983), Frank Horn (1961-1968), Ruben Pantoja (1979-1982), Hubie Phillips (1937-1942), Al Ruiz (1978-1985), Guillermo Sevilla (1989-1991), Pat Shanahan (1984-1994), and very special guest Grace Jester. Grace was the widow of the late Harland Jester (late 1930s). Grace and Harland were both in the Victor McLaglen Light Horse drill team. Harland tried to get Grace's attention and impress her by also riding in the motorcycle team. I guess it worked because when he proposed, she accepted.

Back Row (L-R): Mickey Minor. Scott Griffin, Devin Griffin, Paul Lach, Harry Fisher, Jake Elmore, Moe Elmore, Mike Betschart, Bruce Chubbuck, Frank Hicks, Maria Willers, Mark Frymoyer
Front Row: Tylor Hicks, Dan Welch, Marty Fisher, Tim Hutchings, Sue Hutchings

Paul Lach from Kawasaki presents giffts to the team.

New Retirees: Tedd Farrell, Bob Nugent, Bob Jenson Mike Betschart and Harry Fisher present their plaques.

New Retirees: Ted Farrell Bob Nugent Bob Jensen

The Old Timers brought photo albums and shared pictures from "back in the day" and believe me, they had lots of stories to tell of the times when they were in the team.

"Old Timers"

Tony & Dela Ayala

Frank & Joan Horn

Chuck & Delores Caldara

In 2003, the team performed at the CHOC Ride again. It was near Riverside, California, and I remember it as being extremely hot. The good part was that we were able to spend the day with our good friend, Mickey Jones. Harry had talked Mickey into standing on the Pyramid and all Mickey could say was, "standing on that Pyramid is pretty scary!"

Tylor Hicks, Scott Griffin, Mark Frymoyer, Jake Elmore, Mike Betschart, Mickey Jones, Bruce Chubbuck, Frank Hicks, Maria Willers, Sue Hutchings, Mickey Minor

The "High Pyramid"
Motormen: Mike Betschart, Mark Frymoyer
Standing: Mickey Jones, Frank Hicks
Safety: Scott Griffin
Top: Mickey Minor

Actor, Mickey Jones

Yuma Prison Run

The Corps started off 2004 as usual by performing at the Yuma Prison Run. The team put on an exciting performance, showing young and old alike, what can be done on those beautiful Harley-Davidsons.

And once again, as the team's announcer, I warned everybody, "Don't have a couple of beers and try this in front of your friends. There are a few details that you'd want to know first, but you can learn 'em by joining the team."

RIGHT:
Front Row: Josh Allen, Sue Hutchins, Mark Frymoyer, Mickey Minor, Devin Griffin
Back Row: Tylor Hicks, Bruce Chubbuck, Mike Betschart, Harry and Ruth Fisher, Moe Elmore, Scott Griffin, Frank Hicks

"Street Vibrations" Sparks, Nevada

In September 2005, we traveled to Sparks, Nevada, to perform for Street Vibrations at the Nugget Resort Casino. This was the same event where we had performed a few years back. The really cool part was that – there we were – on their huge electronic billboard. What a thrill to see our Motor Corps up on that big billboard, especially when it was all lit up at night.

LEFT: Mark Frymoyer riding the front crashbars The "One Motor Pyramid"

RIGHT:
Motormen: Mike Betschart; Middleman: Frank Hicks
Safety: Moe Elmore; Top man: Mickey Minor

We even made the FRONT PAGE of the newspaper!

The "Spread Eagle" Driver (L): Mike Betschart
Center (spread): Scott Griffin; Driver (R): Sam Watson, Jr.

LEFT: Mark Frymoyer doing his interesting "Walk-over" trick. Driver: Mike Betschart

Rip's B.A.D. Ride

In 2005, we once again performed at Rip's B.A.D. Ride (Bikers Against Diabetes). Yep, we performed on grass, complete with gopher holes!

LEFT: Bruce Chubbuck led the team on his 1936 EL Harley.

They look pretty good from the rear, too!

They always finish the show with the High Pyramid.

RIGHT: Sorry. Mickey Minor, I just had to include this one because you hardly ever let this happen.

Redding, California

In 2006, we made a trip to Redding, California, to do a couple of shows. The motorcycles were trucked in Harry's 53 foot transporter and we showed up looking very professional.

LEFT: Back Row: Tedd Farrell, Mike Betschart, Sam Watson, Harry Fisher, Jake Elmore, Scott Griffin, Tylor Hicks, Mickey Minor, Bruce Chubbuck,
Front Row: Mark Frymoyer, Marty Fisher, Josh Allen-Kohler, Frank Hicks, Devin Griffiin, Sue Hutchins

RIGHT: "High Pyramid"
Motormen: Sam Watson, Harry Fisher, Mike Betschart, Marty Fisher
Safety: Frank Hicks, Moe Elmore, Scott Griffin
Chariot: Devin Griffin, Josh Allen-Kohler
Top: Mickey Minor

Setting up and getting ready in front of our own personal transporter truck.

The Four Corners Tour

The Four Corners Tour is a motorcycle ride that's sponsored by the Southern California Motorcycle Association (SCMA). Requirements are to ride to the four cities of the United States: Blaine, Washington; Madawaska, Maine; Key West, Florida; and San Ysidro, California. Each rider takes a picture of his/her motorcycle, with the registration towel provided by the SCMA at each of these landmarks, obtains a gas receipt from each city, completes the SCMA entry forms for each city, and mails it all from home after completing the ride. The entire ride is approximately 7,000 miles and must be completed within 21 days. The rider can take any route desired, start with any city and do it all at any time during the year. At the end of the year, a banquet is held and those who complete the requirements are honored. There's no monetary award, just bragging rights.

The SCMA banquet in 2006 was held in Ontario, California, on February 4th and Harry was asked to be the speaker. Wendell Perry, writer for *ThunderPress*, wrote: "Casual conversation with Harry can be interesting and amusing and leave the recipient of Harry's wisdom and humor anticipating the next opportunity for discourse."

"The opportunity to listen to the Colonel share the story of his involvement with the Motor Corps, as he addressed the assembly that evening, was one not to be missed," according to Edward H. Waldheim, who is commissioner of Off-Highway Motor Vehicle Recreation for the State of California Department of Parks and Recreation, president of the California Off-Road Vehicle Association and an old friend who attended just to see and hear Harry.

One of the pictures shown during Harry's presentation

Vintage Motorcycle Days, Ohio

In 2007, we were invited to go to Ohio to perform at AMA Vintage Motorcycle Days. This was a huge event with a custom bike show, racing, motorcycle swap meet, and the world famous Victor McLaglen Motor Corps!

We performed several times over the three-day event, and in between, found time to visit the beautiful American Motorcycle Hall of Fame.

BELOW:
We visited the Motorcycle Hall of Fame, since we were that close!
Back Row (L-R): Bruce Chubbuck, Tedd Farrell, Ken Graeb
Front Row: Sherry Graeb, Sue Hutchins, Ruth Fisher, Marty Fisher, Tylor Hicks, Mark Frymoyer

VINTAGE MOTORCYCLE DAYS – MID-OHIO (Cont'd)

"DC-10"
Top: Art Wales
Handlebars: Sue Hutchins
Front Fender: Mickey Minor
Drive: Sam Watson, Jr.
Safety: Jake Elmore

Mark Frymoyer performing his "One-Legged Ride"

Tylor Hicks, Sam Watson,
Sue Hutchins, Mike Betschart, Scott Griffin,
Mickey Minor, Tom Kelley, Mark Frymoyer

"High Pyramid"
Drivers: Scott Griffin, Harry Fisher, Sam Watson, Jr., Marty Fisher
Standing: Tom Kelley, Moe Elmore, Scott Griffin, Art Wales
Top: Mickey Minor,
Safety: Ken Graeb

Rip's B.A.D. Ride -2007

It's 2007, and time to do Rip's B.A.D. Ride again. As usual for this venue, the show is on a grassy, gopher-ridden spot, at a park in Irvine, California. Mark Frymoyer and Mike Betschart wow the crowd with their "Walk Over" stunt and get a big chuckle from their audience, too.

I gave a little preview of this stunt, so the crowd knew what to expect.

"Have you ever been riding your motorcycle out in a big old parking lot, with no one in sight, except for one couple, who is just meandering along without a care in the world and no thought about you? Well, we've had that experience ourselves and the way we dealt with the problem --- we just drive right underneath them. Something like this!"

Marks steps up on the front fender, onto the handlebars, onto Mike's shoulder and down over the rear fender. Of course, he likes to pick a cute gal out of the audience, to help him with this stunt, just to make it more interesting!

Rip's B.A.D. Ride – on the grass and over chuck-holes!

RIGHT:
Building the "High Pyramid" Top: Janice Burgin; Drivers: Sam Watson, Jr., Harry Fisher, Mike Betschart, Marty Fisher; Seatmen: Frank Hicks, Scott Griffin Side Chariot: Tylor Hicks, Mark Frymoyer

BELOW:
"Spread Eagle" Spread out: Mark Frymoyer
Left Driver: Harry Fisher
Right Driver: Marty Fisher

Lined up and ready.

"Pivot Slow Circle" Mark Frymoyer, Rear Rack: Tylor Hicks

Building the "Sunflower" Driver: Harry Fisher
Left: Janice Burgin; Right: Mickey Minor
Safety: Sam Watson, Jr.

Rip's B.A.D. Ride (Cont'd)

More of Rip's B.A.D. Ride. The team parked in front of the stage and made an impressive sight as they got ready to perform.

Marty Fisher knows the drill –he's been doing it since he was 15 years old!

LEFT: Colonel Harry Fisher blows the whistle and the show begins.

Christmas Party 2007

Every year, the Motor Corps hosts a Christmas Party and invites special friends. In 2007, it was at the Fishers' house. Everyone brought a potluck dish, put on holiday garb, and those who wanted to participate in the gift exchange, brought a present. It's a good excuse to just kick back and enjoy telling stories about what happened in the past year and, of course, poke fun at the ones who screwed up the stunts or drill!

ABOVE: Harry Fisher, Frank Hicks, April, Darlene Griffin, Marty & Allison Fisher, Sherry Graeb, Bart & Wendell Perry, Ruth Fisher, Hollywood Moore, Steve & Kimmy Schapiro

RIGHT: Hollywood Mike and Tylor chit chat

2010-2014

By 2014, the Motor Corps had been entertaining fans all over the world for the past 79 years. During that time, we only had three leaders and most of the members had individually performed with the team for more than 10 years; many, for more than 20 years. Our legacy is something to be proud of. We've had more than 400 members during that time, we've helped raise thousands of dollars for well-deserving charities, and we'd always set a good example of good sportsmanship and gentlemanly behavior so as to be a good example to youngsters growing up.

Commander Harry Fisher and the woman behind the man, his wife, Ruth Fisher.
This "Dynamic Duo" led and managed the Victor McLaglen Motor Corps from 1978-2014.
Did I mention how much fun we had?

The 2010 decade brought more activity. The team performed the usual shows at Yuma, the Santa Maria Elks Rodeo Parade in Northern California, and the Love Ride at Lake Castaic, California, as well as other usual venues. One ongoing problem, however, was attracting new members. Members were retiring, having health issues, moving out of state, and dropping out. New members were needed. It was difficult to find a motorcycle rider who (1) owned a 74 or 80 cubic inch Harley, (2) had the desire to become a member, and (3) had the time and funds to commit to either practices or shows, almost every weekend. Harry, our leader, however, had a unique strategy for attracting and attaining new members.

For instance, Butch Swanson came to watch practice a couple of times. His Dad, James Swanson, had been a member when Butch was just a little boy and Butch thought it was "pretty neat". Harry started his usual chitchat with anybody that showed up and said, "Butch, why don't you stand on the rear rack of my bike for a spin around the lot." "Butch, ride my bike through the cones a bit and see what you think." "Butch, stand on the front axle while I do the Slow Circle." "You're a natural for this stuff. Have you ever considered joining the team?" It didn't take long before Butch was out looking for a bike of his own, riding in the drill, and participating in some of the stunts! He eventually became a very good stuntman and a very close friend of Harry's, too.

Soon after Butch became more proficient with the stunts and drill, we had a show to perform in Phoenix, Arizona, for the Phoenix B.A.D. Ride (Bikers Against Diabetes). Harry transported the bikes and the team flew into Sky Harbor International Airport in Phoenix. Butch had never flown in an airplane and was terrified to fly. His daughter, Christina, finally talked him into taking the plunge and he boarded the plane in California. While they were parked at the gate, getting ready to taxi out, another plane clipped the wing of Butch's plane. Well, that set off a panic attack with poor Butch, and it took a bunch of talking to get him calmed down. The flight crew checked things out, there was no damage, and the plane was ready to go. When they arrived in Phoenix, I saw Butch's face when he stepped off the plane. I swear, he had no color in his face and was still shaking! Since then, he's taken a few more flights and is getting somewhat comfortable, however that first time was definitely traumatic for him and it gave the rest of us something to tease him about!

Butch enjoys a soft drink to calm his nerves!

Yuma Prison Run - 2010

In 2010, the team did their usual first show of the season, at the Yuma Prison Run in Yuma, Arizona. It was the Centaurs Motorcycle Club's 75th anniversary for the Yuma Prison Run and a big deal for this event. The Motor Corps had some recent additions and changes in membership which increased the anxiety levels for the members. After being on our usual winter vacation for a few months, the members were always a little rusty in executing the stunts. So the fans sometimes got more than they expected from the show.

One major change for the team was that Mickey Minor, at 77 years old, had decided to retire and we had no one to climb to the top of the "Pyramid," and no one to do all the headstands involved in some of the other stunts. Mickey had been a key member and finding a replacement was a challenge.

We were, however, lucky in that Janice Burgin had joined the team a couple of years prior and she started bringing her teenage son, James, to practice. James was agile, enthusiastic, strong, and had great balance, so he was a terrific candidate for the top of the "Pyramid". Now we had to ease him into that position without too much anxiety. Harry had James stand on various stunts, working up to the higher and higher positions, and then tried getting him to the top of the "Pyramid" while it was not moving (static). You may have all the physical qualifications needed to do these stunts, but confidence is key. Being a teenager, and the youngest member among all these long-time Harley riders, was not conducive to building confidence. I think, after James saw the prestige of being the "top man" on the "Pyramid", he warmed up to the idea. He practiced and practiced, and it didn't take long before he became the man for the job!

Drivers: Butch Swanson, Mark Frymoyer, Sam Watson, Jr.
Safety: Frank Hicks, Rigo Soto
Top: James Burgin, Janice Burgin

Yuma Prison Run –2010 (Cont'd)

In addition to James Burgin, the team had two new rookie members, Steve Searles and Rigo Soto, riding in the flag unit and performing in some of the stunts. This added much-needed membership to the team.

Right after the Motor Corps' performance, all the motorcycle riders line up to get ready to be escorted through the town of Yuma and out to the old territorial prison. The Motor Corps and the local police department do the escorting.

A tour of the old prison is fascinating. It was built in 1876, and closed in 1909. It is now a State Park.

Burgin and son James perform the P-38 stunt

Thunder Press, June 2010

The old Yuma Prison

Run-A-Mucca, Winnemucca, Nevada

In May, 2010, the team traveled to Winnemucca, Nevada, for the Run-A-Mucca event. This event had been an annual event for nine years and the team was happy to finally get "On the Road Again," as singer Willie Nelson would say.

On May 23rd, everyone helped get the motorcycles and equipment loaded into the truck and Harry left a couple days later for the 575 mile drive to Winnemucca. On Friday, May 28th, the team boarded a plane in Ontario, California, and landed in Reno, Nevada. There, we piled into rental cars and drove the remaining 165 miles.

The next day, we put on three performances. Everything went really well until the last show, when the "Pyramid" came tumbling down. No one got hurt (except for egos), but there always seems to be a photographer nearby to catch the action and this one even made the local news!

The Victor McLaglen Motor Corps perform a rare trick: falling

For the diehard Harley-Davidson riders, there was the traditional "Burning Bike" event. A Honda was mounted on a stand about ten feet in the air, pallets stacked high and liberally doused with diesel fuel and the whole thing was set on fire. As it burned, the heat ignited fireworks hidden in the frame and the whole thing was spectacular. It made a great front cover For the July *Thunder Press* Magazine.

Top: "The Victor McLaglen performs a rare trick: falling down."

ABOVE: "Ladder Ride"
Driver: Harry Fisher
Stunt guy: Jeremy Norton

LEFT: Burning the Honda motorcycle.

Transporting the Motorcycles

In the early 1980s, the team began making long trips across country to perform in shows. Harry foresaw that transportation for the motorcycles was going to be a key issue. The first long trip was to Daytona Beach, Florida, for the annual Bike Week festivities. We procured a sponsor with a truck. Then, we had to figure out how to safely secure the Harleys inside. That meant there needed to be an abundance of tiedown straps, furniture blankets, and a ramp to load the motorcycles into the trailer.

Since some of the guys were professional truckers anyway, it was figured out and the bikes arrived in excellent shape.

Our first transporter, in the 1980s

For our trips in the later years, Harry Fisher's "show" trailer and Peterbilt were set up to transport not only the motorcycles, but all the equipment. It also provided a changing room for the team to get ready for the shows. This truck looked like a professional show truck, too.

Looking professional in the 21st century!

"An American Treasure" Documentary

"An American Treasure" is a documentary DVD created by Mickey Jones in 2012, Mickey Jones is a well-recognizable actor and musician. As a drummer, he toured with Bob Dylan in 1966, then spent ten years with Kenny Rogers and the First Edition. Mickey then began his acting career. Some of his many roles have been in television series such as: Bones, Entourage, Home Improvement, and the Beverly Hillbillies, but he has over 150 more roles to his credit. This DVD was about the history of the Victor McLaglen Motor Corps. The DVD is a little more than an hour long and traces the Motor Corps from 1935 to 2012.

Mickey did all the creative stuff and narrated throughout the film. Just for fun, he asked me to narrate the performances for the DVD and finally, Mickey interviewed Harry. Making the film was fun for us, but Mickey spent many hours before he even let us see it.

Mickey Jones

Mickey and Harry in the sound-proof room doing their recording.

DVD front cover

DVD back cover

On September 1, 2012, a special screening was held at the Simi Valley Cultural Arts Center in Simi Valley, California, to show off the new documentary. All the Motor Corps current and "Old Timers" were invited, along with local dignitaries such as the Mayor of Simi Valley and sponsors who had been very supportive over the years.

Simi Valley Cultural Arts Center

"An American Treasure" (Cont'd)

Some of the "Old Timers" arrived early to go through a quick practice and participate in the performance prior to the actual screening. They had not lost their touch and did a great job. After the performance, Mickey and Harry said a few words inside the theater and the movie began.

Each guest received a complimentary copy of the DVD and Mickey Jones was surprised with an Honorary Motor Corps Membership presented to him complete with an official Motor Corps jacket. Another highlight was when "Old Timer" member, Guillermo Sevilla, then presented his son, Rene Sevilla, with the keys and title to his old Motor Corps bike so that Rene could join the team.

Wendell Perry gave the event a whole page write-up in *Thunder Press*, which was distributed nationwide, along with some great photos furnished by Wendell's husband, Bart Perry, aka: "Bart at Large."

It was a very successful event and everyone went home happy. THe DVD is available at www.thevmmc.com.

Our World Championship Trophy

In 1993, the 1936 Victor McLaglen Motor Corps World Championship trophy was delivered to Tom Scott, who owned Anaheim-Fullerton Harley-Davidson. Tom was remodeling and expanding his facilities and thought maybe he had a good place to display our trophy. Tom said, *"That trophy sat in someone's garage for many years and it was a mess. In fact, it was in pieces. The original wood base was split, and it was in poor condition. I told Harry that I work with metal plating folks who worked with gold and silver, plus chrome, etc. We got all the pieces refinished and some of my guys rebuilt the wood base with most of the original pieces. Other pieces were replaced. At the time, we were just starting the remodel, where we added the second story. On completion of the new buildings, the trophy was finished and we built the case to show it off."*

We are very proud of this trophy and very grateful to Tom and his wife, Barbara, for their efforts.

In 2012, Tom and Barbara decided to sell their business and retire. Mark Ruffalo, owner of California Harley-Davidson in Harbor City, California, asked if we'd like to display it in his showroom. Of course we did. It was moved to Mark's business, and he had a custom display case made for it. Mark was not only the owner of California Harley, but also President of the Southern California Dealers Association and he wanted very much to support the team. Naturally, we were more than happy to accept this new location for our beloved trophy.

Subsequently, Mark had a new, huge display case built, with plenty of room for the trophy to sit center-stage, with pictures and artifacts surrounding it.

In December 2013, Mark Ruffalo held a "Customer Appreciation Day" at California Harley. There were special discounts, photos with Santa, a buffet lunch and the unveiling of the new display case, showing off our treasured trophy.

As Wendell Perry wrote in Thunder Press (January 2015), *"He announced that California Harley-Davidson, long a supporter of the Motor Corps, would now proudly carry on the tradition of Harley-Davidson dealerships, most recently Anaheim-Fullerton H-D and owners Tom and Barbara Scott, to act as the home for the Victor McLaglen Motor Corps. Mark thanked the Motor Corps for 77 years of great shows and for representing Harley-Davidson in such a positive way."*

"Harry thanked all the VMMC members present for their many years of dedication. He shared a letter he had received from a former member, a Los Angeles police officer who had ridden with the VMMC in 1949. Then he introduced Mickey Minor, the most recent Motor Corps retiree, a very slight man who has thrilled crowds for many years by climbing to the top of the rolling pyramid. He then brought James Burgin forward, a very young man who has ridden with the Motor Corps for a couple of years now, and who has proved himself capable of filling the place at the top of the pyramid. And so, the torch is passed."

The new Victor McLaglen Motor Corps display case showing off our 1936 World Championship Trophy

Mark Ruffalo presents the new display case. Harry Fisher, Frank Hicks, and Mickey Jones look on.

The team attended the unveiling of the new VMMC display case, new home for the 1936 World Championship Trophy. Back Row: Bob Jensen, Frank Hicks, Rigo Soto, Mickey Jones (Honorary Member), Guillermo Sevilla, Mark Frymoyer, Rene Sevilla, Tedd Farrell, Janice Burgin, Sam Watson; Front Row: Steve Schapiro (Honorary Member), Mickey Minor, Harry Fisher, Ruth Fisher, James Burgin, Mark Ruffalo, Ruben Pantoja, Butch Swanson, Dodo Widodo, Sue Hutchins

(L-R) Mickey Jones, Harry Fisher, Mark Ruffalo

2014 Annual Awards Banquet

In 2014, the Annual Awards Banquet was held. Actually, "annual" isn't exactly correct, because the last banquet was held eleven years ago! Everyone was busy, they didn't have the dollars to put on a banquet, no one volunteered to head up the project, etc. Those are some of the excuses I can think of, and I'm sticking to them!

Finally, I decided enough is enough. A banquet is way overdue and we'd better get this project underway. After all, Harry and I had moved to Santa Fe, New Mexico, and were attempting to retire from the Motor Corps. This might be our last banquet as "active members." We volunteered (!) new members Rene and Susana Sevilla to head up this event and they did a superb job. The banquet was held at the beautiful Monterey Hill Restaurant's Luminarias Room in Monterey Park, California. Invitations were sent to the current active members, the Old Timers (anyone who had ever been a member), our sponsors, and special guests. Tickets were $30 each and, for the first time ever, each member had to pay for his or her ticket. We were definitely watching the budget.

Presentation of the 2014 Executive Board was made, and the usual membership certificates and cards were awarded. Since the last banquet was held in 2003, there was a lot of catch-up awards to be presented.

(L-R) Back Row: Mickey Minor, Mickey Jones, Harry Fisher, Gene French, James Burgin, Janice Burgin, Butch Swanson, Rigo Soto, Mel Minor, Frank Hicks, Ruben Pantoja, Guillermo Sevilla Sr., Mark Frymoyer, William Sevilla, Mark Ruffalo, Oliver Shokouh;

Front Row: Tylor Hicks, Luis Camarena, Fernando Camarena, Tom Scott, Rene Sevilla

2014 Annual Awards Banquet (Cont'd)

An Honorary membership was awarded to a surprised Steve Schapiro, local motorcycle attorney and one of our sponsors for several years. Special awards were also given to: Wendell Perry for writing such great stories about the team in Thunder Press; Bart Perry for supplying Wendell with the fresh photographs; Susan and Rene for doing all the work for the banquet; Butch Swanson for bringing water and refreshments for all our practices and shows, and Tylor and Mark for providing assistance when Harry was unable to attend events.

A presentation of this year's Blooper Award was made to Mark Frymoyer. In fact, the perpetual plaque was then retired and Mark became the final owner.

Here's just a little background history on how this infamous award came to be.

It was introduced at the Motor Corps Banquet, in 1994, by Big Mike Betschart. In the previous year, Big Mike saw Commander Harry dump his bike pretty good in a parade in the little town of Lake Isabella, California, and thought that was a good enough reason to poke a little fun at the Commander. It would also show the new guys that even an experienced rider like their Commander, could dump his bike now and then.

The award was a surprise to the Commander, but in giving it some further thought, Harry decided it was a good idea for the future, too, and the tradition was carried on. Each year thereafter, a member was awarded the Blooper Award, for whatever interesting slip-up he or she had accomplished that year. Mark Frymoyer was awarded the "honor" at this banquet and since he was the one who had "won" it more than anyone else, it was retired and given to him to keep. Commander Harry Fisher presented several Lifetime Membership Awards. If the member joined the team prior to January 1, 2005, he/she was eligible to receive the lifetime membership after 15 years active membership. If he/she joined after that date, eligibility was available after 25 years active membership. Eight life-time membership certificates were awarded at this banquet.

Bruce Chubbuck (35 year member)
Bruce joined the team at the time of the reorganization in 1979 and was a valued liaison with the Harley Factory. He was also a stuntman and led the shows with his 1936 bike carrying the American Flag.

Mickey Minor (29 year member)
Mickey joined the team in 1985 and soon became the top man on the High Pyramid.

Mark Frymoyer (35 year member)
Mark joined the team in 1978 with the new reorganization and became the team's solo expert, as well as the Stunt Leader and Assistant Drill Leader

Frank Hicks (34 year member)
Frank joined the team in 1980 and held many responsible positions, most recently as secretary/treasurer as well as the flag unit leader and safety man on many stunts.

Tylor Hicks (45 year member)
Tylor first joined the team in 1969, then again in 1972, then 1978, then in 1997 and has been an active full-time member ever since. He was a climber on many stunts.

Tedd Farrell. Tedd joined the team in 1985. He rode in the Flag Division, performed stunts, clowned around a bit and was a very talented artist.

Sam Watson Jr.(19 year member)
Sam initially joined in 1963, then quit to join the Army. He rejoined in 1995. Sam was an exceptionally talented and good, reliable motorman.

Ruth Fisher
After more than 40 years as administrator, publicist, travel agent, and right-hand to the Commander, the team presented me with my own Lifetime Membership card. Surprise!

Tom Scott surprised us all with a beautiful cake for dessert, commemorating the team's 79th Anniversary.

By Tedd Farrell

2014 Annual Awards Banquet (Cont'd)

Some of the "Old Timers" who joined the party

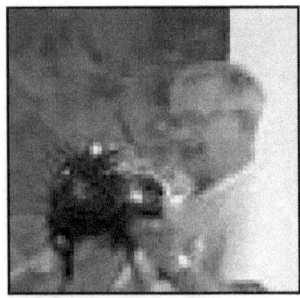
George Anderson 1978-1981

Gene French 1978-1981

Frank Horn 1961-1968

Maria Willers-Hartman 2000-3

Pat Shanahan 1984-1999

We had door prizes for the raffle, but the most sought-after item was a handmade quilt with the Pyramid logo embroidered in the center. All the members present at the banquet signed the quilt. It was designed by Betty Kult and Ruth Fisher, but sewn by Mickey Jones' wife, Phyllis. Each person received a raffle ticket when they checked in and additional tickets were offered with an additional donation to the Motor Corps. The winners of this special prize were Tom and Barbara Scott, recently retired from their Harley shop in Fullerton. They were overjoyed and everyone else was very disappointed! The nice thing was that when Harry Fisher passed away shortly after this banquet, Tom and Barbara gave the quilt to Marty, Harry's son. What thoughtful, first-class people Tom and Barbara are. They are definitely the best!

Tom & Barbara Scott
Winners of the quilt

Mickey & Phyllis Jones. Phyllis made the quilt

Who would have guessed that less than three weeks later, the Motor Corps would lose their beloved leader, Commander Harry Fisher, who suddenly passed away from a massive heart attack.

A few days after the banquet, in California, Harry had loaded his 53 foot trailer with new 2015 factory Harley-Davidsons, kissed me goodbye, and climbed into his Peterbilt truck to transport those new Harleys to Daytona Beach, Florida, for the annual Bike Week event. The Harleys were to stay on display in Daytona Beach and be used for journalists and celebrity photos. Harry had lots of free time for a few days to hang out with old friends and ride a motorcycle around Daytona until the bikes were ready to be reloaded into the truck at the end of the week. He loved it and had been providing this service for Harley for a number of years.

Harry did get to ride a bit with his friends for a couple of days and attend some of the events, but then the heart attack occurred and ended many years of riding, racing, stunting, drilling, escorting, and promoting this sport that he loved so much.

Harry passed away at 68 years old. He will be missed by many, from the east coast to the west coast, young and old, the rich and famous, and the downtrodden. He was a good man and friend to many.

The funeral was held at St. Basil's in downtown Los Angeles, and attended by several hundred people from across the country. The interment was at Glen Haven Memorial Park in Sylmar Park, California and the procession of cars, traveling the 25 miles to the cemetery with about 15 motorcycle escorts, was quite a spectacle. Father Frank Hicks, who is also a member of the Motor Corps, officiated. Mickey Jones prepared a wonderful video showing Harry's life and several friends spoke kind words. There wasn't a dry eye in the place.

I lost my loving husband, Marty lost his admired and loving dad, and the team lost their long-time leader. But life goes on.

The team has regrouped and intends to continue what they do best – riding their Harleys, building human pyramids, showing their skills at riding drill maneuvers at slow speeds, and meeting other terrific riders and fans. Our Founder, Victor McLaglen, would be proud and I'm sure, Harry is proud.

When life gets me down and I start feeling really sorry for myself, I remember this advice I read somewhere:

"When life throws you a curve – lean into it and turn on the throttle!"

Rest in peace, Harry.
We miss you.

APPENDIX A
Members & Dates

The following is a list of nearly 300 members of the Motor Corps, from 1935 to 2014. The members' names and dates they were voted into membership are shown, but many times there was no record of the year they dropped out so that information was left blank.

ABRAMS, WILLIE 1979-1992
AGUIRRE, ERNIE 1936-
ALBRIGHT, JIM 1956-1957 & 1967-
ALFRING, GEORGE 1936-
ALLEN, FRANK 1957-1960
ALLEN, GT 2003-2004
ALLEN, JOSH 2004-2007
ALLEN, REX 1930s-
ALLUM, BILL 1940s -
ANDERSON, ED 1963-
ANDERSON, GEORGE 1978-1981
ANDERSON, KEVIN 1981-1981
ANDERSON, MIKE 2008-2010
AUGUSTON, FRED 1980-1985
AYALA, TONY 1959-1965
BAKER, CARL 1975-
BARRERA, DAVID 1987-
BARRIOS, JESS 1988-
BARWICK, ED 1972-
BAUM, DOC 1960-1962
BEHLING, HARVEY 1938/1980-1996
BEMBARON, JOE 1973-1975
BENGSTON, BING 1949-1952
BERDAHL, DENNIS 1966-
BEST, LEO 1964-1964
BETSCHART, ALLEN 1994-
BETSCHART, MIKE 1988-2007
BETTLEMAN, HAROLD 1949-
BIRDAHL, DENNIS 1966-
BLANCHETTE, BOB 1974-1977
BOGDA, WILLIAM 1956-
BRADLEY, ROBERT 1958-
BRECHT, JACK 2008-2011

BREWER, MONTE 1973- (Honorary)
BRILL, JACK 1950-1959
BROADBENT, JAMES 1962-1962
BROOKS, LARRY 1969-
BROSELL, DOC 1978-
BROW, FRANK 1955-
BROWN, CHARLIE 1973-1979
BROWN, FRANK 1956-1956
BROWN, KEN 1980-1985
BUCKNER, CHUCK 1979-1987
BUIE, LEE 1961-1961
BURGIN, JAMES 2010-2012
BURGIN, JANIS 2008-2012
BUTTERFIELD, PAUL 1954-
CALCO, FRED 1962-
CALDERA, CHUCK 1961-1964
CAMARENA, FERNANDO 2013-
CAMARENA, LUIS 2013-
CARMODY, LARRY 1980-1981
CASTRO, LARRY 1981-1987
CATES, SKEETS 1936-
CATFORD, MIKE 1965-1971
CHAVEZ, BEN 1985-1987
CHUBBUCK, BRUCE 1978-2013
CLAYTON, CHUCK 1975-
COHEN, JAY 1986-1992
COOK, BUD 1936-
COSTA, LEO 1940s-
COWEN, TOM 1978-
CRAWFORD, JIMMY 1935-
CRAWFORD, JOHN 1956-
CUPPETT, LES 1962-1965
DAVIES, ROGER 1978-1985

DAVIS, HARRY 1950s-1956
DAVIS, RUSS 1990-
DAY, SONNY 1970s-1981
DELEO, RON 1975-1977
DENIKE, GENE 1960-
DeRUSH, NICK 1935-1953
DESCOTEAUX, ART 1954-1957
DIZACOMO, JOE 1961-1963
DOAKS, FRED 1969-
DOTZENROD, BILL 1986-1988
DOUGLAS, CURLEY 1955-
DOYLE, STEVE 1987-1990
DRAHOS, HARVEY 1946-
DUMONT, ANDY 1980-1981
DUNHAM, WAYNE 1941-
ELLIS, LES 1993-2000
ELMORE, JAKE 2002-
ELMORE, MOE 1999-
ERICKSON, BAKER 1957-
ERICKSON, PHIL 1948-
EVANS, TED 1987-
EVORS, EARL 1956-1956
FARRELL, BUTCH 1969-
FARRELL, TEDD 1985-
FARRELL, WARREN 1985-1987
FENTON, JIMMY 1940-1949
FERRY, DENNIS 1970-1974
FISHER, HARRY 1962-2014
FISHER, MARTY 1989-2008
FISHER, RUTH 1978-2014
FISK, NEWTON 1957-1958
FITZGERALD, WAYNE 1935-
FREEMAN, LLOYD 1953-
FREEMAN, RALPH 1956-1957
FRENCH, GENE 1978-1981
FROST, KENNY 1964-1967/1991-1992
FRYMOYER, KENNY 1984-1986
FRYMOYER, KIRBY 1978-1995
FRYMOYER, MARK 1978-2014
FUDGE, ROY 1957-1958

GALUSHA, BOB 1978-1980
GARZA, GEORGE 1982-
GEORGESON, LES 1963-1974
GERRY, DICK 1957-2001
GIVENS, LEE 1957-1958
GRAEB, KEN 2007-2008
GREEN, RAY 1966-1968
GREENWOOD, JOHN 1940s-1960s
GRIEST, RONNIE 1954-1969
GRIFFIN, DEVIN 2003-2005
GRIFFIN, SCOTT 2002-2014
GRIFFINS, PAUL 1959-1960
GRIGGS, CHARLES 1940s-
HALL, NATE 1978-1979
HAMER, CLIFF 1961-1967
HAMMACK, DELMAR 1961-1962
HANCOCK, ALBERT 1962-1963
HARDIN, HARRY 1954-1957
HARKER, HERB 1953-1978
HARRIS, TEX 1995-
HASEROT, LES 1937-
HICKS, FATHER FRANK 1980-2014
HICKS, TYLOR 1969-2015
HILL, MIKE 1985-
HILL, DICK 1984-1987
HOLBROOK, BOB 1980-
HORN, FRANK 1961-1968
HOWELL, CHUCK 1937-1942
HUTCHINGS, SUE 2002-2007
IRVING, NEIL 1956-1963
JACKSON, JERRY 1979-
JAMES, NEIL 1958-
JENSON, BOB 1978-2001
JERNIGAN, JIM 1960-1962
JESTER, HARLAN 1930s-
JOHNSON, LARRY 1983-1985
JONES, MICKEY (Honorary) 2012
KATTHOEFER, DENNIS 1978-1979
KAZIAN, JOHNNY 1964-1965
KELLER, BOB 1971-1981

KELLEY, TOM 1971-1971
KEMP, STANLEY 1948-
KENYON, MIKE 1956-1958
KERLEY, ROGER 1930s-
KLEIN, BOB 1936-
KOKOL, GIL 1960-1960
KREIDER, BILL 1949-
KULT, RAY 1992-1993
LATCHAT, CARMEN 1974-1976
LATZ, JAY 1961-1963
LAUERS, BOB 1981-
LAUSCHE, DENNIS 1979-1980
LEE, TROY 1993-1994
LOCKE, OTTO 1949-
LOMAS, BILL & RONNIE (Honorary)
LOWER, BOB 1981-1982
MACIAS, AL 1980-1985
MAINE, EARL 1967-1970s
MANSHARDT, RALPH 1935-1942
MARGRAVES, STANLEY 1935-1930s
MARTIN, ALVIS 1981-1985
MARTIN, RONNIE 1959-
MATHIS, ERNEST 1957-1958
MAY, GARY 1964-1964
McCARTNEY, FRANK 1935-
McCOOL, RON 2010-2014
McLELLAN, GEORGE 1964-1967
McDONALD, BILL 1979-
MEHLBAUM, RAY 1993-2000
MEYERS, KELLY 1937-1941
MILITELLO, JOE 1964-1973
MINOR, MEL 2007-
MINOR, MICKEY 2010-2010
MULDOON, PATRICK 1957-1958
MURPHY, BILL 1969-
NEWSOME, TOM 2007-2007
NOBLE, HARRY 1970-
NOE, KEITH 1995-1996-
NOLAN, JERRY 1980s-
NORTON, JEREMY 1999-

NUGENT, BOB 1984-2002
O'BRIEN, BUB 1969-
ODA, RON 1992-
OLIVER, NICK 1978-1981
PACKINGHAM, SAM 1954-
PANTOJA, RUBEN 1979-1982/2013-2014
PARSONS, JAMES 1948-
PEROTT, JOE 1958-1959
PERRY, BILL 1963-1964
PETERSON, LARS 1957-1957
PHILLIPS, WILD BILL 1937-
PHILLIPS, EDDIE 1937-1940s
PHILLIPS, HUBIE 1937-1942/1988-1990
PHILLIPS, RAY 1940s-
REESE, JAMES 1985-
REEVES, BILL 1966-
REID, SAMUEL 1963-1964
RESLEY, JEFF 1965-
RICKS, ART 1935-
RISLEY, JEFF 1965-
ROACH, MRS. HAL 1939 (Honorary)
ROBERTS, CHARLES 1936-
ROBERTS, JOHN 1961-1961
ROMERO, JAVIER 1993-1993
RUGGLES, HAP 1935-
RUIZ, AL 1978-1985
RUIZ, ALBERT 1979-
SALSBURY, RED 1955-1956
SCHAEFER, FRED 1960-1960
SCHAEFFER, JOHN 1988-1992
SCHAPIRO, STEVE (Honorary) 2012
SCHIMMEL, ROB 1983-1984
SCHOBERT, CHUCK 1954-1957
SCHOOLEY, SHOOLEY 1970-
SCHRUERS, QUINTON 1954-1956
SCOTT, TOM & BARBARA
    (Honorary) 2012
SENTER, JOHN 1954-1959
SESSLER, LEE 1958-
SEVILLA, GUILLERMO, SR. 1989-1991

/2013-2014
SEVILLA, GUILLERMO JR. 1989-1991/
   2013-2014
SEVILLA, MICHAEL 1989-1991/2013-2014
SEVILLA, RENE 1989-1991/2013-2014
SHANAHAN, PAT 1984-1999
SHERMAN, GARY 1953-
SMITH, BILL 1955-1957
SMITH, SMITTY 1970-1980
SNOW, BOBBY 1962-1962
SNOW, DON 1965-1971
SOTO, RIGO 2011-2014
SPOON, CHUCK 1963-1966
STACKEM, GERALD 1957-
STAFFORD, LEO 1970-
STAGNER, WALT 1969-1970
STAPERT, JOHN 1957-
STARKEY, JACK 1957-1957
STERR, BILL 1967-1969
STEWART, JOEL 1935-
STILTZ, BUD 1960-
STILTS, TOM 1960-1961
STINT, OB 1953-
STOCKWELL, RONNIE 1961-1962
STUTTS, JOHN 1938-
SUSSLER, LEE 1958-
SWAN, BILL 1936-
SWANSON, JIM 1965-
SWANSON, BUTCH 2007-2014
TANURAHARJO, BEN 2011-2011
TATRO, WILFRED 1954-
TAYLOR, CLIFF 1959-1962
TEMPLET, BILL 1965-1965
THOMAS, ALVIN 1935-
THOMPSON, JERRY 1978-1985
TURNBULL, WILLIAM 1966-1969
VASQUEZ, TOM 1966-
VIRGIN, GLENN 1981-1982
WADDELL, LOUIE 1981-1982
WALES, ART 1984-1990
WALKER, JOHNNY 1992-
WARREN, DON 1975-1993
WATCHBORG, MARSHAL 1954-
WATKINS, DENNIS 1966-
WATSON, RAY 1958 & 1963-1965
WATSON, SAM JR. 1963-1965/1995-2014
WATSON, SAM SR. 1955-
WEAVER, RICHARD 1975-1976
WEISBERG, SAM 1962-1963
WELCH, DAN 1994-2002
WELCH, PAIGE 2003-
WELDEN, JIM 1961-1963
WEST, BILL 1953-
WHITE, HARVEY 1974-
WHITESELL, ERNIE 1981-
WIDDUP, VERN 1949-
WIDODO, DODO 2011-2012
WILLAMAN, DAN 1992-
WILLERS-HARTMAN, MARIA 2000-2003
WILLIAMSON, BILL 1964-1964
WILMOTT, THERON 1955-1957
WOLFE, KYLE 1958-
WOOD, RICH 1993-
WOODARD, WOODY 1984-1989
WRIGHT, JOHN 1986-
WYRICK, BILL 1976-
YAWN, WADE 1957-
ZELENAK, DICK 1963-1965

APPENDIX B
1995/1996 Cycle World International Motorcycle Shows (IMS)

In 1995, Harry Fisher was contacted by Terry Carpenter, Operations Coordinator for Advanstar Expositions, regarding the possibility of providing entertainment for the upcoming Cycle World International Motorcycle Shows (IMS). This would involve the team traveling to eight cities on eight weekends, from December to March, performing nine shows at each venue; two shows on Friday evening, four on Saturday, and three on Sunday. Whew! This was going to take a lot of stamina on the part of the members and a lot of coordination for the team's organizers.

After about two nano-seconds of thought and a lot of discussion with each Motor Corps member, Harry told Terry he would throw some figures together and let him know what it would take for the team to accept this invitation. Basically, we estimated the cost and that's what we charged. We didn't plan on making any money on this venture. We just wanted to do the tour (but don't tell Terry that!).

Generally, the traveling team consisted of only 14 travelers: three squads, a leader, and an announcer. The travelers would be selected based on seniority, ability, and their value to the performance. Harry and one other member would transport the motorcycles from city to city, via truck. The rest of the team would fly by commercial airliners. They'd depart Southern California on Friday, arrive at the next city in time for the first show, perform all weekend, then fly home on Sunday, after the last show. Most of the members had regular jobs, so they had to take a vacation day on Friday and make sure they were at work on Monday morning.

The plan became pretty routine real fast. The members would meet at the airport (or sometimes at a member's home to carpool to the airport) and Ruth would dole out the tickets at the airport terminal. We didn't want any member to arrive at the airport without his ticket, so Ruth was in charge of them. This was not yet the age of electronic ticketing and each person had to have a paper ticket and a paper boarding pass. Yep, back in the "olden days!" After we all met and each person had a ticket in hand, we lined up together at the counter to get our boarding passes, then we followed Big Mike in a caravan toward our assigned airport gate. Mike was great at figuring out where we were supposed to be, and all we had to do was follow. This worked out well.

In planning this adventure, The first thing we did was to share some rules for everybody.
- **Always carry your uniform and luggage onto the aircraft.** Helmets and boots were sent in the truck, but the uniforms traveled back and forth with the member. After all, they DID need to be cleaned after doing nine shows in a weekend! We never checked our luggage, because we definitely didn't want to take a chance on the luggage being lost in transit.

- **Mark all luggage with your name and address.** We were carrying our luggage onboard, but there was still a possibility it could be lost or misplaced – Murphy's Law, you know.
- **Have your luggage packed and ready to go before the last show.** We didn't have much time between the ending of our last show and getting to the airport, so every minute counted.

Routing for the transporter

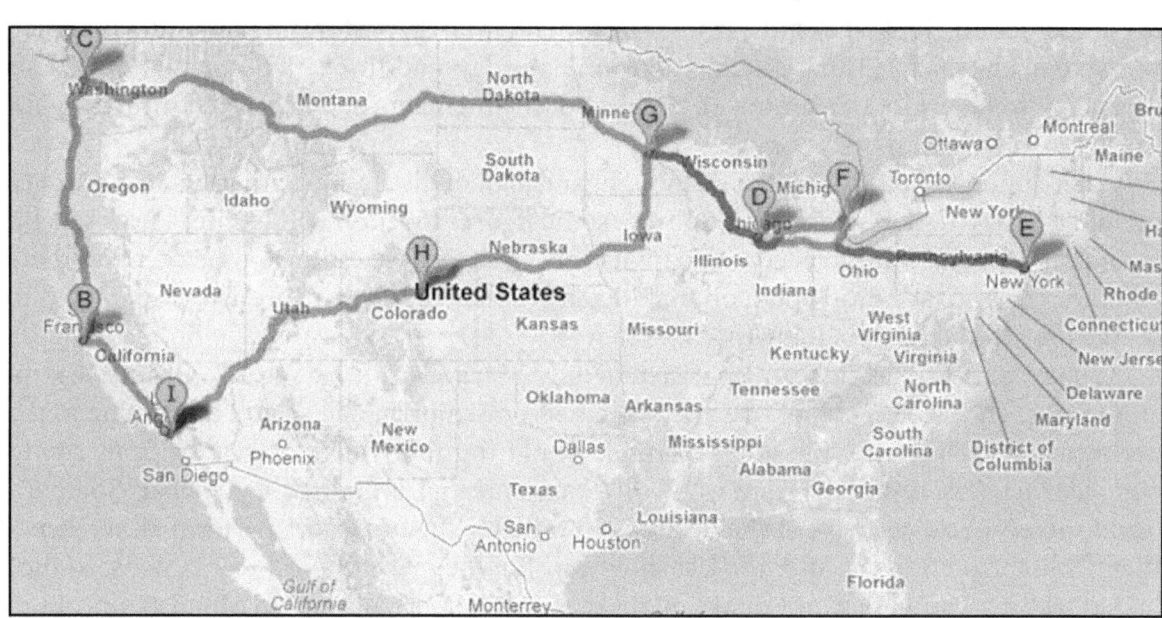

The show schedule:
A. December 15-17, 1995   Anaheim, California
B. January 5-7, 1996   San Francisco, California
C. January 12-14, 1996   Seattle, Washington
D. January 19-21, 1996   Chicago, Illinois
E. February 9-11, 1996   New York City, New York
F. February 23-25, 1996   Pontiac, Michigan
G. March 1-3, 1996   Minneapolis, Minnesota
H. March 15-17, 1996   Denver, Colorado

"Our" truck, with the San Francisco Bay Bridge in the background. Did we go in style or what?!!! This was our dressing room –when there was nothing else available, a place to keep our precious motorcycles safe, and a way to move all our equipment safely from city to city.

Anaheim, CA

The first IMS event of the season was held at the Anaheim Convention Center (near Disneyland) in Anaheim, California. We were lucky that this show was local and all the members could attend, without worrying about hotel and airline expenses. Lots of our friends and relatives attended, the motorcycle crowd was terrific, and we felt pretty proud of ourselves. We did think that the 120'x 80' area with a post in the middle, was really tight for our performances. Little did we know that it would be the second largest area we were going to have on this tour! The good news was that no one fell down, everyone did great, and the shows were a success.

Here are the rules Harry gave us for "showtime":

- **At the end of the show, be sure to spend time shaking hands, signing autographs, and talking with your audiences.** Also, any help you can provide selling pins, posters, videos, and T-shirts at our booth, would be appreciated.
- **Stay with the group.** Don't wander off where we can't find you, in case we need to talk to you about something, or change a schedule. Walking around the convention hall in your uniforms is good, it gives us great exposure. Do not, however, go down the street three blocks away, for a quick sandwich. Check in first and make sure it's OK.
- **Be polite and helpful to everyone** – not only our own members, but the convention hall workers, the vendors, the promoters (especially them!) and, of course, those folks who come to see you. (You wouldn't think this would have to be said, but a reminder never hurts.)
- **Don't get a swelled head** – We return to our ordinary jobs after the weekend, just like everyone else.
- **If you're having a problem with something the team is doing, or something is happening that will affect the shows or the team's effort, talk to me.**

San Francisco, CA

We had a break for Christmas and New Years Day, before preparing for our first out-of-town shows. We had begun referring to these out-of-town trips as "the tour." Actually, it wasn't San Francisco, it was San Mateo, and the IMS events were at the San Mateo County Expo Center. Harry and Marty Fisher departed in the 18-wheeler to get everything set up early. There were 13 show bikes, all the equipment, and extras of everything: Tools, battery charger, spark plugs, air compressor, duct tape, and bailing wire (of course, these are Harley's, you know!). Then each rider had a plastic bin with his/her name on it, which consisted of a helmet, boots, and belt. Lastly, the infamous "Hot Dog Wagon" went on board. The Hot Dog Wagon got its name because that's what everybody thought it looked like! Actually, it contained all our saleable items. We'd set up for a show, roll out the wagon, and we were open for business.

The famous "Hot Dog Wagon" with Tylor Hicks selling and Scott Griffin buying

The Hot Dog Wagon concept started after we'd gone to a bunch of shows in California, and had T-shirts to sell. We had boxes of T-shirts, then a table, then a table cloth so it would look purdy and a cash box for change and a couple of other little boxes for pens, business cards, etc. We were having a late lunch and iced tea in a Denny's Restaurant after one of the shows, and I started thinking. I drew a sketch on a napkin of what I had in mind and handed it to Sam Watson. Sam was an expert in woodworking.

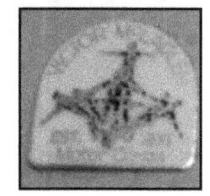

He built his own house, built all the cabinets, a beautiful staircase, and more; not only for his house, but for lots of other folks up in the San Gabriel Mountains in Southern California. So I knew that if anybody could do the job, Sam could. We told him that it needed to be on wheels, that we needed a place for the posters, videos, toy trucks, and T-shirts, a drawer for the cash and to be able to lock it up. Oh, and also it needed to fold out, so that we had a table-top area.

A couple of weeks later, Sam arrived at practice with a gorgeous custom-made oak wagon. It had wheels, a handle from a Red Flyer Wagon, and a place for everything. It was just perfect. The Hot Dog Wagon was born.

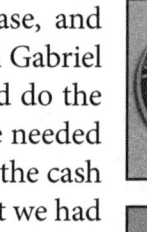

Pins $5 each

Model-T Toy Car $35

The Hot Dog Wagon contained items we wanted to sell: Motor Corps T-shirts, pins with stunts on them, posters of the "High Pyramid," videos (remember, DVDs weren't yet invented) and a little Model-T toy truck, with the "High Pyramid" picture and "Victor McLaglen Motor Corps" name on the sides. We were all set up to make a few extra bucks at the shows! After each show, we'd sell our wares in a fast frenzy that was over in about 15 minutes! Usually, some of the wives who'd traveled with us, would handle the sales and then direct the buyers to the members, who would autograph their purchase. This worked really well and the help from these ladies was very, very much appreciated. It also added a few extra bucks to our treasury, to help with expenses and, occasionally, a dinner out for the team. We signed autographs and, best of all, met some great motorcycle enthusiasts across the country.

T-Shirt $15

The San Francisco shows went very well and we finally got into a good routine, but new rules were added:

- **Go to the restroom before the show** (not funny –that's really important!) How would you like to be in the middle of, say, the DC-10 with an audience of a couple hundred biker-dudes and have your motorman say, "Hey guys, climb down, I've got to go to the restroom?" Not so funny, I'm thinking.
- **Be at the show area, dressed and ready to perform, thirty minutes before show time.** That way, if there's a problem, we have time to fix it.
- **Start talking to people before the show and build a little rapport with the crowd.**

Great. No problem.

The only real problem was – the performance area in San Mateo was 70'x 40'. Everyone thought that the Anaheim area was small – remember, it was 120'x 80', almost twice as large. This was not good, but we learned real quick about going even slower than usual, turning sharper, and making it look easy! We did Serpentines, Figure 8s and even a couple of Cross-overs and really wow'd the audience. If you can take a 600 pound Harley, go six mph on a slippery cement floor, follow the drill pattern, ride handlebar to handlebar and keep it all on two wheels –man, you can impress even the biggest, baddest biker!

Oh yeah, by the way, we stayed at a Best Western hotel. We couldn't afford the high priced "host" hotel and, remember, we were on a low-income budget. We had two people to a room, sometimes three or four and usually had to walk several blocks to get to the convention center! Not everyone arrived by air. Eight members of the team vanpooled, which is at least a six-hour ride, all jammed into a Ford van, with Tex Harris driving. We were definitely not high-rollers!

Seattle, WA

The next weekend the team was in Seattle, Washington. The event was held at the Washington State Convention & Trade Center, and they had a 70'x 30' work area. Good grief – the work areas were getting smaller and smaller. They also had a pillar located in the middle of the show area!

I've got to admit, those shows in Seattle were not the best ones we'd ever done. In fact, they might be the worst! Here we were, trying to show off and make a big impression on our friends and competitors, the Seattle Cossacks motorcycle stunt team. We were performing on their home turf and we were slip-sliding all over the place!

Our good friends, the Seattle Cossacks, are an excellent motorcycle stunt team, and they were around to support us. Harry said, "Why don't you guys jump on and we'll do some shows together." Their announcer, Paula, was also there and I invited her to help me announce. Sounds like a good plan, eh? Well – maybe not so good. Since they had not practiced together, AND the area was so small, AND the floor was so slick, things didn't exactly go according to plan.

The Sunflower stunt started off pretty good. Dave Eady, their #1 motorman, hopped on Harry's '51, a couple of their guys jumped on the back and left side, a couple of our guys jumped on the right side and front, and away they went.

I don't know what happened, but there they were – flopping around the deck like fish out of water –and laughing their heads off with everyone else scurrying to help pick them up. It was great fun!

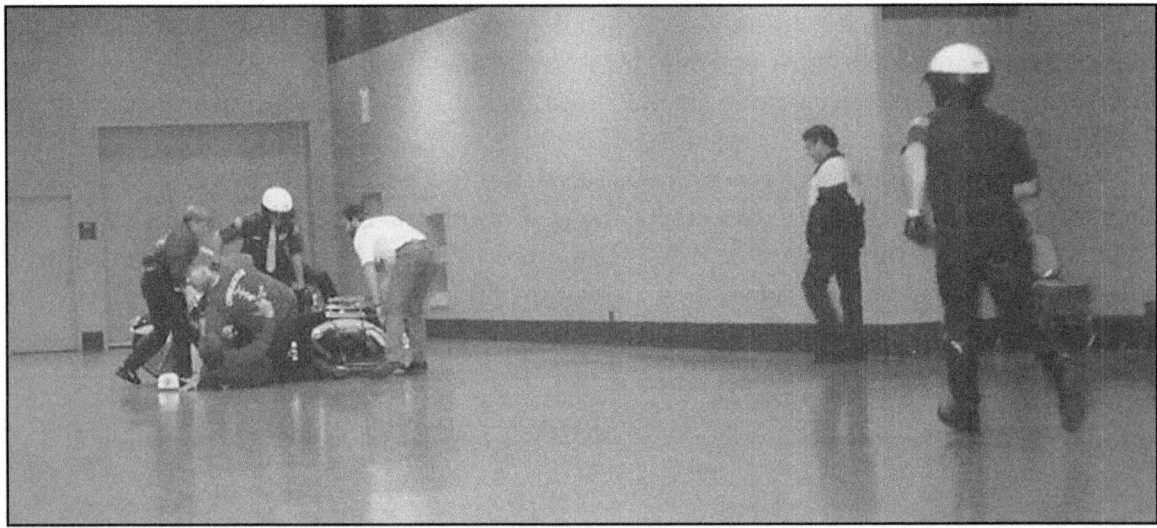

The last show on Sunday finished at 5:15PM and we had to be at the airport to check in at 6:00PM. No sweat – it was only about 15 miles. As long as we didn't hit any traffic, we'd have plenty of time. Did I mention that this was Seattle – known for it's heavy traffic? Well, we made it, and arrived in Ontario, California, at 10:40PM. Everyone returned to work on Monday morning, bright-eyed and bushy-tailed!

Drivers: Bob Jensen, Harry Fisher, Marty Fisher, Mark Frymoyer
Safety: Pat Shanahan, Tex Harris
On Top: Dan Welch, Mickey Minor

Driver: Harry Fisher
Rider: Marty Fisher

Driver: Marty Fisher
Upside down: Dan Welch

Driver: Harry Fisher
Rider (Rt): Dan Welch
Rider (Lt): Marty Fisher
Upside down: Mickey Minor
Safety: Pat Shanahan

Look how small the area is – 70'x 30'. They turned that 4-Motor Chariot stunt in that small space on a slippery floor. Wow! Are you impressed or what?!

Chicago, IL

The next weekend we met at Ontario Airport, in California, at 5:50AM for a 6:50 flight, nonstop with breakfast (remember when they used to serve breakfast and we complained about it?) and we arrived in Chicago at 12:47PM. This allowed plenty of time for check-in at the Chicago Niles Thrift Lodge (remember, we were still on a budget).

Weather proved to be a problem for the truck that was transporting our bikes and equipment. Tex and Harry were driving the transporter from Seattle to Chicago, and were held up by a huge snowstorm. They got as far as Fargo, North Dakota, and that's where they were stuck. Fargo had one of the worst snowstorms ever and the truck was parked at a truck stop. Wind chill factor put the temperatures way below zero and no one was going anywhere. They called us Friday afternoon after we'd arrived in Chicago, and gave us the bad news. The bikes definitely would not be there in time for the Friday night shows. Bummer.

The team regrouped and decided we'd better go to the show area, notify the promoters about the situation, and post a sign saying the show was canceled due to the snowstorm in the Northwest. We took a little tour of the city, found a great little place for a Chicago-style pizza (and beer) and kicked back for the evening, while Harry and Tex toughed it out in Fargo.

Meanwhile, Harry and Tex were finally able to get back on the road. They drove all Friday night and were met on the outskirts of town by Marty, Mark, and Dan, who led the way into town and the Convention Center. Our super-hero truck drivers were a welcome sight to see and very much appreciated. Marty, Dan, and Mark ran the route a couple times the night before, so they knew the quickest way to get to the Convention Center without getting lost. At 8:30AM, the truck pulled into the Convention Center loading dock and everyone chipped in to help unload. Those bikes were so iced up and cold they would hardly roll! The guys found some heaters and fans and started thawing them out, one by one. Most of the bikes were ready to do our first show at 12:30.

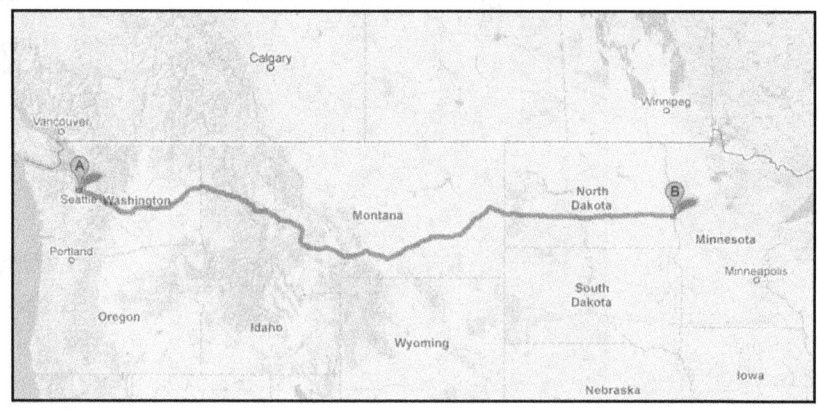

Everything happened just in the nick of time.

Cleveland, OH

Cleveland was on the original schedule. We planned to go there the next weekend, but the Fire Marshall had other plans. No matter what we told him and no matter what Advanstar told him, he wasn't about to let those dangerous motorcycles into his convention center. So, we had a weekend off. Our next stop would be New York City.

New York City, NY

The television media couldn't seem to get enough of this IMS event. It was kicked off on Friday morning by WABC-TV's morning news program. The station spent two hours in the morning letting over four million people in the tri-state area know what the weather would be like and where to find the 1996 motorcycle models from all the major manufacturers. They talked about it on *Good Morning America* and aired it again on the evening news. The Motor Corps was seen. We were HOT! CNN came out to do some interviews and get footage for another motorcycling program they were doing for April, and WNBC spent Saturday afternoon filming the show. We were unaware that any of this was going to happen. Late Thursday afternoon, Harry was notified that the television cameras would be there early Friday morning to film the team and he had to think quickly – what was he going to do? The team wouldn't get there until Friday morning and this was a great opportunity for some exposure. The problem was, there was only Harry and Tex to do stunts. As luck would have it, Kenny Frymoyer, a former member who had moved to Pennsylvania a few years prior, showed up unexpectedly and Harry put him to work. Without practice for at least a couple of years, Kenny jumped on the "½-P38", "Horse", "Swan", "Slow Circle", "Push-up" and anywhere else he was needed, to entertain the TV cameras. Kenny was trying to get nervous, but Harry didn't give him time to think!

Due to the 3,000 mile journey and three-hour time change, it was an all-day project just to get to NYC. The team took the red-eye, departing LAX on Thursday evening at 8:00PM and arriving at Kennedy Airport at 6:09AM Friday morning. Marty immediately paged Harry (remember, this was too early for cell phones) to keep him apprised of the team's arrival. With the help of Music Express and the perseverance of the team, we arrived at the hotel in Newark, New Jersey. The hotel was coincidently hosting a dog show, and the halls and elevators were constantly filled with gorgeous, beautifully-groomed, purebred dogs. We arrived just in time to check in, leave our bags with the concierge, hop on a ferry right outside the hotel lobby door and ride across the Hudson to the Jacob K. Jarvitz Convention Center. Harry and Tex had the bikes warmed up and running, with uniforms ready. We were just in time for the team to get suited up, jump on the bikes and perform our "High Pyramid," to show off for Good Morning America's FIVE MILLION VIEWERS! Whew!

We just loved those New Yorkers, too. Marty will never forget one old biker codger, who came up to him before the first show on Saturday. Marty was polishing up his 1964 Panhead and the guy came over and asked him what his job was with the team. Marty said, "I ride." The old guy said, "Sure, kid. Maybe you ride them in from the truck, but what you really do is polish and clean them – right?" Marty said, "No, I ride." The old guy still didn't believe him. After all, Marty was only 21 years old and looked 17. The old codger probably thought there was no way this kid could actually ride in this elite team. Marty didn't get too upset. He just said, "Come on back at 12:30 and see the show." So the guy did come back for the 12:30 show – and the 3:00 show – and the 6:00 show – and the 8:00PM show. After that last one, he came over to Marty and said, "You know, I've got to apologize to you. I've been riding for more than 40 years and I saw you do things with your bike that I know I couldn't do. You're one helluva rider, son," and he shook Marty's hand. Great story.

A couple of the wives had a great time, too. Cheryl Wood and Claudia Watson had booked a really tight schedule to tour New York City that weekend while we were doing the shows. They saw three Broadway shows, rode through Central Park in a buggy, went up to the top of the Empire State Building, took the ferry over to the Statue of Liberty, went to the Metropolitan Museum of Art, the J Paul Getty Art Museum, St Patrick's Cathedral, China Town, shopped 'til they dropped, and had lunch at Trump Tower and the World Trade Center. Claudia said, "For me, the high point of the trip (no pun intended) was standing on the roof, not the observation floor but the roof, of the World Trade Center with only a three foot railing between us and ... The steps to the roof are occasionally opened for small numbers of people (a dozen or so) when the weather is clear and no wind. We got lucky, it was a thrill." We didn't see these two adventurers for 72 hours – not until we all met at the airport to come home – and they did look tired (but happy)!

Another great story that came out of this NY visit.

We sold more T-shirts, pins, posters, and videos than in any other city, and our cash drawer was pretty fat. I had a habit of putting most of the cash in my fanny pack underneath my sweatshirt for safety. This way, it was close to me at all times and less likely to be stolen.

I had about $400 when I entered the ladies room. I removed the fanny pack and hung it on the stall door hook. When I left, I forgot to take it with me.

It was about an hour later, when I discovered the fanny pack was missing and quickly went into panic mode. I immediately remembered what had occurred and figured I would never, ever see the money again. I did want to cover all my bases, though, so I went to the information booth and asked if, by chance, anyone had turned in the black leather fanny pack.

The Christian Motorcycle Club was manning the booth and, to my extreme surprise, they had my fanny pack. Someone had turned it in – money and all! I am so grateful to them for being so honest and to whoever turned it in to them. It would have been easy money for someone, but they were very honest, and it was very much appreciated. It's so nice to know there are some really honest and good people out there. Don't you just love bikers?!

Pontiac, MI

We had the thrill of performing at the famous Pontiac Silverdome stadium in Pontiac, Michigan! This is the home of the Detroit Red Wings hockey team and the Detroit Lions football team. Wow! We'd seen this on TV and now we were right in the middle of it. Pontiac, Michigan, home of General Motors, originally known as Pontiac Springs Wagon Works. Pontiac, named after a great Ottawa Indian Chief. We were stoked. Last week, New York City, this week, Pontiac.

This was another "red eye" flight. We departed Ontario, California, at 11:30PM Thursday night and arrived in Detroit at 10:15AM, after changing planes in St. Louis, Missouri. We then took a shuttle van for 30 miles to the Silverdome and checked in at the Hilton. You notice I said "Hilton." We must have gotten a really good deal to upgrade to a Hilton.

Now, Harry Fisher had a good friend, Tom Davies, whom he had worked with at Rapid Blue Print Co. in Los Angeles. Tom now lived in the Detroit area, so Harry dug out his phone number and gave him a call. He let Tom know what was happening and where he'd be. Tom said he'd come by to help unload and set up. Great! Tom and his brother-in-law, Jody, met our truck and chipped in to help unload, fuel the bikes, air the tires, and get brake fluid. Jody even put his staff at City Disposal Service on call, in case we needed anything else. Later, Harry and Tex went to the coffee shop where all Tom's motorcycle buddies hung out – shop owners, teachers, engineers, engine builders of exotic machines, etc. They told these guys about the shows and they all showed up to watch.

Everything started looking up. Our show area was now 85'x 30'. We had the routine down perfectly, until Sam Watson ran out of gas! This happened in the middle of the "DC-10" stunt! Gas was somewhere in the $1-$2 range, so what was your problem, Sam? After that, the guys on Motorman Sam's stunts each chipped in a quarter, to make sure the gas tank was full! I know we were on a budget, but come on – Oh, and did I mention that this was where Mark somehow ran into Big Mike's bike, just before they started the "High Pyramid stunt?" Yep – bent the axle and pissed off Big Mike big time! Harry just said, "Does it run?" Big Mike said, "Well, yeah." So Harry said, "Then roll 'em" and the stunt went out – bent axle and all!

We also were fortunate to have former member, Kevin Anderson, from Columbus, Ohio, come to the show. Kevin participated in the shows during the entire weekend, which added more depth to our overall look. Kevin had been in the Motor Corps with his dad, George Anderson, several years before, so he knew the routine. He was especially instrumental when we all arrived back at the airport to fly home. Pat Shanahan then discovered he didn't have his airline ticket with him! Apparently, he'd dropped it at the Silverdome, Kevin found it, and rushed to the Detroit airport to hand-deliver it to Pat. Pat received it just in time to catch the plane!

This was pretty cool —our name right up there on the marque of the Pontiac Silverdome!

Pretty good view of the team from the catwalk. Mickey Minor and Dan Welch in deep discussion.

Dan Welch doing a handstand on the handlebars!

It's difficult to know who is in charge of this interview – the camera guy or Harry? Meanwhile, Ray Mehlbaum is just standing there patiently waiting for someone to ask him a question.

We arrived at the airport, with only ten minutes to spare, but still had to return the rental van. There was no way we could do that and get to our plane on time. The best option we could think of was to park the rental van in front of the entrance at TWA, lock it up, and leave the keys inside. That's what we did and just made it to the plane with seconds to spare. We did try to do the responsible thing and called the rental agency, but it was Sunday and no one answered. You know, we found out later that the van sat there in front of that lobby for 24 hours without a ticket or being towed! That sure wouldn't happen today.

Larry Huffman is a "primo" announcer and knows how to keep things interesting

Harry, "Are you ready to do the show?" Ruth, "Absolutely"

Minneapolis, MN

With just four days to recover from the Pontiac trip, we left bright and early the next Friday morning to fly to Minneapolis, arriving at 1:41 p.m. Tedd Farrell had relatives in the area, so we had lots more fans. In addition, Tedd was able to visit with them a bit, before we had to go to work. Again, Harry and Tex had the bikes unloaded and our area set up when we arrived. We were "good to go." The show area was 80'x 50', so things were lookin' up.

The Minneapolis Convention Center was connected to the hotel by what we called a "Habitrail" system. This was a series of plastic-tube type hallways, that went from the Hyatt Regency to several other buildings at the Convention Center. This was great, because it was COLD outside. There was snow, wind, and temperatures far below what our Southern California bodies could handle.

We also had an opportunity to meet the Dick Gerry and Tedd Farrell families, while we were there. A lot of the families of our members had heard of the team and sort of knew what we did. It was great that they came to our shows in Minnesota, and helped with some of the logistics. Their help and support was very much appreciated.

It was at one of our shows that Jesse "The Body" Ventura showed up. Initially, he was supposed to just promote the IMS shows and talk with the crowd, but with much urging by the IMS main announcer, Larry Huffman, he conceded to standing on the "High Pyramid" during one show with Ray Mehlbaum talking him through it all the way. Jesse stood on the rear rack of two bikes and Ray was right beside him on the shoulders of those two drivers, saying, "You're doing fine, Jesse, just stand tight, don't wiggle, hold the rope, just a few more feet to go, you're doing good, just another 30 seconds, they'll bring the bikes to a slow roll and stop, just keep standing there, you're doing good– there you go, you're all finished. You did good. We'll help you get down." Poor Jesse was shaking like a leaf, but he didn't pass out, didn't panic (too much), and finished the stunt like a Pro!

Jesse Ventura on the "High Pyramid"

The group poses with Jesse Ventura in the back, center

Jessie had little choice except to strap on a Motor Corps helmet and be part of the World Famous Victor McLaglen Motor Corps show!

SUCCESS! He did it! There Jessie is, first time ever, standing on the team's biggest stunt – the "High Pyramid!"

Dan Welch, Sam Watson, Jr., Tedd Farrell, Bob Jensen, Mark Frymoyer, Ruth Fisher, Jesse Ventura, Larry Huffman, Tex Harris, Ray Mehlbaum, Mike Betschart, Rich Wood, Dick Gerry, Mickey Minor. (Kneeling) Harry & Marty Fisher (and mascot Patches)

Denver, CO

At last we had a weekend off, before heading to the last show of the tour. We'd gotten so used to arriving home late Sunday night, throwing our clothes in the washer/dryer, going to work tired Monday morning and packing to leave again on Friday, that the thought of not going anywhere was unthinkable. What in the world would we do with all the free time? Yard work? House maintenance? Nah –we'll just not think about it.

Friday arrived and we flew out of separate airports. Mickey Minor flew out of John Wayne Airport in Santa Ana, California, Marty Fisher flew out of San Diego, California, and the rest of us flew out of Ontario, California. We were all scheduled to arrive in Denver around the same time and made our way to La Quinta to check in. Yep, we were back to staying at the "budget" hotels! Besides, it was right next to Denny's and Baskin Robbins. We were living right!

The Channel 4 news came out on Friday afternoon and did a live broadcast of the "2-Motor Pyramid." Dick Gerry coordinated all this, while some of the rest of us tried to find Marty at the airport! Remember, he'd had to take a separate flight out of San Diego, but arrived a bit later than planned. He was found and brought to the convention center, so all was well.

A HUGE area for the performance

The show area? Well, this one was 120'x 80'! This was about twice as large as any of the others! It was SO big that it threw off our timing. Mickey Minor went upside down on a stunt and all the blood rushed to his head for twice as long. Frank Hicks held up Art Wale's legs on a "Push-Up" stunt and figured his arms were going to break before he got to the other end of the arena. Let alone Sam Watson's neck muscles were overly-strained, from Art laying on his head doing the "DC-10" stunt for longer than they were used to! Being one mile high in Denver, Colorado, didn't help with the energy level or the performance of the motorcycles, either. We definitely needed that extra oxygen. Therefore, after that first show on Friday evening, at our 6:30 show, we moved some of the fencing and shortened the area down closer to what we'd gotten used to–about 80' x 70'–and the rest of the shows went much better. The news commentator after our shows said, "the crowds love the Victor McLaglen Motor Corps." We were diggin' the attention!

Mark, Harry and mascot, Patches scoping out the area. Notice the St. Patrick Day hat?

We were in Coors Beer territory, so of course we had to take advantage of that. So, between shows on Saturday afternoon, some of us made a mad dash to the Coors Brewery facility in Golden, Colorado, about 15 miles away. We took their tour, had a tasting of their product and made it back in time for the next show. This was probably the fastest tour Coors ever experienced! Golden is beautiful and the Brewery was very clean, modern, and interesting. Oh, and I learned an important fact – don't drink beer and expect to be a great announcer for the show!

This was St. Patrick's Day weekend, so we figured we had to go downtown and check things out. We were all packed into a big van, touring the city, looking for a pub or restaurant for corned beef and cabbage and green beer. We pulled up to one intersection and a drunk – excuse me, partying citizen –came out of the bar and yelled, "Hello –Top of the evening to ya. I'm Irishman, Tim O'Malley" in the best Irish brogue that he could muster. Marty leaned out the window and said, in his California Irish brogue, "Pleased to meet ya, I'm Marty FulO'Shit". The guy didn't know what to say to that! We never did find that corned beef and cabbage and green beer, but we had a great time.

Marty doing the "Roman Ride" with burros.

Now that's a BIG jug of beer. It makes Marty Fisher look tiny.

Back home in California

Our infamous 1995 IMS Tour was over. It was one of the greatest Motor Corps experiences of our lives. We met terrific people across this great country, we perfected our skills, until those stunts could practically be done blindfolded, and we had such camaraderie in the team that we were like a close-knit family. No one could come close to putting on a show like we did. We had that 20 minute show timed perfectly and could even do it in a 50' circle.

Traveling Teams

ANAHEIM
1. Mike Betschart
2. Tedd Farrell
3. Harry Fisher
4. Marty Fisher
5. Ruth Fisher
6. Mark Frymoyer
7. Dick Gerry
8. Tex Harris
9. Frank Hicks
10. Bob Jensen
11. Ray Mehlbaum
12. Mickey Minor
13. Pat Shanahan
14. Sam Watson
15. Dan Welch
16. Rich Wood

SAN FRANCISCO
1. Mike Betschart
2. Tedd Farrell
3. Harry Fisher
4. Marty Fisher
5. Ruth Fisher
6. Mark Frymoyer
7. Dick Gerry
8. Tex Harris
9. Frank Hicks
10. Bob Jensen
11. Ray Mehlbaum
12. Mickey Minor
13. Pat Shanahan
14. Sam Watson
15. Dan Welch
16. Rich Wood

CHICAGO
1. Mike Betschart
2. Harry Fisher
3. Marty Fisher
4. Ruth Fisher
5. Mark Frymoyer
6. Dick Gerry
7. Tex Harris
8. Bob Jensen
9. Ray Mehlbaum
10. Mickey Minor
11. Sam Watson
12. Dan Welch
13. Rich Wood

DENVER
1. Mike Betschart
2. Harry Fisher
3. Marty Fisher
4. Ruth Fisher
5. Mark Frymoyer
6. Dick Gerry
7. Tex Harris
8. Bob Jensen
9. Ray Mehlbaum
10. Mickey Minor
11. Sam Watson
12. Dan Welch
13. Rich Wood

NEW YORK
1. Mike Betschart
2. Harry Fisher
3. Marty Fisher
4. Ruth Fisher
5. Mark Frymoyer
6. Dick Gerry
7. Tex Harris
8. Bob Jensen
9. Ray Mehlbaum
10. Mickey Minor
11. Sam Watson
12. Dan Welch
13. Rich Wood

SEATTLE
1. Mike Betschart
2. Harry Fisher
3. Marty Fisher
4. Ruth Fisher
5. Mark Frymoyer
6. Dick Gerry
7. Tex Harris
8. Frank Hicks
9. Bob Jensen
10. Ray Mehlbaum
11. Mickey Minor
12. Sam Watson
13. Dan Welch
14. Rich Wood

MINNEAPOLIS
1. Mike Betschart
2. Tedd Farrell
3. Harry Fisher
4. Ruth Fisher
5. Mark Frymoyer
6. Dick Gerry
7. Tex Harris
8. Bob Jensen
9. Ray Mehlbaum
10. Mickey Minor
11. Sam Watson
12. Dan Welch
13. Rich Wood

PONTIAC
1. Mike Betschart
2. Harry Fisher
3. Ruth Fisher
4. Mark Frymoyer
5. Dick Gerry
6. Tex Harris
7. Bob Jensen
8. Ray Mehlbaum
9. Mickey Minor
10. Pat Shanahan
11. Sam Watson
12. Dan Welch
13. Rich Wood

Recap

Number of cities on this tour	8
Total number of shows	71

Estimated Attendance at each show:

Anaheim	37,556
San Francisco	27,378
Seattle	26,723
Chicago	44,488
New York City	52,215
Pontiac	24,417
Minneapolis	27,472
Denver	16,522
TOTAL	256,771

Booth (Hot Dog Wagon) Sales total $6,402

With our sales at the Hot Dog Wagon, we were able to give each traveling member a few bucks at each show for food and refreshments. It wasn't much, but it certainly helped and was appreciated. It also gave us a bit to pay for the flyer, business cards, and posters that we needed to replenish.

We did pretty good with our budget, too:

	Plan	Actuals
Meals –Driver	$2,120	$2,120
Meals –Team	$5,280	$4,680
Hotel	$8,199	$8,079
Airfare	$24,571	$19,566
Ground Trnsp	$1,440	$1,076
TOTALS	$41,610	$35,521

I think we did pretty good. We had money left over for insurance for the next season and replenishing the uniforms,.

After we returned home, we had a wrap-up pizza party. We watched Evelyn Jensen's videos from the IMS shows, looked at more pictures, told stories –about lost airline tickets, leaving the van at the airport, Harry getting his whistle caught in the front spokes doing the Floorboard Ride (!), watched the 15-second debut on Good Morning America, and debuted the new 20-minute Motor Corps video we had made professionally, to promote the team.

What a time! What fun! What an absolutely extraordinary, remarkable team we have!

A Special Note From Our Commander

I would like to take this opportunity to tip my helmet to all of you. You were all an integral part of this effort. Many, many thanks ---

To the members who took time off from your jobs (some at no pay) and away from your families,

To you who made special arrangements for tests and classes at college,

To those of you who closed down your shop or businesses so you could leave on Fridays for the weekend,

To all of you who made the shows so professional and dynamic.

To those who didn't get to travel, but who are also a very important part of what this Motor Corps is today –who helped in the preliminary effort, who were there to help whenever we called to say we needed something,

To the wives who helped in the booth and helped their guys go on these trips,

To those who helped load the truck, run errands, pick up T-shirts, get advertising flyers, pack posters, carry booth supplies to the airports, etc. etc.

To Evelyn who spent several trips from Redlands to Anaheim, to get those posters made up in a hurry, then made arrangements with a friend for a loan, to pay for them on a 30-day agreement,

To Nancy, who kept track of the money, went to the bank, made hotel and van reservations, and coordinated the airport vanpool arrangements.

You ALL made it happen!

More thanks will be sent to our sponsors, Kendall, Tsubaki, Monarch, and Accell; to Team Expo, who have the power to move us in front of these new crowds and gave us the chance to do what we've been wanting to do for a long time. More thanks to Larry Huffman (Voice of the Expo), and Ruth (Voice of the Motor Corps), who put everything they had into making the crowd react to our performance. I'll never forget some of those jokes! Thanks to Patches, who has her own unique way to draw a crowd and helped break the ice for some people to talk to us who would not have dared before. (By the way, she'll be in doggy uniform from now on!) Thanks to Cathy Reed, our Travel Agent at AAA. She made everything work out perfectly and got us the best prices possible.

A special thanks to my wife, Ruth, who took care of all the airplane tickets, coordinated the team travel, and was the focal point for all the activities.

One last thanks –to Doug Domokos. We would not have had this opportunity without his recommendation to Advanstar to hire us. Thanks a million, Doug.

Many times in my Motor Corps career I have heard guys say that we are "Just a club", that we could not work a professional circuit –Well, hell AND THEN SOME, we did 71 shows, 4 TV appearances, and 3 radio spots, while we were in 7 states in 2 ½ months. Not a person was late, or missed a performance. I'd say that we are one VERY PROFESSIONAL TEAM.

Congratulations on a job well done!

Harry Fisher, Commander

A letter from Harry to the team after the tour was completed -April 7, 1996

APPENDIX C
2000/2001 Cycle World International Motorcycle Shows (IMS)

Glenda Yost, promotions manager at Advanstar, contacted us about doing the entertainment for the 2000-2001 season tour of Cycle World's International Motorcycle Shows (IMS). Excellent! We had so much fun in 1996, that everybody was gung-ho to do it again. Maybe me -not so much. There's a lot of work coordinating this event – airplane tickets, hotel reservations, rental cars, airport shuttle, etc. -however, I dug in and did it anyway. It must be those winning personalities in the Motor Corps – or Harry's persistence!

For this tour, instead of nine cities, we only went to five. That was okay and we were all eager to do it. This gave us time to get the bikes running tip-top, to get the paint touched up, re-chrome some of the really bad parts, get fitted for new uniforms and practice, practice, practice.

Our Basic Team

1. Mike Betschart
2. Harry Fisher
3. Marty Fisher
4. Ruth Fisher
5. Moe Elmore
6. Mark Frymoyer
7. Tylor Hicks
8. Bob Jenson
9. Ray Mehlbaum
10. Mickey Minor
11. Jeremy Norton
12. Sam Watson
13. Dan Welch
14. Maria Willers

We were fortunate to have Jeremy along this time to help Harry with the transporter truck. He'd had years of experience with truckloads of motorcycles, so he was an expert at loading, unloading, driving AND doing stunts, too. It was a win-win situation.

Our Schedule

Dallas, TX	December 15-17, 2000
Minneapolis, MN	January 26-28, 2001
Cleveland, OH	February 3-4, 2001
Chicago, IL	February 9-11, 2001
St. Louis, MO	March 23-25, 2001

Equipment loaded in the truck:

Cooler (we went through about three cases of water at each venue)
Decking Bars (to keep the motorcycles separated and locked down)
Hot Dog wagon (stocked with T-shirts, posters, pins, videos)
Extra boxes of Hot Dog wagon supplies
Gas Cans (we kept remembering that Sam ran out of gas last time!)
Generator
Hand truck, brooms, trash bags
Helmet Boxes (and helmets)
Ladder, Stunt Ladder
Motorcycle Jacks
Motorcycles (Duh!)
Plastic supply tubs
Plywood (for double-decking the trailer)
Stunt Ropes
Tie-downs, Soft-ties, Bungee straps
Tool Box (and tools!)
Uniform Closet (and uniforms!)

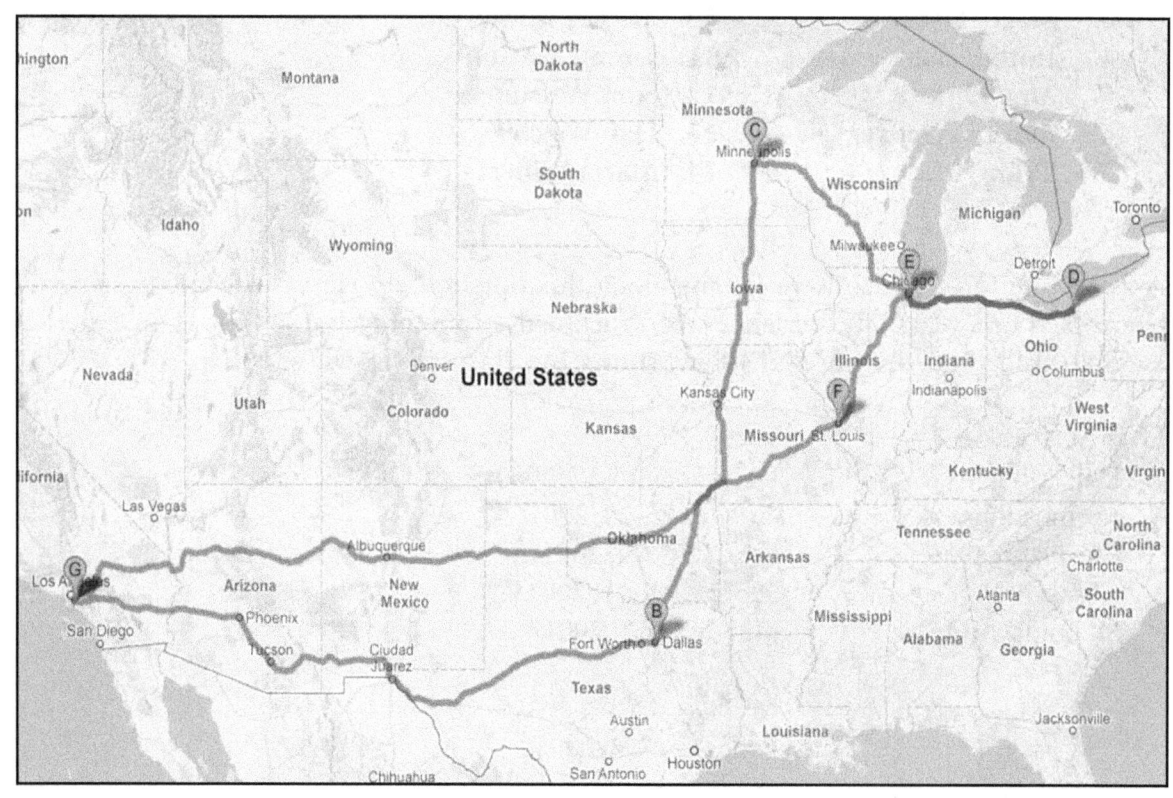

We were also very fortunate to have legendary professional announcer, Larry Huffman, helping us with these shows once again. Larry was the official announcer and public relations guy for the IMS show and was perfect for the job. He always arrived at the next city ahead of the rest of us, and did radio and television spots to promote the IMS shows. At the opening of each show, he introduced the team, got the audience warmed up, and helped me to keep the audience "in the know" as to what the team was doing.

It seems that even though the spectators could see what's happening, the stunts still needed to be explained! I would describe the moves before they made them, then the audience could follow along to see the stunts built up, then broken down.

Larry Huffman

In between stunts, Larry would talk to the audience and keep them interested. It was fun and I learned a lot from him on these two IMS tours. Larry is a great guy and a strong supporter of the Motor Corps. I can still hear him say, "Mark's an excellent rider –keep your eye on him –he executes his solo stunts flawlessly 99% of the time" which, of course, caused everyone to step back, waiting for that 1% time to happen.

We were honored to have Larry Huffman help with the announcing.

Larry watching Mark do "Walk the Hog" –flawlessly 99% of the time!

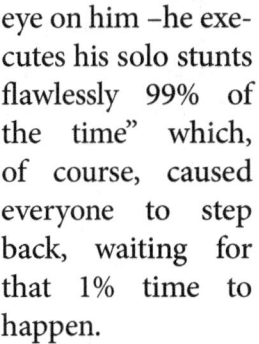

Larry tries out our Whizzer bike.

Dallas, TX

This was the first IMS show for some of the team members. We talked Art Wales and Moe Elmore into joining us this time. We also hired Jeremy Norton to drive the truck and do stunts. It was fun having some "new blood" on the tour. On the other hand, we were a little sad because our long-time member and good friend, Dick Gerry, wasn't with us this time. Dick had passed away on Feb. 25, 2001 and we missed him tremendously. Dick was 78 years old and had been in the Motor Corps for about 44 years. He had completed the entire tour in 1996, was a terrific rider, good friend, and a lot of fun to have around. He was everybody's best buddy.

We flew out of the Long Beach airport for our trip to Dallas, Texas. The LGB airport is small and simpler, easier to park, easier to get through the lines and just overall easier. Same procedures as the previous IMS Tour – except NOW we had electronic ticketing! There was no chance of losing those tickets this go-around. And cell phones – most everybody had them - and we could call someone if there was a hitch in the get-away!

We stayed at the "Host Hotels" this time. We figured that even though the daily rate was more, we saved by not renting cars or shuttles. Since the Host Hotels gave us discounts and were generally right next to the convention centers, it was more convenient. So, at Dallas, we stayed at the Hyatt Regency. Very nice.

We always "double-up" when we do an "away" show and this was how it generally went:

Room #1 – Harry and Ruth Fisher
Room #2 – Mike Betschart and Bruce Chubbuck
Room #3 – Tylor Hicks and Mo Elmore
Room #4 – Marty Fisher & Mark Frymoyer
Room #5 – Bob Jensen and Mickey Minor
Room #6 – Art Wales and Sam Watson
Room #7 – Tedd Farrell and Jeremy Norton

Of course, when the wives would go, there was a little rearranging done and often times, additional rooms booked. Sometimes we'd have three people to a room. It all worked out.

The Dallas shows went well – no accidents, no problems. Sam even had a full tank of gas! We all flew home on Sunday, after the last show, while Harry & Jeremy packed up the truck and headed back to California, to celebrate the holidays with our families.

Signing Autographs

One of the best parts of doing those shows was talking to the folks who came to watch. The team had their autograph pens with them at all times – and just had a great time signing posters, T-shirts, programs, videos, and anything else they were asked to sign.

Minneapolis, MN

On Sunday, January 20, everyone met at the truck with motorcycles and plastic bins containing their uniforms, ready to load into the trailer. It may have been only 13 motorcycles in that 53' trailer, but with all the equipment and extra tires, parts, etc., that truck was full. The truck headed out toward Minneapolis the next morning.

On Friday, January 26, at 7:00 a.m., the team met at the Ontario Airport, to depart to Minneapolis. This was Maria Willers' first time to travel with the team to perform at the IMS shows. She was also the first WOMAN to do these shows with the Victor McLaglen Motor Corps. I'm sure she really felt the pressure, but she came through it all admirably.

It didn't help that before the first show on Friday, Harry got the team together and gave them a little pep talk, "You know, the news media will be here. They will have all their cameras up on the catwalk, there'll be CNN, NBC, CBS, ABC – all the big stations – and they'll be doing interviews right after the shows, so be sure to say the right things, don't fall down, don't cuss..."

I could see that Maria was white and about to pass out, so I just put my arm around her and said, "Maria, he's just kidding!" Then she started breathing again!

The only other problem we had, was that Big Mike came down with a wicked cold. He was suffering –fever, coughing, sore throat, headache, the works. He found a drugstore close by and bought some meds, tried not to breathe on the rest of us, and did the shows anyway. We were a close-knit, well-oiled machine by this time and Big Mike was an instrumental part of the show. He, Sam Watson, Harry Fisher, and Bob Jensen, were the key motormen. All the stunts were built on their bikes. It would have seriously hampered the show if one person had to drop out. Yeah, Big Mike should have stayed in his room all weekend, drinking O.J. and sleeping, and yeah, we probably should have made him do it – but we had shows to do, damn it, and he just had to ride. Actually, I'm sure that no matter what we said, he still would have ridden anyway. He was tough and stubborn, and not prone to listening to any of us! It all worked out OK, though. The shows went off well, Mike survived the cold and we were back home in LA at 10:05PM Sunday night. We were ready for work the next morning. Well, sort of ready.

Cleveland, OH

Can you believe it? The team met at Mark Frymoyer's house in Downey, California, at 4:30 a.m. to be shuttled to LAX! Mark talked his good friend, Walt Braico, into driving us to the airport and we all piled into a big 15-passenger van to make the trip. We had 13 people, plus the driver. It all looked do-able on paper, however, we forgot about the luggage! No problem, everyone either slid it under the seats, or just held their luggage in their laps. In fact, Walt drove us a couple times during this tour. Also, Mark's neighbor, Elias Noriega, drove us sometimes. This turned out to be a community project!

We flew out of LAX, which is always cumbersome, but we were able to get a good rate and it was a nonstop flight. Whenever possible, we booked nonstops. There was less chance of any delays in getting to our destinations. By the way, the roundtrip ticket for this flight was $189.70 each. All our flights were booked through Marrietta, at Tri-Community Travel in Wrightwood, California, and she did a marvelous job getting us the best deals possible.

Three sets of the "2-Motor Chariot"

This was the second city for Maria Willers. I think she was still a bit nervous, but getting more used to the pressures. She was a big hit with the fans. We performed at the IX Center and the show schedule was the usual one:

Friday: 5:30PM, 7:45PM
Saturday: 11:30AM, 2:30PM, 5:00PM, 7:30PM
Sunday: 11:30AM, 1:30PM, 3:30PM

Getting ready for the "6-Motor Chariot"

"The Fan"
Driver: Big Mike Betschart

Center Safety: Bob Jensen Left: Art Wales- Right Mickey Minor

"DC-10" Driver: Sam Watson., Front Fender: Mickey Minor
Handlebar: Jeremy Norton. Top: Art Wales
Safety: Moe Elmore

Another interesting story came out of our shows at Cleveland . . .

Bob Jensen, as many of you might already know, has only one eye. It doesn't really slow him down. He's been compensating for that loss for a lot of years and as far as I know, the team has never had to do anything different to accommodate his lack of two eyes. Oh, they might put him on the right side of a line-up, but that's about it.

Well, at one of the Cleveland shows, a mother with her little girl came up to Bob after the show and told Bob about her little girl having a visual impairment and she had noticed that Bob had the same problem. Her mother told her that, just because she had a vision impairment, that doesn't mean she can't do things like riding a motorcycle someday. Bob picked up on that conversation and started talking to the little girl and told her not only could she ride a motorcycle one day, but she could do anything she wanted to do and not to let her eye problems slow her down. Then the little girl was all smiles and her mother thanked Bob profusely for his words of encouragement. It was a very touching experience – not only for the little girl and her Mom, but for Bob and the rest of us, too. I doubt that Bob will ever forget that little girl.

Our last show was done by 4PM and we immediately started loading everything into the truck, because we had to leave no later than 6PM for the ride to the airport.

We made it to the airport and arrived at LAX at 9:46PM. Walt shuttled us to Mark's, house where we got into our cars and drove home. We were exhausted, but we had big smiles on our faces!

Chicago, IL

Chicago was another early flight. We met at Ontario Airport in Ontario, California, at 5:30AM for a 6:30AM departure. This was a nonstop flight to O'Hare Airport in Chicago and we arrived at 12:28PM and checked in at the Hyatt Regency, ready for our shows.

Air travel was going well; however, Harry Fisher and Jeremy Norton, were about to experience some issues with unloading the truck. Apparently, they have a really strong union at this Convention Center. This was Chicago, after all. The only way those motorcycles were going to get from the truck to the show area was if one of their Union guys pushed it. Of course, they didn't necessarily know HOW to get it out of gear or actually push those big Harleys. It took at least two of them on each bike to get the job done, but they were closely watched by Harry and Jeremy, and the bikes got placed. You know how it is with you Harley owners – NO ONE touches your bike and when it's a "show bike" to boot, well, this was not a good scene. This was when some of the guys met up with the chief security officer at the Cen-

ter and he was quite a character. He showed how they could check out everything happening at the Center on the many surveillance cameras and he let us know he was serious about his job and about all the people who worked for him. We weren't about to try any "funny stuff!"

The Union guys strung the extension cord for our speaker system and plugged it in for us, even though we were capable. We'd sneaked the fencing back a bit when no one was looking, to give us a tad more room to ride, and the shows went on without a hitch.

When it came time for the last show on Sunday, we had a plan to get past the Union guys. As we finished our last ride around the arena, the team waved to the crowd and before anyone (specifically,

the Union guys) knew what was happening, we rode right out of the arena and into the back of the truck. The truck just happened to be parked at the loading dock with its back doors open! Our new best buddy chief security officer helped with this ploy and it went off without a hitch! Don't mess with our guys. We'll outsmart you every time!

At this show, we met the Regional Manager, Ron Klimke, and showed him how to do the "Push Up." Ron was a good sport and I think he had a lot of fun trying out his new talent!

Ron Klimke,
Suzuki Motorcycles

Art Wales (up)
Ron Klimke (pushing)
Harry Fisher (driving)
Mike Betschart (driving)
Marty Fisher (supervising)

Harry Fisher and Jeremy Norton got to be friends with lots of other workers and vendors during the tour, new friends and old friends from the last tour in 1996. I have a feeling there was a lot of standing around yapping, too! By the way, it's always important to be on the good side of the forklift driver!

THE TEAM – Back Row: Jeremy Norton, xx, Mickey Minor, Ruth Fisher, Ron Klimke, Mike Betschart, Maria Willers, Moe Elmore, Sam Watson, Bob Jensen, Mark Frymoyer, Bruce Chubbuck.
Front Row: Tedd Farrell, Harry Fisher, Marty Fisher, Art Wales

St. Louis, MO

Here we go. It's Friday and time to travel. We met at Mark's at 6:15 a.m., and flew out of LAX at 8AM., nonstop on TWA. Remember TWA? Who knew they wouldn't be around much longer. We arrived in St. Louis at 1:30 p.m., ready to check in at the hotel and go to the Transworld Dome, home of the St. Louis Ram's Football Team! The best part was, we used their locker room to change into our uniforms! How great is that? The team walked in the same place where some of their heroes walked! (I think it's a "guy thing." Look at the big smile on Marty's face, standing in front of the locker room doors!)

We were all very honored to have this special lady come watch our show. Elizabeth Harker made the trek from Illinois to watch the show and we made sure she had a seat right up front, along side her sister. Liz was the widow of our second leader, Herb Harker. Liz had always been the Motor Corps' best supporter, not only during the 25 years when Herb was riding and then was in charge, but afterward, when Herb retired. She always tried to keep up with what we were doing and helped if we needed anything. We loved her and will be eternally appreciative for all she's done for the team.

Liz must have liked the show – she left with an autographed poster!

The Wales Family: Dan on the front, Becky on the shoulders, Brandon on the back and of course, Dad (Art) driving. Who said we aren't a family-oriented motorcycle team?

This was our last IMS show!

Our second "IMS tour" was over and everyone returned to being ordinary, everyday citizens. Back to our regular jobs, mowing the lawns, washing the cars, and taking out the trash. No longer "stars." Nobody asked for our autographs, except maybe our tax accountants. Man, reality sometimes sucks!

We did have one helluva time, though, and we will always remember "The 1995/1996 and 2000/2001 IMS Tours!

The "Whizzer" is a motorized bicycle built by Harley-Davidson. Harley-Davidson of Anaheim-Fullerton gave us one to travel with. One of the team members would ride it around the show area, prior to our shows, to get people's attention for the show that was just minutes away.